Best Practices in Professional Learning
and Teacher Preparation

VOLUME 3

Best Practices in Professional Learning and Teacher Preparation

Professional Development for Teachers of the Gifted in the Content Areas

Edited by Christine L. Weber, Ph.D.,
& Angela M. Novak, Ph.D.

PRUFROCK PRESS INC.
WACO, TEXAS

a service publication
NATIONAL ASSOCIATION FOR
Gifted Children

Library of Congress Cataloging-in-Publication Data

Names: Novak, Angela M., 1963- editor. | Weber, Christine L., editor.
Title: Methods and strategies for gifted professional development / edited by Angela M. Novak and Christine L. Weber.
Description: Waco, TX : Prufrock Press Inc., [2018] | Series: Best practices in professional learning and teacher preparation ; volume 1 | Includes bibliographical references.
Identifiers: LCCN 2018013789| ISBN 9781618217721 (paperback) | ISBN 9781618217745 (epub) | ISBN 9781618217738 (ebook)
Subjects: LCSH: Teachers of gifted children--Training of. | Gifted children--Education.
Classification: LCC LC3993.25 .M48 2018 | DDC 370.71/1--dc23
LC record available at https://lccn.loc.gov/2018013789

Copyright ©2020, National Association for Gifted Children

Edited by Katy McDowall and Andilynn Feddeler

Cover design by Micah Benson and layout design by Shelby Charette

ISBN-13: 978-1-61821-972-5

No part of this book may be reproduced, translated, stored in a retrieval system, or transmitted, in any form or by any means, electronic, mechanical, photocopying, microfilming, recording, or otherwise, without written permission from the publisher.

For more information about our copyright policy or to request reprint permissions, visit https://www.prufrock.com/permissions.aspx.

Printed in the United States of America.

At the time of this book's publication, all facts and figures cited are the most current available. All telephone numbers, addresses, and website URLs are accurate and active. All publications, organizations, websites, and other resources exist as described in the book, and all have been verified. The authors and Prufrock Press Inc. make no warranty or guarantee concerning the information and materials given out by organizations or content found at websites, and we are not responsible for any changes that occur after this book's publication. If you find an error, please contact Prufrock Press Inc.

Prufrock Press Inc.
P.O. Box 8813
Waco, TX 76714-8813
Phone: (800) 998-2208
Fax: (800) 240-0333
http://www.prufrock.com

Table of Contents

INTRODUCTION 1

SECTION 1: CURRICULUM FROM THE BIGGER PICTURE

CHAPTER 1:
Engaging Gifted Teachers in Professional Learning
About Content Curriculum 7
BY CHRISTINE L. WEBER AND EMILY MOFIELD

CHAPTER 2:
Professional Learning Through a Growth Mindset Lens 27
BY MARY CAY RICCI

CHAPTER 3:
It's a Marathon, Not a Sprint: Gifted Professional
Learning and the Change Process From the
Administrator's Shoes. 41
BY KAREN D. JONES AND ANGELA M. NOVAK

SECTION 2: CURRICULUM THROUGH A CONTENT LENS

CHAPTER 4:
Professional Learning Practices in Literacy Education
for Gifted and Talented Students 73
BY MARY L. SLADE AND TAMMY BURNHAM

CHAPTER 5:
Research-Based Essentials in Professional Learning:
Social Studies. 91
BY KIMBERLEY L. CHANDLER

CHAPTER 6:
Foreign Language Education and Professional Learning
for Teachers of Advanced Language Learners 109
BY BRONWYN MACFARLANE

CHAPTER 7:
Research-Based Essentials in Professional
Learning in the Arts. 129
BY HOPE E. WILSON

CHAPTER 8:
Professional Learning in Science for Teachers of the Gifted: A Focus on Science and Engineering Practices and Crosscutting Concepts **149**
BY KIM A. CHEEK

CHAPTER 9:
Crafting Professional Learning Experiences for Teachers of Gifted Students in Mathematics **175**
BY ERIC L. MANN AND REBECCA L. MANN

CHAPTER 10:
Using the CLEAR Curriculum Model's Language Arts Units to Support Professional Learning in Gifted Education **191**
BY TRACY C. MISSETT, CAROLYN M. CALLAHAN, AND CHERYLL M. ADAMS

ABOUT THE EDITORS **213**

ABOUT THE AUTHORS **215**

Introduction

This book is the third volume of a three-book series related to professional learning and teacher preparation in gifted education. Volume 1 focuses on methods and strategies for gifted professional development. Volume 2 explores professional learning strategies for special topics in gifted education. Volume 3 provides a twofold focus: Curriculum From the Bigger Picture and Curriculum Through a Content Lens. The purpose of this series is to present various topics supporting strategies and best practices in teacher training, focusing on identifying and meeting the needs of gifted learners, as outlined and required in the Every Student Succeeds Act (ESSA, 2015) for Pre-K–grade 12 administrators and supervisors, coordinators of gifted programs, Pre-K–grade 12 educators and teachers of the gifted, and other stakeholders in the field. These books continue the discussions started in *Using the National Gifted Education Standards for Pre-K–Grade 12 Professional Development* (Johnsen & Clarenbach, 2017) and offer expert suggestions for exemplary practices that maximize professional learning.

In this volume, authors present practical suggestions for organizing professional learning opportunities specific to advancing teachers' understanding of content knowledge, along with resources and materials to guide facilitators. Section 1: Curriculum From the Bigger Picture highlights the importance of content in the educational context of professional learning. Section 2: Curriculum Through a Content Lens focuses on different disciplines and the implications for gifted professional learning in each.

Section 1 begins with Weber and Mofield highlighting the need to support teachers' pedagogical content knowledge through professional learning. An emphasis on leveraging high-quality curricular and instructional materials when providing professional learning opportunities enhances the rigor and challenge needed by learners in gifted programs. The authors remind educators to use a critical eye when selecting appropriate curriculum for gifted learners and suggest using the National Association for Gifted Children's Curriculum Studies Rubric for Rating Outstanding Curriculum Material, which distinguishes features for promoting rigor and meeting the needs of academically advanced students.

The second chapter by Ricci sets the stage for applying growth mindset thinking when engaging in any professional learning opportunities, which is an especially helpful strategy when teachers expand content knowledge in areas with which they may be unfamiliar or uncomfortable. She provides suggestions for professional learning facilitators to help those who demonstrate fixed mindset thinking. An educator mindset reflection tool that could be used prior to professional learning is shared to help facilitators understand each participant's knowledge base of the principles of growth and fixed mindsets. She concludes the chapter by emphasizing that implementing a growth mindset can allow one to be a more effective presenter and, in turn, provide more effective professional learning.

Chapter 3, written by Jones and Novak, takes the reader from the growth mindset to considering systemic and people-focused change at the school level from an administrator's perspective. Written from the perspective of a principal recognizing a lack of knowledge in gifted pedagogy and practice, personally and on the part of the faculty, the authors walk through the administrator embarking on self-directed professional learning and conducting action research. This chapter addresses content from the administrator's point of view: the change process and professional learning in gifted education.

In Chapter 4, which begins Section 2, Slade and Burnham discuss the need for training to include significant content related to the necessary differentiation of literacy education for gifted and talented students. They organize the chapter around three components, (1) the relevant literacy content and pedagogical skills most likely to impact student achievement, (2) the necessary modifications to or adaptations of traditional literacy education programming to address the needs of gifted students, and (3) the unique aspects of literacy education for gifted and talented students.

Looking at social studies content in Chapter 5, Chandler focuses on professional learning for teachers in K–12 as it relates to instruction in this discipline. Included is information about the standards that drive such professional learning; key strategies with a focus on the College, Career, and

Civic Life (C3) Framework for Social Studies State Standards; and sample professional learning plans for developing expertise in social studies for teachers of the gifted.

MacFarlane explores foreign language education and professional learning for teachers of advanced language learners in Chapter 6. Competencies for the professional expertise learning and training needs of foreign language teachers are provided, along with an emphasis on the need for educators to understand the characteristics of these learners. Examples of designing foreign language professional learning opportunities, as well as additional resources and materials, offer the guidance needed to plan meaningful professional learning experiences that impact diverse gifted students.

In Chapter 7, Wilson discusses research-based essentials in professional learning for the arts, as well as the challenges this discipline encounters in pursuing and making such opportunities available to educators. She describes the different types of art educators and their specific needs, the qualities of professional learning in the arts, and the potential challenges. Wilson shares strategies and helpful resources to enhance the planning of training in this area.

In Chapter 8, Cheek describes the Next Generation Science Standards, their structure, and why they can serve as a framework in which to design professional learning for science teachers of the gifted. She also discusses professional learning in science and highlights two strategies (immersion and examining student work) that developers of professional learning in this area may find useful. Finally, Cheek shares how implementing both strategies can help science teachers of the gifted be more generative and better meet the needs of high-ability learners.

In Chapter 9, Mann and Mann emphasize that it is essential that teachers have an in-depth conceptual understanding of what they teach. This begins with a need for transforming the learning of mathematics. Teachers also must accept students who use nontraditional methods for solving problems. This occurs when there are continued learning opportunities through properly focused professional learning communities.

The third volume of the series concludes with Chapter 10 and an example of content in practice: a curriculum model. Missett, Callahan, and Adams discuss the CLEAR Curriculum Model, which emphasizes the development of curriculum characterized by evidence-based and appropriate learning experiences for gifted learners. The theoretical underpinnings of the model are explored. Lesson component examples from the CLEAR language arts units provide a better understanding of how the model can be implemented by teachers.

References

Every Student Succeeds Act, 20 U.S.C. § 6301 (2015). https://congress.gov/114/plaws/publ95/PLAW-114publ95.pdf

Johnsen, S. K., & Clarenbach, J. (Eds.). (2017). *Using the national gifted education standards for pre-k–grade 12 professional development* (2nd ed.). Prufrock Press.

Section 1
Curriculum From the Bigger Picture

CHAPTER 1

Engaging Gifted Teachers in Professional Learning About Content Curriculum

Christine L. Weber and Emily Mofield

As educators and professional learning facilitators embrace the tenets of professional learning—which emphasize opportunities that are interactive, continual, and relevant to the content-based needs of teachers and their students—educators need to consider the impact of these tenets and how they support teachers' pedagogical content knowledge, particularly as it relates to curricular and instructional materials for meeting the needs of gifted learners.

Hirsh (2019) outlined four cornerstones of professional learning for Learning Forward's publication *4 Cornerstones of Professional Learning*. These cornerstones may guide districts toward setting goals. They include:

1. **Lead with equity.** Equity and excellence in teaching and learning is included in Learning Forward's vision statement and "represents the inspiration, challenge, and essential purpose for pursuing more effective ways to serve educators and students" (p. 2).
2. **Invest in team learning.** For every student to succeed, every educator engages in collaborative, job-embedded learning to strengthen capacity and collective responsibility.
3. **Leverage high-quality instructional materials.** Educators use their learning time to understand high-quality instructional mate-

rials and prepare for implementation, advancing their potential to improve student learning.
4. **Advocate with evidence.** To sustain support for professional learning at all levels, educators equip themselves with data from research and practice. They share that data with stakeholders and speak up for their learning and that of their peers.

Many of these suggestions, with a continued emphasis on endorsing research and best practices, are developed in various chapters of Volumes 1 and 2, and now Volume 3, in this series. This chapter focuses specifically on the third cornerstone, as outlined by Hirsh (2019), of leveraging high-quality curricular and instructional materials to provide rigor and challenge for gifted learners. Additionally, this chapter sets the stage for outlining what this cornerstone looks like for those involved in planning and implementing professional learning that strengthens teachers' knowledge and teaching of domain-specific content, and that results in effective pedagogical content knowledge. In order to implement any plans for high-quality professional learning related to teaching gifted learners, educators must first consider: What are high-quality instructional materials and content? Authors in this volume who focus on professional development for teachers of the gifted in the content areas emphasize the need to improve teachers' content knowledge and pedagogical content knowledge, which are both essential for teachers of the gifted (Gubbins, 2008; Little & Ayers Paul, 2017).

In Volume 1 of this series, Novak and Lewis (2018) provided a multitude of professional learning options for educators to explore, such as professional learning communities (PLCs), mentoring, cohorts, and online communities. Gilson (2018) challenged readers to consider differentiated professional learning, drawing on specific principles related to adult learning theories. Other chapters support research and best practices with additional strategies for professional learning, such as using case studies, employing a reflective practice, using coteaching, and implementing new technologies. The latter is especially important when planning technology integration building on Shulman's construct of pedagogical content knowledge (PCK) to include a technology knowledge (Koehler & Mishra, 2009). This model, TPACK, is designed around the idea that content (what is taught) and pedagogy (how it is taught) must be the basis for any technology used in the classroom to enhance learning (see https://www.rt3nc.org/edtech/the-tpack-model). This chapter emphasizes the importance of identifying criteria for selecting high-quality curriculum, which impacts the content identified during professional learning opportunities. This chapter focuses on three questions:

- What is high-quality gifted curriculum, and how does it support gifted students in learning content-specific strategies and methodologies?
- What are examples of high-quality curriculum?
- What role do content standards play in professional learning of gifted educators?

What Is High-Quality Gifted Curriculum? How Does It Support Gifted Learners?

Engaging teachers in professional learning about gifted curriculum must include a clear understanding of what high-quality gifted curriculum actually is and what makes it different from regular curriculum. Professional learning must address (1) the essential components of high-quality curriculum, (2) why these features benefit gifted student learning, and (3) how gifted students best learn the content. When teachers understand the structure, parts, and functions of high-quality curriculum, professional learning experiences can offer opportunities for teachers to interact with and evaluate exemplary gifted curriculum. Further, the understanding of these essential components will strengthen teachers' skills in developing their own high-quality curriculum. In essence, high-quality gifted curriculum allows gifted students opportunities to develop their strengths and talents. Gifted students learn information quickly, process content at high levels, and make abstract connections across concepts. In response to these characteristics, impactful gifted curriculum embeds opportunities for students to engage in the thinking processes inherent in a discipline and practice applying these processes to real-world problems and issues (Renzulli et al., 2000; Tomlinson et al., 2009; VanTassel-Baska & Baska, 2019; VanTassel-Baska & Wood, 2010). Thus, in professional learning, teachers must consider the role of *content-specific* curriculum (the *what*) as an opportunity to develop gifted students' strengths and talents.

Within a content area, gifted students need experiences that allow them to apply the core ideas, structures, and processes of the discipline (Tomlinson, 2004; VanTassel-Baska & Wood, 2010). The more complex these experiences are, the more likely students will have to integrate background knowledge, decision making, problem solving, creative thinking, and critical reasoning. When providing professional learning on designing gifted curriculum, teachers need to learn how various content areas require different ways of applying thinking processes, such as critical thinking and creativity. For example, creative thinking in science may involve developing multiple solutions to a real-world problem (e.g., "How can we prevent honeybees from dying?"), while creative thinking in the language arts may include using flexibility and elaboration in a creative narrative. Further, critical thinking in social studies involves examining bias, perspective, and context within a primary source document, while critical thinking in math includes verifying the reasonableness of a solution through applying a mathematical model.

In the context of talent development in particular, gifted curriculum is an opportunity for identified potential to be transformed into achievement within a domain (Subotnik et al., 2011). Ericsson's (1996) work on expert performance explains that experts have developed a sophisticated understanding of domain-specific patterns and that they can apply these patterns to reach solutions. This notion is highlighted particularly in cognitive psychology as the building of "schema," and, for novice learners, it is critically important to make such concepts and patterns explicit in order to facilitate understanding of the organization of knowledge. Defined, schema is the "interpretive frameworks, built out of past knowledge and experience, that allows us to make sense out of the bits and pieces of information presented to us in given situations" (Mitchell, 1989, p. 277). Relevant to gifted curriculum, the thinking processes within these domains can be explicitly taught (Stambaugh & Mofield, n.d.; VanTassel-Baska & Wood, 2010). Thus, as teachers engage in professional learning about content curriculum for gifted learners, whether through learning how to use a published curriculum or develop their own curricula, they should consider the question, "How do experts think about this content differently than novices?" The National Research Council (1998) noted that when novices solve problems, they spend considerably more time defining the problem than experts do and have stronger metacognitive skills. Additionally, experts differ in their skills to:

- develop a mental framework for organizing knowledge,
- retrieve integrated collective facts (rather than piecemeal facts),
- perceive structures of situations in order to know next steps and examine patterns, and
- understand when to revise ideas (Adams et al., 2008, para. 2).

Professional learning related to gifted curriculum should also address how gifted students best learn content and which academic language is most useful to emphasize for content-specific methodologies. *All* learners need the initial building blocks for developing schemas for organizing knowledge, and *all* learners need opportunities to engage in authentic learning and challenging curriculum for meaningful learning to occur. This is facilitated by a variety of instructional strategies that foster creativity and curiosity, allow students to apply learning to new contexts, and differentiate for student readiness and interest (Tomlinson, 2004; Tomlinson et al., 2009). Additionally, meaningful learning is achieved by intentionally planning instruction around academic language, academic discourse, and purposeful talk relevant to discipline-specific vocabulary and syntax so that students can comprehend complex texts as they progress through more challenging content (Frey et al., 2010). However, for gifted students, these instructional approaches need to be applied to more advanced content with opportunities for higher levels of complexity, abstraction, and degrees of generalizability (Beasley et al., 2017).

Professional learning for gifted educators should focus on developing and/or selecting curriculum that intentionally differentiates by readiness for gifted learners by considering how advanced content-specific academic language and discourse can be used within the curriculum to channel learning. For example, although typical middle school students might learn to analyze a speech for an author's purpose, claim, and use of structure as part of learning a grade-level standard, high-quality gifted curriculum should intentionally include activities that allow students to evaluate more sophisticated rhetorical devices, such as syllogisms or use of synecdoche, and require students to apply these techniques in developing their own arguments in response to real-world issues. Indeed, this deliberate planning for use of academic language with gifted students can bridge the learning from novice- to expert-level thinking. As students grapple with more sophisticated concepts via academic discourse, they build more complex mental schemas for pattern recognition and deep conceptual understanding.

NAGC Curriculum Studies Rubric

Professional learning related to curriculum might involve exploring the question, "Can high-quality gifted curriculum be developed or only purchased?" Just because curriculum is published does not mean that it is high-quality. In the same vein, not all teacher-created resources align to best practices in gifted education. So, how might professional learning guide teachers to evaluate the curriculum they use, adopt, and/or create?

The National Association for Gifted Children's (NAGC) Curriculum Studies Network developed a rubric to guide educators in developing and selecting high-quality curriculum for gifted learners that distinguishes features for promoting rigor and meeting the needs of academically advanced students (Beasley et al., 2017; see Appendix 1.1). Among these components, high-quality curriculum units articulate objectives that require students to understand not only the facts within a content area, but also the concepts, principles, methodologies, and dispositions within a field. This means students would apply the work of a practicing professional within the unit of study, using discipline-specific skills related to the content area. This may include using the methodology of ethnography within a social studies unit or the use of scientific modeling to explain phenomena within a science unit. Ultimately, students need opportunities to apply concepts of the discipline and essential understandings of the field in authentic products (Erickson, 2007; Phenix, 1964; Tomlinson, 2004). As stated by Beasley et al. (2017), "a goal for high-quality curriculum is to give students resources to use as tools to solve problems and answer questions authentic to the field or discipline" (p. 55).

Related to the development of schema, problem solving should be taught as it is applied within a field, because approaches to problem solving vary by content area. Problem identification and problem solving in language arts might involve considering: "Why was this text written? How does it relate to the context and problems of its time? What does the author's story or narrative reveal about the problem? How does the author's craft and structure develop the author's message as it relates to a larger societal or personal issue?" The problem-solving process in social studies, however, may involve several aspects of problem identification and analysis, such as evaluating multiple sources in order to develop conclusions about a proposed question like "Was America a democracy before 1919?" Beyond answering "yes" or "no," students take a stance to develop a logical, reasonable conclusion from multiple sources of evidence and perspectives, reasoning through assumptions and implications to substantially defend a position (Stambaugh & Mofield, n.d.). The solution stage would include exploring alternatives to decisions made during a period in order for students to understand that the past, present, and future are the results of multiple decisions and factors interacting across time.

Applying processes of experts within a discipline has a high impact on gifted learners because it involves making complex connections across multiple sources and developing conceptual understanding of the content-related ideas and principles. When applying discipline-specific methodologies and models for thinking, gifted students also have opportunities to think of content from whole-to-part rather than part-to-whole, an approach that is particularly suited for gifted learners because of their ability to think abstractly (Rogers, 2007). As such, when supporting teachers in using high-quality gifted curriculum, training should emphasize conceptual understanding within content-specific professional learning.

The integration of technology (as previously suggested in the TPACK model) is also an important feature of high-quality curriculum, especially when students learn how real practitioners engage with it as an authentic tool to solve problems in their field. As teachers select and develop gifted curriculum, they might ask, "How would a historian, scientist, mathematician, literary scholar, etc., use technology to deepen their understanding of concepts, produce new knowledge, and share this knowledge with the world?" Through the development of authentic products, teachers should encourage the use of technology to guide students not only to access content, but also to create content (Heitin, 2016). Students might have opportunities to network with experts in a field of study through the use of digital online platforms to gain insight into the problems and methods used in real-world contexts. As part of product development, students may share their new knowledge and ideas through media productions using green screen technology, platforms such as Sway (https://sway.office.com) or Story Spheres (https://www.storyspheres.com), or even self-made TED talks. Technology also affords the opportunity to address real-world issues related to the content studied; for example, students may learn to apply coding systems to develop an innovative app to address a local community issue or join with other students to address real-world issues through online global projects, such as the Sustainable Development Goals (https://sustainabledevelopment.un.org). Further, students may seek opportunities to get feedback and publish their work within author communities, such as Underlined (https://www.getunderlined.com).

Gifted curriculum is an opportunity for students to explore content, which leads to the discovery of emerging talent. Whether selecting curriculum or developing curriculum, professional learning might include time to consider the question, "Does this unit provide opportunities for students to discover that they might have strengths in a content area?" For example, students may start to see themselves as scientists after using a simulation model to learn about gravity and make scientific arguments (e.g., Stambaugh & Mofield, 2018). Additionally, curriculum should include opportunities to interact with professionals in the field or mentors (in person or through video conferencing) who can provide insight into the nature of how they apply their knowledge to real-world problems and issues. For example, students might interview wildlife professionals to learn about how they measure changes in the ferret population, how they think about the larger context of the ecosystem, and how their authentic products (e.g., a scientific model or proposal) address the problem (e.g., Gallagher & Plowden, 2013). Students also need opportunities to self-reflect about their own learning and strengths throughout the unit so that they might start to see themselves as capable and confident producers of knowledge within a domain. Experiences such as these pave the way for potential to transform into ability, ability to competence, and competence to creative contribution (Subotnik et al., 2011).

Overall, the NAGC Curriculum Studies Rubric is a tool that can be referred to during professional learning and other collaboration efforts to design, select, and evaluate gifted curriculum and how it is implemented in the classroom. Program leaders and administrators may use it to evaluate the extent to which students are actually exposed to high-quality instruction. Additionally, during PLCs, teachers may consider, "How can we extend and enrich the learning for students who have demonstrated proficiency?" (DuFour et al., 2010, p. 199), referring to these curriculum features to guide next steps for instruction. It might also be used to facilitate instructional coaching, guiding teacher reflection on the extent to which their lesson planning includes these components and what adjustments in instruction are needed. Further, the rubric might be used during coplanning or coteaching to design effective differentiated lessons for identifying and developing talent. In sum, the features on the rubric can provide a rationale and standard for training on gifted content-based curriculum and are steeped in the foundations of what is known about how gifted students learn.

What Are Examples of High-Quality Gifted Curriculum?

The NAGC Curriculum Studies Rubric highlights appropriate pedagogical practices (the *how*) as part of a unit's learning activities and the use of instructional practices, like modeling, shared inquiry, problem-based learning, mentoring, and constructivist approaches. Curriculum should provide opportunities for problem-based/real-world application to learning and opportunities to apply a concept or methodology within a field. As discussed previously, these processes and methods are applied differently in a variety of content areas; therefore, teachers who use curriculum units for gifted learners should know and understand the content at a level that allows for such in-depth instruction and exploration of advanced concepts. Since 1997, the NACG Curriculum Studies Network has recognized exemplary units that meet the criteria for high-quality curriculum by scoring high on the rubric (Purcell et al., 2002). A list of these curriculum units can be found on the Curriculum Studies Network page at https://www.nagc.org/curriculum-awards. This list includes a number of published curriculum units from various universities that provide guidance for teachers on implementing content pedagogical knowledge.

To illustrate, the units authored by the Center for Gifted Education at William & Mary are designed with the Integrated Curriculum Model (ICM; VanTassel-Baska & Baska, 2019; VanTassel-Baska & Wood, 2010), which emphasizes the advanced content, process, and issues/concepts in a content area. In these units, students are taught the scientific research process, a critical thinking model, and/or an analysis model for text applied to advanced content and theme. The advanced curriculum series by Vanderbilt Programs for Talented Youth (e.g., Stambaugh & Mofield, 2018) also uses the ICM and is intentionally designed to expose students to the content as part of a trajectory toward expertise in the field. For example, students are taught content-specific processes for organizing knowledge of a domain in order to think about literature, science, and social studies as experts do. In literature, beyond discerning the isolated components of plot, theme, and conflict, students examine how literary elements interact to create meaning and evoke interpretation. These models have been vetted by experts in the field to substantiate the validity of their structure and use.

Curriculum from the University of Connecticut has been recognized repeatedly for math units (e.g., Gavin et al., 2008) that emphasize real-world problem solving and mathematical thinking processes. The Project M^2 and Project M^3 math curriculum encourages students to "grapple with challenging problems, discuss and write about their thinking, and justify their answers as mathematicians do" (Gavin, 2016, p. 165). University of Virginia's CLEAR curriculum (e.g., Missett et al., 2016) provides opportunities for students to apply critical literacy by reading diverse texts and creating authentic products related to the language arts (see Chapter 10 of this volume). Curricula written by Gallagher and others (e.g., Gallagher & Plowden, 2013) provide opportunities for students to engage in applications of content knowledge through problem-based learning.

These are just a few of the many high-quality gifted resources available. Professional learning related to content curriculum may highlight how curriculum developers take varied approaches to designing units around advanced content. The NAGC Curriculum Studies Rubric can serve as a structure in professional learning, providing a guide for developing or purchasing gifted curriculum. Leaders, instructional coaches, and teachers in gifted education may consider which approach best suits the district's goals and programming for gifted education and/or advanced academics.

What Role Do Content Standards Play in Professional Learning of Gifted Educators?

With the adoption of Common Core State Standards (CCSS), educators are reminded about the need to reflect on their role in educating gifted learners (VanTassel-Baska, 2016). As previously emphasized, educators must consider the connection between characteristics of gifted learners and content-specific standards that drive differentiation. In the present era of accountability, districts want curriculum to be aligned to standards because students are assessed on how well they learn them (even if the learners might be above grade level). As a result, gifted educators need professional learning opportunities to design instruction that might align to above-grade-level standards, combine *multiple* standards (for compacting), and add depth and complexity to the standards. VanTassel-Baska (2016) provided three major strategies worth considering about curriculum planning:

- Provide pathways to accelerate the CCSS for gifted learners.
- Provide examples of differentiated task demands to address specific standards.
- Create interdisciplinary product demands to elevate learning for gifted students and to efficiently address multiple standards at once (pp. 75–76).

Gifted curriculum may be designed as a more complex version of grade-level standards-based curriculum. Professional learning through coplanning, instructional coaching, and coteaching may involve using the standards as a base for adding depth, complexity, and other differentiation features to student tasks (Mofield & Phelps, 2020). Because standards establish a starting point for preassessing and planning for what students know, do, and understand, they lay the groundwork for differentiation, which may involve using above-grade-level standards, combining multiple standards, or eliminating portions of standards. In many school districts, rigid pacing guides dictate what and when standards are taught, but unfortunately, such rigidity can ignore individual needs of students (Johnsen, 2016). Professional learning might emphasize the need for flexible pacing where grade-level standards are not the destination of the lesson; rather, they serve as a map for understanding where a student is in relation to the learning goal.

Summary

Strengthening teachers' knowledge of content pedagogical knowledge is key to planning and implementing effective professional learning related to the content areas. Ultimately, when teachers know the content better, they teach it better. Teachers must have an understanding of the conceptual underpinnings, which would guide more appropriate essential questions and development of learning experiences that require more in-depth processing (Erickson, 2007). This is especially crucial when content, strategies, and technology are combined in professional learning. We end this chapter with a few final thoughts on moving forward in developing teachers' practices and competencies in implementing high-quality gifted curriculum.

One of the most authentic ways to develop teachers' knowledge on content-specific methodologies is to provide opportunities for teachers to collaborate with experts in the field to discuss and develop lesson content as part of their professional learning. For example, in *Space, Structure, and Story: Integrated Science and ELA Lessons for Gifted and Advanced Learners in Grades 4–6*, the authors consulted with an astronomer to discuss and review the science content related to black holes, gravity, and Einstein's theory of relativity (Stambaugh & Mofield, 2018). The astronomer was able to help address misconceptions, provide insight as to how astronomers collect data, and affirm or disaffirm the validity of the source materials. Students also benefit when mentors or professionals within a field are invited to guide students through thinking within the discipline. As alluded to before in this chapter, this may also be in the form of videoconferencing for feasibility. When mentors engage with students over time, this can expose students to firsthand perspectives within a particular domain and perhaps inspire a talent trajectory.

To implement curriculum successfully, professional learning for high-quality curriculum should involve opportunities to understand teachers' perspectives and belief systems regarding the nature of gifted students and what they need in terms of content curriculum. Assessing the prior attitudes of teachers can help bridge connections to new pedagogical content (Zhao et al., 2002). Additionally, teachers must understand why the curriculum should be used, particularly the link between the characteristics and needs of the gifted learner and the way the curriculum addresses these needs. As teachers adopt and/or modify gifted curriculum, teachers need to see explicit connections to the differentiation features within the unit. For example, within professional learning sessions, teachers may be asked to examine curriculum for learning activities that incorporate features of the NAGC Curriculum Studies Rubric. Teachers might note opportunities for students to practice problem solving as a scientist through the use of designing models to explain a phenomenon. This review process may help teachers discern between simple lesson activities and true opportunities for talent development through the learning experiences related to the discipline. Finally, as teachers implement high-quality curriculum, they would benefit from feedback about its implementation through one-on-one coaching and sufficient time to plan for such high-level instruction (Brighton et al., 2005). Opportunities for reflective practice in order to promote the understanding of what teachers do and why they do it is a necessary component to any professional learning plan (Slade, 2018). Educators need to question current practices, implement research-based practices, and evaluate the impact of such practices on the overall education of students. The follow-up aspects of a professional learning plan are critical in supporting teachers as they apply newly learned strategies related to a content domain. As educators strive to improve their pedagogical content knowledge, they can better address the intellectual and educational demands of gifted students.

References

Adams, W., Wieman, C., & Schwartz, D. (2008). *Teaching expert thinking.* http://www.cwsei.ubc.ca/resources/files/Teaching_Expert_Thinking.pdf

Beasley, J. G., Briggs, C., & Pennington, L. (2017). Bridging the gap 10 years later: A tool and technique to analyze and evaluate advanced academic curricular units. *Gifted Child Today, 40*(1), 48–58. https://doi.org/10.1177/1076217516675902

Brighton, C. M., Hertberg, H. L., Moon, T. R., Tomlinson, C. A., & Callahan, C. M. (2005). *The feasibility of high-end learning in a diverse middle school* (RM05210). University of Connecticut, The National Research Center on the Gifted and Talented.

DuFour, R., DuFour, R., Eaker, R., & Many, T. (2010). *Learning by doing: A handbook for professional learning communities at work* (2nd ed.). Solution Tree.

Ericsson, K. A. (Ed.). (1996). *The road to excellence: The acquisition of expert performance in the arts and sciences, sports, and games.* Erlbaum.

Erickson, H. L. (2007). *Concept-based curriculum and instruction for the thinking classroom.* Corwin.

Frey, N., Fisher, D., & Nelson, J. (2010). Lessons scooped from the melting pot: California district increases achievement through English language development. *Journal of Staff Development, 31*(5), 24–28.

Gallagher, S. A., & Plowden, D. L. (2013). *Ferret it out: A problem about endangered species and animal ecosystems.* Royal Fireworks Press.

Gavin, M. K. (2016). Mathematics curriculum for gifted learners. In K. R. Stephens & F. A. Karnes (Eds.), *Introduction to curriculum design in gifted education* (pp. 151–174). Prufrock Press.

Gavin, M. K., Chapin, S. H., Dailey, J., & Sheffield, L. J. (2008). *Project M^3: What are your chances?* Kendall Hunt.

Gilson, C. M. (2018). Moving toward differentiated professional learning for teachers learning to differentiate for gifted students. In A. M. Novak & C. L. Weber (Eds.), *Best practices in professional learning and teacher preparation: Methods and strategies for gifted professional development* (Vol. 1, pp. 93–120). Prufrock Press.

Gubbins, E. J. (2008). Professional development. In J. A. Plucker & C. M. Callahan (Eds.), *Critical issues and practices in gifted education: What the research says* (pp. 535–562). Prufrock Press.

Heitin, L. (2016). *What is digital literacy?* Education Week. https://www.edweek.org/ew/articles/2016/11/09/what-is-digital-literacy.html

Hirsh, S. (2019). *4 cornerstones of professional learning: Fundamental principles pave the way for educators' actions.* Learning Forward. https://learningforward.org/wp-content/uploads/2019/02/4-cornerstones-for-download-1.pdf

Johnsen, S. K. (2016). Aligning curriculum to standards. In K. R. Stephens & F. A. Karnes (Eds.), *Introduction to curriculum design in gifted education* (pp. 63–91). Prufrock Press.

Koehler, M. J., & Mishra, P. (2009). What is technological pedagogical content knowledge? *Contemporary Issues in Technology and Teacher Education, 9*(1). https://www.citejournal.org/volume-9/issue-1-09/general/what-is-technological-pedagogicalcontent-knowledge

Little, C. A., & Ayers Paul, K. (2017). Professional development to support successful curriculum implementation. In J. VanTassel-Baska & C. A. Little (Eds.), *Content-based curriculum for high-ability learners* (3rd ed., pp. 461–483). Prufrock Press.

Mitchell, J. B. (1989). Current theories on expert and novice thinking: A full faculty considers the implications for legal education. *Journal of Legal Education, 39*, 275–297.

Mofield, E., & Phelps, V. (2020). *Collaboration, coteaching, and coaching in gifted education: Sharing strategies to support gifted learners*. Prufrock Press.

Missett, T. C., Azano, A. P., & Callahan, C. M. (2016). *Research and rhetoric: Language arts units for gifted students in grade 5*. Prufrock Press.

National Research Council. (1998). *How people learn: Brain, mind, experience, and school*. The National Academies Press.

Novak, A. M., & Lewis, K. D. (2018). Tools of the trade: Finding the best fit for your professional learning needs. In A. M. Novak & C. L. Weber (Eds.), *Best practices in professional learning and teacher preparation: Methods and strategies for gifted professional development* (Vol. 1, pp. 51–69). Prufrock Press.

Phenix, P. H. (1964). *Realms of meaning: A philosophy of the curriculum for general education*. McGraw-Hill.

Purcell, J. H., Burns, D. E., Tomlinson, C. A., Imbeau, M., & Martin, J. (2002). Bridging the gap: A tool and technique to analyze and evaluate gifted education curricular units. *Gifted Child Quarterly, 46*(4), 306–321. https://doi.org/10.1177/001698620204600407

Renzulli, J. S., Leppien, J. H., & Hayes, T. S. (2000). *The multiple menu model: A practical guide for developing differentiated instruction*. Prufrock Press.

Rogers, K. B. (2007). Lessons learned about educating the gifted and talented: A synthesis of the research on educational practice. *Gifted Child Quarterly, 51*(4), 382–396. https://doi.org/10.1177/0016986207306324

Slade, M. (2018). Reflection as an essential practice in professional learning for gifted education. In A. M. Novak & C. L. Weber (Eds.), *Best practices in professional learning and teacher preparation: Methods and strategies for gifted professional development* (Vol. 1, pp. 39–50). Prufrock Press.

Stambaugh, T., & Mofield, E. (n.d.). *Advanced content models for differentiating curriculum: Simple tools for complex thinking* [Manuscript in preparation]. Prufrock Press.

Stambaugh, T., & Mofield, E. (2018). *Space, story, and structure: Integrated science and ELA lessons for gifted and advanced learners in grades 4–6*. Prufrock Press.

Subotnik, R. F., Olszewski-Kubilius, P., & Worrell, F. C. (2011). Rethinking giftedness and gifted education: A proposed direction forward based on psychological science. *Psychological Science in the Public Interest, 12*(1), 3–54. https://doi.org/10.1177/1529100611418056

Tomlinson, C. A. (2004). *How to differentiate instruction in mixed ability classrooms* (2nd ed.). ASCD.

Tomlinson, C. A., Kaplan, S. N., Renzulli, J. S., Purcell, J. H., Leppien, J. H., & Burns, D. E. (2009). *The parallel curriculum: A design to develop high potential and challenge high-ability learners* (2nd ed.). Corwin.

VanTassel-Baska, J. (2016). Gifted education in the age of content standards. In T. Kettler (Ed.), *Modern curriculum for gifted and advanced academic students* (pp. 69–76). Prufrock Press.

VanTassel-Baska, J., & Baska, A. (2019). *Curriculum planning and instructional design for gifted learners* (3rd ed.). Prufrock Press.

VanTassel-Baska, J., & Wood, S. (2010). The integrated curriculum model (ICM). *Learning and Individual Differences, 20*(4), 345–357. https://doi.org/10.1016/j.lindif.2009.12.006

Zhao, Y., Pugh, K., Sheldon, S., & Beyers, J. L. (2002). Conditions for classroom technology innovations. *Teachers College Record, 104*(3), 482–515.

Appendix 1.1

National Association for Gifted Children Curriculum Studies Rubric for Rating Outstanding Curriculum Material

High scores on each component reflect high-quality.

	1	2	3
Nature of Differentiation	Open-ended activities are included in the unit and allow for students' differing needs.	Open-ended tasks provide student support through one or more of the following adjustments: pacing, depth, breadth, level of abstraction, level of complexity, degree of generalizability, or talent development.	Activities and assignments that accommodate the learning needs of high achieving students are explicitly described. These include adjustments to content, process, product based on student readiness, interest, and learning profile throughout the unit.
Opportunities for Talent Development	The unit includes at least three of the activities listed below. • Opportunities for "kid watching" and "talent spotting" • Opportunities for students to engage in some activities aligned with their individual strengths, preferences, or interests • Opportunities to foster the connection between unit activities and potential career fields, leadership opportunities, or real-world applications • Opportunities to interact with role models, community resources, mentors, or professionals in the field • Opportunities to explore advanced content in that field • Opportunities to acquire the skills, methodologies, and dispositions of the practicing professional in that field • Opportunities to investigate real-world problems and to develop authentic products and services in that field	The unit not only includes at least three of the activities listed below but data from these activities are used to drive future instructional decisions within the unit.	The unit uses more than three of the activities below, uses data from these activities to drive future instruction AND includes student self-reflection on how tasks impacted their learning/perception of self as a learner.
Clarity of Objectives	Objectives are stated but require assumptions on the part of the reviewer as to outcome goals.	Objectives are reasonably clear; reader is fairly confident he/she understands what students need to know and be able to do.	Objectives are clearly stated, specific, and unambiguous.

Nature of the Objectives	The objectives are aligned to state and/or national standards. They are concerned with details and factual knowledge and include basic skills requirements.	Objectives are aligned to state and/or national standards and focus on students' learning and incorporating concepts and skills within a field of study.	Objectives are aligned to state and/or national standards and focus on students' learning and incorporating concepts, principles, cognitive skills, methodologies, and dispositions within a field of study.
Evaluation Components	The assessment model is limited to paper and pencil evaluation instruments (i.e., tests, quizzes).	The assessment model includes at least two approaches to evaluation design, such as student portfolios, observational checklists of student behaviors, paper/pencil evaluation, product evaluation, or self/peer evaluation with evaluation data being used to drive future instruction.	The assessment model includes at least three different evaluation measures including, for example, student portfolios, observational checklists of student behaviors, product evaluation, or self or peer evaluation. Assessment data is used to monitor student growth, provide student feedback, allow for student self-reflection, or to differentiate content or instruction.
Learning Activities	Learning activities within the unit support different learning profiles and readiness levels.	Learning activities throughout the unit, allows teachers to utilize student learning preference information in student task assignment decisions.	Learning activities within the unit provide opportunities for student centered, problem based/real world application learning.
Instructional Strategies	The instructional strategies are described and provide opportunities for concept and methodology of a field exploration.	Instructional strategies require students to use concepts & methodology in a product to demonstrate learning.	Instructional strategies require students to apply concepts and methodologies to address a real world problem.
Student Products and Assignments	The author describes a minimum of three different options for student projects or assignments. The majority of these assignments involve convergent thinking, recall, and practice.	The author describes different kinds of student products or assignments that are embedded in the lesson plans. These assignments are open-ended and allow for personal interpretation and/or accommodate varying levels of expertise.	The author describes different kinds of student products or open-ended assignments, including the development of student driven creative products, or the development of products related to real-world applications or problem solving.
Resources and Level of Student Engagement with the Materials The unit Contains:	Primary and secondary information sources to support student learning are provided.	Students are engaged with print and non-print materials, i.e., books, video tapes, audio tapes, hands-on materials, software, Internet sources.	Students engage with resources that are authentic to the discipline/field of the unit. Students find and use appropriate resources to answer questions and solve problems authentic to the discipline/field of the unit.

Alignment of Curricular Components	The curriculum unit contains a minimum of 5 lessons, each lesson describing the following instructional components: objectives, assessment, introduction, teaching strategies, learning activities, products, resources, differentiation strategies, and talent development activities.	The curriculum unit not only includes all curricular components, stated in #1, but also demonstrates a clear sequence and alignment of these components to support a variety of learners.	The curriculum unit demonstrates all components as stated in level 2 and is clearly sequenced, is aligned to support learners, and provides options for increasing rigor and challenge to meet students' different learning needs.
Evidence of Effectiveness	The unit has been used at least once with students; anecdotal evidence is included – such as teacher impressions of success.	The unit has been used at least once with students; evidence that supports general student growth is provided such as anecdotal evidence, pre/post test data, student self-assessment of growth, and product examples. This information is used to make unit revisions.	The unit has been taught more than once. Developers describe a systematic effort to assess growth and change in gifted education students. This includes a clear plan for documenting student growth/change with work examples provided (actual student products and/or photos of student work). Reflections on effectiveness with students are provided and utilized to drive unit revisions.
Ease of Use by Other Educators	Unit components are explained so teachers could implement it easily within their classroom setting.	Unit components are explicit, well-sequenced and support teachers in differentiating learning within the unit tasks.	Unit components are explicit, well-sequenced and support teachers in differentiating learning within the unit tasks. Reflections on field test results are included as data driven revision suggestions for planning, implementation and use by others.

Total Score: _____/36

CHAPTER 2

Professional Learning Through a Growth Mindset Lens

Mary Cay Ricci

Educators often attend professional learning sessions and think, "There is no way I can do what they are asking in the timeframe they have given me," or "This makes no sense to me; I will never be able to do this," or perhaps something like, "My students will not be able to make that growth goal in one semester." Professional learning sessions will not be very effective if participants do not apply growth mindset thinking. What exactly does that mean? Dweck (2006/2016) identified two belief systems that learners apply to a variety of situations: a *growth mindset* belief and a *fixed mindset* belief. When people apply grow mindset thinking, they believe that with perseverance, resiliency, some mistakes along the way, and a cache of strategies, they can understand and accomplish just about anything. With a growth mindset, participants in professional learning sessions consider the possibilities, embrace growth, and welcome any perceived challenges. A fixed mindset is the belief that people only have the capacity to understand, accomplish, and/or achieve in certain areas. They believe that they were born with intrinsic strengths and weaknesses that cannot be changed.

Therefore, if a teacher is attending a professional learning session focused on learning how to set up a virtual classroom for their students and they do not consider technology a strength, they might immediately feel intimidated, feel that they will not be successful, and/or wonder if they can get someone else to set it up for them.

Overview

The field of education continually changes, and educators must be open to new learning, particularly in gifted education. Applying growth mindset thinking is important, as is being ready and open to learn things that might be counter to what was previously believed. The field of gifted education goes through philosophical and instructional shifts. For example, many years ago, tic-tac-toe assignment sheets and cubing were considered gifted education strategies because they allowed for choice. Educators now know that choice is good for all students, not just advanced and gifted learners. Educators need to be open to changes and growth, which requires a growth mindset.

Think about all that the field of gifted education has always believed about the social-emotional needs of gifted learners. What most educators do not realize is that there is little to no recent empirical research that actually proves that certain behaviors are more prominent in gifted learners. In recent years, gifted education scholars, such as Olszewski-Kubilius and Steenbergen-Hu (2017), have presented research about the lack of research in this area. Basically, some of the social-emotional characteristics that the gifted education field has always espoused to be found in gifted learners may not be as prevalent in gifted cohorts as once thought. For example, a little-known fact is that Dabrowski's theory of overexcitabilities was never intended to be focused on gifted learners; Dabrowski was simply looking for a way to look at exceptional personality development (Olszewski-Kubilius & Steenbergen-Hu, 2017). These social-emotional differences may exist, but there is no solid evidence of that in the field of gifted education yet.

Many educators can think of students they know who have demonstrated some of these personality characteristics, such as perfectionism or emotional overexcitabilities. Participants in a professional learning session focused on social-emotional learning of advanced and gifted students may hear about the lack of research-based evidence and tune out. They may think things like, "I don't care that there is limited research that supports this; I know it is true," or "I have observed these traits in gifted learners"—and they certainly may have observed these social-emotional behaviors in the gifted children that they parent or teach, but these traits may not be exclusive to gifted learners. There is simply not enough information yet.

This is just one example of how adult learners can display fixed mindset thinking during professional learning sessions and why there is a need for growth mindset professional learning. How can professional learning facilitators help those who demonstrate fixed mindset thinking? Consider the following suggestions:

- Facilitate professional learning sessions that focus on the difference between fixed and growth mindsets.
- Let participants know that they may find what is being presented counter to what they have always thought to be true. Challenge them to have an open mind and adopt growth mindset thinking.
- Allow time for participants to question, wonder, and reflect on the content that is being presented.
- Create an exit card that asks participants to reflect on the learning, share concerns, and identify perceived barriers for implementation (this information should also be used to adjust future professional learning sessions).
- Embed information about the principles of growth and fixed mindset thinking within the sessions.

Professional Learning Strategies

Establish Norms

Before beginning any professional learning, establish norms or ground rules for the sessions. If time permits or if norms have not typically been used before, the participants should have input when establishing these norms. More details about establishing norms from the National Staff Development Council can be found be found at https://learningforward.org/wp-content/uploads/2006/09/nsdc-tool.pdf.

Here is a sample of norms to consider:
- Honor time limits.
- Be present.
- Have an open mind and consider the possibilities.
- Minimize distractions (mobile phones, laptops, side conversations).
- Ask questions.
- Have a growth mindset!

Differentiate

Professional learning sessions should always model best practices in teaching and differentiation. Just like the classroom, teachers enter sessions with a wide range of understandings and backgrounds. Consider the following sample (using growth mindset thinking as the professional learning content) when planning for differentiated ongoing professional learning:

- **Content for the school year:** Focus will be on learning about the principles and concepts of growth and fixed mindsets. Educators will apply learning to themselves as well as their students.
- **Logistics:** Entire staff will attend a half-day session during preservice week and each quarter during professional learning days. There will be five sessions in total.
- **Preassess:** Gain an understanding of each participant's knowledge base regarding the principles of growth and fixed mindsets. Because mindset work affects a person's belief system, a reflection and/or preassessment should be given. It is also a good idea to try to capture what the team's beliefs are prior to any professional learning sessions—this will create a baseline that can be compared to at a later date. Educators may complete an online survey that includes scenarios of situations that may occur in the classroom. Send out this survey (electronically through Google Surveys, Survey Monkey, etc.) before the staff hears any discussion about mindsets in order to obtain true baseline data. Sending the same survey out again after at least a year of transforming practices will help measure growth. Figure 2.1 is an example of an educator mindset reflection tool that can be used prior to professional learning.
- **Evaluate the preassessment data and plan for the sessions:** If there is a large gap in knowledge, consider working with the group that needs to catch up on the learning first, and then work with the entire group.
- **Assess formatively:** As the presentation is happening and after each session, use the information to tweak the next session.
- **Engage learners by creating interactive sessions:** Ask questions, pause for reflection time, and build in time for conversation/discussions and hands-on learning. Have a "bin" or "parking lot" on the board or wall for questions that are specific to a teacher's situation. Circle back and address questions/comments in the "bin" at the end of a session.
- **Use examples from their content or grade level:** If the presentation is for multiple grade levels and content areas, choose examples that are generic or are in the middle of the grade range. With K–5

Educator's Mindset Reflection Tool

Please respond to the following scenarios according to what you personally would do if there were not outside influences or constraints (system or school expectations) on you. What do you feel is the BEST answer?

1. You have a child who is reading significantly below the rest of the class. Your English language arts class is about to start a text in which she has expressed significant interest. You plan to do the following:
   a. Give her a book on her reading level that deals with the same topic.
   b. Have her read the same book as everyone else—she's in this grade level and she has to read this.
   c. Have her read the book with a small group and provide frequent feedback.
   d. Have her read the abridged or graphic novel of the same text.

   Explain why you chose this response.

2. A student who consistently gets A's in other content areas fails one of your math tests. After determining the student is not having family or personal problems, what feedback do you give him?
   a. Math may not be your thing. Just try to pass!
   b. I'm here to help if you want it.
   c. You might want to change your strategy on how you're studying. You can do this!
   d. Nothing—the student will have to face the consequences of his actions.

   Explain why you chose this response.

Figure 2.1 Growth mindset tool. Developed with Claire E. Hughes-Lynch. From *Create a Growth Mindset School: An Administrator's Guide to Leading a Growth Mindset Community* (pp. 54–57), by M. C. Ricci, 2018, Prufrock Press. Copyright 2018 by Prufrock Press. Reprinted with permission.

3. Gifted education should:
   a. Identify students who are truly gifted and give them enrichment or acceleration opportunities.
   b. Provide differentiated enrichment and accelerated educational opportunities for all students.
   c. Identify students' interests and talents and provide development opportunities.
   d. Not exist—all students are gifted.

   Explain why you chose this response.

4. Special education should:
   a. Identify students with disabilities and provide remediation.
   b. Provide differentiated activities for multiple ways of learning for all students.
   c. Identify students who are struggling and provide supported education.
   d. Not exist—all students are special.

   Explain why you chose this response.

5. You have a student in your class who is normally well-behaved. This week, however, she does not stay on task and rarely finishes her work. You are currently studying current events, and you know that she is interested in science. How would you respond to her?
   a. Tell her that maybe current events isn't her "thing" and that next week, you will move on to a different topic.
   b. Give her work to do in science instead.
   c. Tell her that you appreciated the effort she put forth in the discussion.
   d. Ask her how she can see a connection between science and current events.

   Explain why you chose this response.

Figure 2.1. Continued.

6. You have a child who has been struggling significantly in your class. On today's test, he did very well. What do you say to him?

   a. Look how smart you are!
   b. I knew that you could do it!
   c. Looks like your hard work paid off!
   d. Nothing—he should be doing this well all the time.

   Explain why you chose this response.

7. You have an identified gifted child who is struggling with reading at grade level. You plan to put her in the following reading group:

   a. The low reading group, so that you can focus on her reading skills with similar students.
   b. A heterogeneous group, so that collaborative learning can be used.
   c. Self-selected groups, each focusing on a different text of interest.
   d. The high reading group, so that she can read challenging material.
   e. I don't group; all children get the same education based on the standards.

   Explain why you chose this response.

8. You have a child in special education who is reading just above grade level. You plan to put him in the following reading group:

   a. The low reading group, so that you don't pressure him and you can focus on his special needs.
   b. A heterogeneous group, so that collaborative learning can be used.
   c. Self-selected groups, each focusing on a different text of interest.
   d. The high reading group, so that he can read challenging material.
   e. I don't group; all children get the same education based on the standards.

   Explain why you chose this response.

Figure 2.1. Continued.

9. You have children with the following pre- and posttest scores:

Child	Pretest	Posttest
Noah	70%	85%
Jason	90%	95%
Ryan	10%	60%

Which child do you highlight as doing good work?
  a. Noah
  b. Jason
  c. Ryan
  d. None of them
  e. All of them

Explain why you chose this response.

10. You have a child who is identified as gifted and is struggling in your math class. You plan to do the following:

  a. Teach him the math at his level, or collaborate with another teacher to help him at this level.
  b. Teach him the math that everyone else is working on—he's in this grade level and has to keep up.
  c. Have the rest of the class work on the regular assignment and show him more advanced math and explain how the skill you're working on is important for understanding the advanced math.
  d. Have the rest of the class work on the regular assignment and reteach him the original instruction.

Explain why you chose this response.

Answer Key for #1–#10: A = Fixed, C = Growth

Figure 2.1. Continued.

teachers, choose a third-grade standard as an example—try to apply knowledge relevant to the specific group at the session.
- **Evaluate and monitor:** Provide an opportunity for participants to provide feedback about each session—don't wait until after the last session. Also, plan for ways that will evaluate understanding and monitor application of the learning.
- **Use a web service:** Collaboration tools like Google Classroom provide support to learners between sessions. Participants can use the space to ask questions, have conversations, and share ideas about implementation. Resources can also be stored in the space for participants to view and download. Google Classroom is set up for teachers and their students—but also works well for professional learning facilitators and their participants.

If possible, do preliminary planning for your growth mindset professional learning sessions with your leadership team. The team may discuss some of the following:
- Who will facilitate the professional learning sessions . . . the school administrator, a member of the school staff, central office staff, or an outside speaker or consultant?
- Are there funds available to hire an outside consultant/speaker?
- Should we partner with a neighboring school or district?
- Can we use a book study format (e.g., *Mindsets in the Classroom*; Ricci, 2017)? Will the book study be face-to-face, through an online discussion, or a hybrid?
- Will the calendar allow for at least quarterly professional learning sessions?
- What are some ways that we can monitor the application of what has been learned?

These questions can be discussed among a leadership team. Decide when the sessions will take place and make clear the expectations for attendance. If possible, invite every adult who works in the office or school to the sessions: the secretary, building service workers, cafeteria workers, etc. Consider inviting PTA (Parent Teacher Association) or PTO (Parent Teacher Organization) parent leaders. Sessions should be informative and interactive with time to reflect and plan. If some members of the staff already have a healthy knowledge of mindsets, then differentiate the learning, ask them to participate in planning the sessions, or have them develop a tool or platform that will help the school or district move forward with growth mindset thinking (Ricci, 2018).

Implications

What are the implications of planning for professional learning through a growth mindset lens? How might sessions look and feel different if growth mindset principles are front and center during planning and facilitating?

Here are a few questions to reflect upon during the planning process for professional learning sessions:
- What are some ways to gauge understanding of the topic before the session begins?
- Will there be time for participants to think about anticipated challenges or barriers and ways to address them?
- Do the plans include examples of ways to problem solve (persevere) if participants cannot easily implement the new learning?
- Will there be time for reflection throughout the session?

Once mindsets have been considered during the planning phase, it is time to consider mindsets during training. During the session, be willing to switch gears if what was planned is not meeting the needs of the group. Be prepared to eliminate entire sections and/or add new content to the presentations if the content does not meet the needs of the group, especially in the first meeting. I am usually prepared to do this, particularly if it is my first time with a group. For example, I was once invited for a second consecutive year to speak to a group of principals at a state education administrators' conference. I had already laid the groundwork the year before at this particular conference and was asked to facilitate a *Growth Mindset 2.0* presentation for the upcoming year. The conference planners asked that I present new content related to leading with a growth mindset, as well as go deeper into the content that was presented the year before. I planned an interactive, engaging session for the group and was excited about the session. However, after about the first 15–20 minutes, I learned that most of the group were new to the subject—there was a significant turnover in the principals that attended this conference and about half the group had not attended the session the year before. For half of the group, it was like asking them to start on Chapter 5 of a book without having read the first four chapters. I had to switch gears and create a balance of content for the newbies as well as content for the more experienced group.

During professional learning sessions, consider the questions and possible responses in Table 2.1.

What about your own mindset? Do you believe that all teachers can be effective? Do you believe that struggling teachers can improve with professional learning, constructive feedback, coaching, and practice? Reflect

Table 2.1
Professional Learning Questions and Possible Responses

Question to Reflect Upon	Possible Responses
◆ Does the group lack the prerequisite understanding of the content?	◆ Back it up to a place where they need to be. ◆ Ask big questions to ascertain understanding.
◆ Has the topic been "forced" upon the educators by the school or district administration?	◆ Acknowledge this possibility, and then connect the need for the session to a national or larger need in education. ◆ Get participants involved, ask questions, and interact with the group.
◆ Is the timing a challenge for the educators?	◆ Acknowledge this possibility, and be flexible if possible—shorten the session, give a follow-up task, and/or arrange for another session.
◆ Does the group already have a solid understanding of the content?	◆ Acknowledge the understanding. ◆ Ask for participants to contribute their ideas and thoughts about the content. ◆ Enrich their understanding by going deeper into the content. ◆ Adjust pacing—facilitate at a quicker pace on the areas where understanding is demonstrated.

on your own beliefs about teachers who participate in your sessions or those whom you work with—if you do not really believe that educators can improve with feedback, hard work, perseverance, and a cadre of strategies, then perhaps your own mindset is leaning toward fixed in this area. Make sure that you communicate (both verbally and nonverbally) to all teachers that you believe that they can grow and improve their skills.

How do you reflect on yourself as a facilitator and presenter? Do you take time to self-reflect? Do you consistently review session feedback from the participants? Does the format of participant feedback really give you the information that you need for growth?

My personal experience went something like this: I always look at feedback and am proactive about making changes to future sessions based on a pattern of feedback. But ... when I first began presenting, I was very hard on myself. Many years ago, I was reviewing feedback provided by school district participants after a session about changes in gifted and talented identification procedures. There were about 100 teachers in the session, and after the session, as I reviewed feedback, I learned that about 95% of them felt that the session was very helpful and they were leaving with a good knowledge of the process. The challenge that I faced was that I was hyperfocused on the 5% that were less favorable; I felt myself getting defensive about the comments that were written and forgot about the other 95% of people who learned during the session. Is it human nature to focus on the negative?

Consider using the following prompts when collecting feedback:
- As a result of today's session . . .
- I am thinking . . .
- I am challenged by or uncomfortable with . . .
- I am planning . . .

For more specific reflection from participants, try prompts like these:
- I have grown in my knowledge of . . .
- My anticipated challenges/barriers for implementation are . . .
- Things I can try to overcome those challenges or barriers . . .

Evaluations that ask participants to agree or disagree to statements like "The session helped me understand revised identification practices" do not provide enough information to reflect on. It is also important to build time into the session for participants to complete the evaluations, whether they are on paper or online. That will increase the number of participants who reflect and provide feedback—an exercise that is good for both participant and facilitator.

Summary

Keeping growth mindset principles front and center when planning and facilitating professional learning is essential in order for participants to get the most out of sessions. In order to maximize time, they need to be in the right mindset to learn. Additionally, facilitators building upon their own growth mindset behaviors will contribute to more effective learning.

There will often be setbacks along the way . . . that is how educators learn, improve, and grow. As a professional learning facilitator, make a concerted effort to apply growth mindset thinking. Growth mindset thinking allows facilitators to be more effective presenters and, therefore, provide more effective professional learning.

References

Dweck, C. S. (2016). *Mindset: The new psychology of success.* Ballantine Books. (Original work published 2006)

Olszewski-Kubilius, P., & Steenbergen-Hu, S. (2017, November 9–12). *How much have we understood overexcitability: The status of research and findings of a meta-analysis* [Conference session]. National Association for Gifted Children 64th Annual Convention, Charlotte, NC, United States.

Ricci, M. C. (2017). *Mindsets in the classroom: Building a growth mindset learning community* (Updated ed.). Prufrock Press.

Ricci, M. C. (2018). *Create a growth mindset school: An administrator's guide to leading a growth mindset community.* Prufrock Press.

CHAPTER 3

It's a Marathon, Not a Sprint:
Gifted Professional Learning and the Change Process From the Administrator's Shoes

Karen D. Jones and Angela M. Novak

Administrators take courses on policy, planning, and leadership. They are trained to enact change, observe teachers, hire and fire staff, and develop budgets. They oversee curriculum development, manage testing requirements, and put out metaphorical fires on a daily basis. But one area that administrators rarely have training is in gifted education. Without representation in federal legislation, special education case law, or national curriculum standards, gifted education is not a standard part of teacher training programs, educational specialist degrees, or administrative preparation programs. Simply stated, none of the typical paths to educational leadership are paved with gifted pedagogy.

Administrators facing gifted program challenges may need to acquire new skills and then push their faculty through the process of change so that the needs of gifted learners are being appropriately met. Change is not easy; it is a process that is more akin to a marathon than a sprint. It requires training, running for distance, cool down, and reflection. If seen as a simple race to the finish line, the change will likely falter or misfire. This chapter addresses gifted professional learning through the lens of the administrator: how the individual administrator learns through self-directed professional learning and how the principal then turns that knowledge into positive change for the school through action research.

From the Administrator's Shoes

Dr. Mikayla Jackson is second-year principal at Lafayette School in Wake Village in the rural Southeast. During her first year, she spent time getting the lay of the land and evaluating the systems in place in the school. In her doctoral program, she learned that it was important to make the changes she needed to make, not wanted to make. As she walked around her diverse school, she noted over the months that the gifted classroom did not reflect the population of the overall school. Dr. Jackson took some time to review the identification data and learned that the district's population is not represented in the overall gifted program for the district either. After a quick review of the research in the field, she determined that although neither her school nor her district is alone in this problem, it is a problem that is in dire need of strong action. In her principal preparation program, she did not focus on gifted learners or programming. Her first challenge was to learn more.

Preparing for the Race

One focus of principal preparation programs is enacting change in schools. In order to start a change process, the school leader needs to review multiple data sources to determine the problem focus and then the root of the problem. A common method for addressing change in schools is action research. This is reinforced by action research presentation strands at national conferences, such as the University Council of Educational Administration (UCEA) and the American Education Research Association (AERA).

Administrators are trained through their master's or doctoral programs in the processes of action research, with professional development or learning embedded in the process. Principal preparation programs teach several methods of professional development; the term *development* is used purposefully, as not all programs in higher education have shifted universally to professional learning-focused models. Self-directed professional learning (SDPL) can be a step embedded in the action research cycle, or its own initial step, prior to beginning the action research cycle. Figure 3.1 shows a model of an administrative approach to professional dilemmas used by Dr. Jackson in the case study presented in this chapter.

As described previously, Dr. Jackson came into the principalship with understandings of the change process from her administrative program. She established a first step of self-directed professional learning and engaged herself in goal setting to facilitate her own knowledge acquisition. This is discussed in the first leg of the marathon of Dr. Jackson's change process, the following section of the chapter (Mile 1: Self-Directed Professional Learning). Her next step will be to establish an action research project, per her training. She will then round out Mile 6 (The Action Research Cycle to Implement and Measure Change) with this plan and begin its implementation. The lengthiest discussion is focused on the professional learning aspects of Dr. Jackson's journey: the self-directed professional learning and the first phase of her action research cycle (Mile 13.2: People Focus). Limited attention is paid to the action research project steps in Mile 26.2, the Reflective Focus, although the steps are outlined for the full context of Dr. Jackson's thought processes and action research journey.

Mile 1: Self-Directed Professional Learning

As with many administrators, Dr. Jackson's first step was self-directed professional learning. She realized she did not have the knowledge base to tackle the issue of gifted disproportionality without acquiring new information. Best practices in professional learning include self-direction when in a school culture of professional learning (Zepeda, 2019). This self-directed professional learning can occur organically or through a more structured method.

Self-directed professional learning (SDPL) is driven from an individual's will to learn (Van Eekelen et al., 2006), and is based on individual needs and

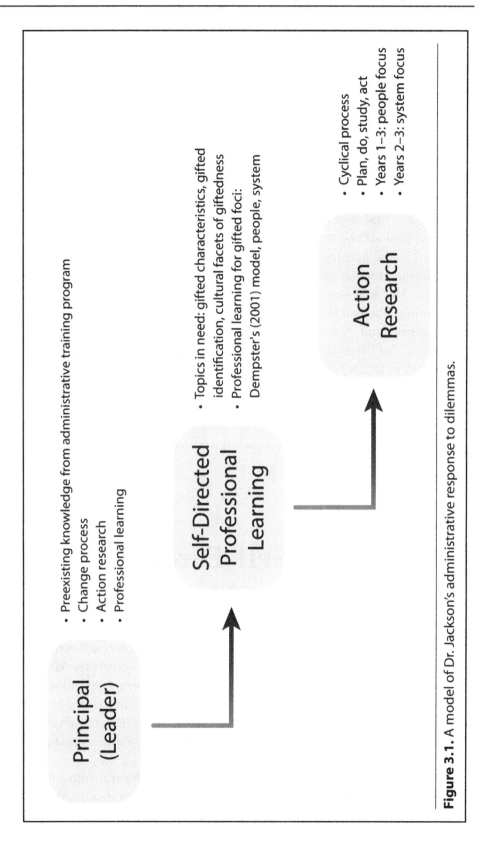

Figure 3.1. A model of Dr. Jackson's administrative response to dilemmas.

situation. An individual's internal processes allow them to build new understandings (Mushayikwa & Lubben, 2009). SDPL has been studied and found successful as a method to improve teaching practices (Beatty, 2000; Meng, 2014). Interestingly, there is a one principal component, self-direction, or the "will to learn," that has been shown to be a predictor of whether individuals are likely to implement new learning (Van Eekelen et al., 2006). Lopes and Cunha (2017) found that effective SDPL required (1) consistent will over several years, (2) implementation of several action research cycles, and (3) an explicit educational intentionality. The explicit intentionality comes when the leader of the professional learning process uses a variety of data to determine the best focus for that situation. Unfortunately, many leaders follow current trends in professional learning and do not explicitly determine their fit for the school's needs.

Croft (2018) described the QUEST model for professional learning for the sole practitioner in gifted education. QUEST is comprised of developing (q)uestions about the topic; listing (u)nderstandings currently held, while acknowledging that some understandings could be misconceptions; considering (e)motions related to the topic, both the practitioner's and others'; researching any published (s)tandards to provide guidance in the research and course of learning; and finally, (t)hinking about a plan of action, including developing goals, that will help thoroughly explore the topic (Croft, 2018). Whether following a systematic model such as QUEST, a more organic "will to learn" venture, or diving into action research with SDPL as the first step, a necessary practice in SDPL is gathering research and resources.

Finding the Right Gear: Research, Resources, and Models

The average administrator is unlikely to have had a great deal of exposure to gifted pedagogy. Those who do may have had experiences as gifted teachers, or they may have accumulated gifted knowledge by reacting to their environments and gained knowledge out of necessity. Access to information is at the fingertips of graduate students, but once they leave the hallowed halls of their institutions, research is not as readily accessible—or so administrators may think. Self-directed professional learning for gifted education, from content to tools, exists in many forms, but the administrator may not know where to turn.

Gifted Organizations. There are several national organizations for gifted education (see Table 3.1 for examples). Joining the organization or perusing the websites for information and resources is a first step for infor-

Table 3.1
Selected Organizations in Gifted Education That Provide Resources

Organization	Finding Resources	Website
National Association for Gifted Children (NAGC)	Information and Publications or Professional Learning tab	https://www.nagc.org
Supporting Emotional Needs of the Gifted (SENG)	Resources tab, then SENG Library	https://www.sengifted.org
The Association for the Gifted, Council for Exceptional Children (CEC-TAG)	Resources tab	https://cectag.com
World Council for Gifted and Talented Children	Resources tab	https://world-gifted.org
Davidson Institute	Search Database tab	https://www.davidsongifted.org

mation. Some organizations have newsletters or LISTSERVs for regular information, although sometimes publications are member benefits, available only if one joins. Other organizations may have a focus on student service but house a wealth of information and resources, such as the Davidson Institute.

The National Association for Gifted Children (NAGC) developed standards in gifted and talented education and, in collaboration with The Association for the Gifted, Council for Exceptional Children (CEC-TAG), on teacher preparation in gifted education. These standards are posted on the NAGC website (see https://www.nagc.org/resources-publications/resources/national-standards-gifted-and-talented-education) and are available for download. Such standards and structural guidance would meet Lopes's and Cunha's (2017) parameters of explicit educational intentionality, and clearly fit into Croft's (2018) QUEST goal of finding standards with which to align professional learning goals. Many states have their own advocacy groups or affiliates to the national organizations that can provide support. Table 3.2 provides websites that are not broad organizations but focus on information and resources around a given topic in gifted education.

In the age of digital information, knowledge abounds on the world wide web, but with the extent, or even excess, of information comes the added challenge of deciphering quality, perspective, and truth. Digital literacy is

Table 3.2
Selected Websites That Provide Resources in Gifted Education

Site Name	Topics	Website
Hoagies' Gifted Education Page	Various gifted topics	https://www.hoagiesgifted.org
The 2e Resource	Twice-exceptionality	https://2eresource.com/
2e News	Twice-exceptionality	https://www.2enews.com
Equity in Gifted/Talented (G/T) Education	Equity in gifted education; focused on Texas but transferable	http://www.gtequity.org
Teaching Tolerance	Teacher support for diversity and equity	https://www.tolerance.org

an important skill for all stakeholders in education, from students to administration to community members.

Local Colleges and Universities. Although the administrator may have finished their last degree, be it an Ed.S., M.A., or Ed.D., it doesn't mean that the resources available at the university library are out of reach. Many local colleges offer local teachers the library cards or teacher resource cards for their online resources. In addition, many local municipal libraries and school systems' libraries have databases that can access research articles. Beyond print and digital resources, local colleges and universities have a depth of human resources. An administrator can approach a local college of education with a gifted degree, endorsement program or experts in the field for support on gifted education pedagogy and practices, and work to establish a collaborative partnership.

School-university collaborations can range from simple to complex, from asking for a one-time training to establishing a long-term research project (Brulles, 2019; Farah, 2019). Brulles (2019) offered several examples of collaboration that benefit administrators and their schools, including "free resources and training, supporting district curriculum and instruction, informing assessments, providing valuable information and unbiased feedback, encouraging close examination of existing services, allowing teachers to learn from experts in the field . . . and building partnerships with leaders in the field" (p. 81). Establishing a collaborative relationship with a university may begin with a goal of self-directed professional learning but can extend far beyond.

There is potential for collaborations between local colleges and universities that benefit a wide array of stakeholders: students, teachers, researchers, curriculum developers, and the broader gifted community through the advancement of the field. A recent special issue of *Gifted Child Today* was devoted to the collaboration between universities and school districts. In one article from this issue, the author described the partnership as mutually beneficial: "This collaboration can be characterized as a win-win situation for both parties, as well as to the field of gifted education. . . . For all the teachers and the students, participating in a research university collaboration is a compelling learning experience" (West Keur, 2019, p. 91). Depending on the level of systemic change, a principal can collaborate with a local college in order to help develop a plan, implement the plan, or even take the action research to a higher level through support and training. Administrators, especially those without a background in gifted education, may find university partnerships valuable resources for social justice and change in their schools.

From the Administrator's Shoes

Dr. Jackson contacted her university mentor, Dr. Jubala, who reminded her that she should not only explore self-directed professional learning on gifted education, but also review professional learning as a topic. Dr. Jubala also reminded Dr. Jackson about Dempster's (2001) model that they studied in class, saying that it sounded like she had both a people focus and a system focus in her problem of gifted disproportionality. Dr. Jackson reviewed the model and continued to look into other professional learning models in gifted education.

Models of Professional Learning. Professional development is the experiential process of gathering skills and professional knowledge (Mushayikwa & Lubben, 2009; Vonk, 1991). Traditional professional development in schools is criticized, in part, because educators are not involved in choosing the content (Gravani, 2007; van Veen et al., 2012). Guskey (2002) identified goals of professional development that included change in attitude and beliefs of teachers and change in learning outcomes for students. A range of activities can move professional development into the realm of professional learning, including reflection, conversation, and peer coaching (Day, 1999; Haigh, 2005; Zwart et al., 2007). As a result of this learning, there may be shifts in an individual's behavior, attitude, and intellect (Evans, 2011).

As administrators learn more about gifted education and accomplish their first goal of self-directed professional learning, they must then set the next benchmark: change in practices at the school level through professional learning of their faculty and staff. Dempster's (2001) model of professional development, based on Burrell and Morgan's (1979) paradigm of social theory, is useful for administrators when considering whether they need to work on changing the system or support their teachers in understanding and working within the system. In Dempster's (2001; Dempster et al., 2012) model, two intersecting continua are used to define four orientations of professional development: System Restructuring, System Maintenance, Professional Sustenance, and Professional Transformation. The x-axis represents a "people focus" versus a "system focus," and the y-axis represents "reproduction" versus "reconstruction" of systems (see Figure 3.2).

In a System Maintenance approach, a principal's learning is competency-based and linked to enduring educational practices set by a central authority. In a System Restructuring approach, professional development focuses on how to make changes in the structure and function of schools. In a Professional Sustenance orientation, learning emphasizes issues arising from "on the job" school management practices and is linked to principals' definition of professional identity. Finally, Professional Transformation concentrates on learning that enables principals to (1) undertake constructive, social, and organizational critique; (2) question taken-for-granted understandings; and (3) reconstruct schooling in alternative ways.

Understanding modes and models of professional learning, as well as the process of teacher change, is an important component of the administrator's journey through self-directed professional learning. These factors can help the administrator understand the faculty and their perspectives throughout the change process, using work such as Guskey's (2002) theory, as well as help the administrator establish a plan for moving forward and determining the focus of the needed change, using Dempster's (2001) model, for example. Understanding where and how to find the resources, and what resources are needed, is an essential first step. Resources alone, however, are not enough; self-directed professional learning is best supported through a structured plan.

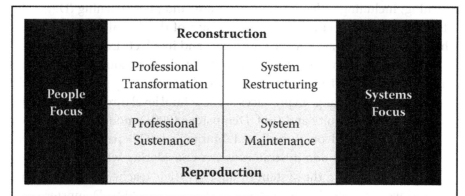

Figure 3.2. Representation of Dempster's model of professional development (Dempster, 2001; Dempster et al., 2012).

The Training Plan: Designing Self-Directed Professional Learning in Gifted Education

Self-directed professional learning should be systematic, sustained, purposeful, and job-embedded (Croft, 2018; Lopes & Cunha, 2017; Van Eekelen et al., 2006). Several of these echo best practices in professional learning in gifted education, specifically sustained, embedded and immediately transferable, and aligned with goals and data-driven. In addition, qualities of collaborative, reflective, and active learning through various modalities are themes in the literature of gifted professional learning (Combs & Silverman, 2016). Thus, for gifted self-directed professional learning for administrators, a plan that enumerates these combined qualities is ideal. (See also Novak [2019] for a discussion of these qualities, as elements of this section have been adapted with permission of the author.)

Establish Goals Based on Current Questions. How individuals acquire new learning is discussed by many scholars. Knowles (1984) proposed that adults have self-direction and approach learning to solve problems. Eraut (2004) indicated that informal learning is a combination of learning from others and personal experience. Another learning example shows learning as reactive and takes place in action, in response to a situation (Mitchell, 2013). All three have a central theme of a goal, question, problem, or experience at the core. The world of gifted education is extensive, and administrators can't learn everything overnight. In order to focus on priorities, a principal might conduct a needs assessment of staff, stakeholders, or a personal inventory. Establishing priorities and setting goals are helpful in determining what path of professional learning research to follow first.

Acquire Understandings Through Multiple Modalities. Research journals and library sources are available and accessible, but not the sole source of knowledge. Administrators can seek new understandings through a variety of modalities and methods—just as they will present the understandings to their staff in various ways. In the presented scenario, Dr. Jackson is struggling with a common issue in schools across the country, the underrepresentation of diverse students in gifted programs. Table 3.3 offers suggested resources that would assist Dr. Jackson, arranged in multiple modalities. Conferences and institutes are offered throughout the year, depending on one's location, and several organizations, such as NAGC and SENG, offer webinars on a regular basis. Social media can also be an informative outlet. The Texas Association for the Gifted and Talented (TAGT, 2019) facilitates a chat on a new topic every week, in which experts and beginners respond to the same prompts using the hashtag gtchat (#gtchat) in order to consolidate responses.

Question, Connect, Reflect. Key components of meaningful professional learning are questioning the knowledge you are receiving, questioning your previous knowledge, making connections to current and past practices, and reflecting on all of the above. Slade (2018) highlighted several essentials in reflective practice in gifted professional learning: reflection-in-action, in which one reflects during a situation, thinking and doing concurrently; and reflection-on-action, in which one considers the outcome of changes made. Slade indicated that "professional learning is enhanced when there is buy-in from participants, which occurs when one is empowered to take charge of his or her own personal learning. Reflection allows educators to take control of their growth and development" (p. 46).

Seek Out or Begin an Administrators' PLC on Topics in Gifted Education. Collaborative reflection benefits the individuals seeking professional learning, as well as having an impact on the organization and community (Slade, 2018). Thus, rather than learning in isolation, administrators may seek out a group of like-minded administrators in their district, or neighboring districts, who have similar questions or concerns, and establish a professional learning community (PLC). Although they can exist in a variety of forms, PLCs generally involve a cyclical approach, based on a common problem or topic, often implementing action research of some kind that is brought back to the group to reflect on and discuss. A book study or discussion group would also be an opportunity for collegial reflection.

Repeat. Professional learning is iterative. It is sustained, ongoing, and cyclical. This is partially due to the research-based best practices of professional learning that embody these very characteristics (Combs & Silverman, 2016; Troxclair et al., 2017). One book, one meeting with an expert, one video, or one webinar is not sufficient. Learning is ongoing; it is a lifelong

Table 3.3
Selected Suggested Resources in
Diversity/Equity Issues in Gifted Education

Books	• *Multicultural Gifted Education* (2nd ed.), by D. Y. Ford (Prufrock Press, 2011) • *Culturally Diverse and Underserved Populations of Gifted Students*, edited by A. Y. Baldwin (Corwin, 2004) • *Effective Program Models for Gifted Students from Underserved Populations*, edited by C. M. Adams and K. L. Chandler (Prufrock Press, 2014) • *Start Seeing and Serving Underserved Gifted Students: 50 Strategies for Equity and Excellence*, by J. Ritchotte, C.-W. Lee, and A. Graefe (Free Spirit, 2020)
Other Readings	• "National Standards in Gifted and Talented Education" (https://www.nagc.org/resources-publications/resources/national-standards-gifted-and-talented-education) • "What Is the Excellence Gap?" (https://www.jkcf.org/our-research/what-is-the-excellence-gap) • *Unlocking Emergent Talent: Supporting High Achievement of Low-Income, High-Ability Students*, by P. Olszewski-Kubilius and J. Clarenbach (https://www.nagc.org/sites/default/files/key%20reports/Unlocking%20Emergent%20Talent%20(final).pdf) • *In Search of the Dream*, edited by C. A. Tomlinson (https://www.nagc.org/sites/default/files/key%20reports/In%20Search%20of%20(2009%20final).pdf)
Webinars	• "Identifying and Serving Gifted Students of Poverty" (NAGC webinar: https://www.youtube.com/watch?v=yZ9yg_bChzU) • "Guiding Gifted Programming from a District Leadership Perspective" (NAGC webinar: https://www.youtube.com/watch?v=w3ZA8wTDWNs) • "Beyond Color Blindness-Effective Instructional Strategies for Culture-Sensitive Classrooms" (NAGC webinar: https://www.youtube.com/watch?v=_O9sIM-l_KM) • "SENGinar: Identifying Under-served Gifted Populations With Leslie Hosey" (https://vimeo.com/ondemand/senginar20160825/191189143)
Movies/Videos	• "Chimamanda Ngozi Adichie: The Danger of a Single Story" (https://www.ted.com/talks/chimamanda_ngozi_adichie_the_danger_of_a_single_story) • "Giftedness Is Not a Number: A Conversation With Nancy Hertzog" (https://www.youtube.com/watch?v=sX6H1qW3Xsc) • *2e: Twice Exceptional* and *2e2: Teaching the Twice Exceptional* • "Rethinking Gifted Education With Scott Peters" (https://www.youtube.com/watch?v=fgmEswWEd6k)

process. In the case of Dr. Jackson, when cultural responsiveness is the facet of the content, a continuum exists, and individuals strive to move forward on the continuum of multicultural pedagogy, but there is always more to learn (Lindsey et al., 2018).

Mile 6: The Action Research Cycle to Implement and Measure Change

Self-directed professional learning can, and often does, incorporate action research. Although initial training provides educational professionals with basic levels of knowledge and skills to begin their careers (Herbert & Rainford, 2014), often that knowledge in preservice programs is theoretical and disconnected from practice (Gomez, 1997). Educational practice is better understood as a reflective practice or a merger of theory and application (Brockbank & McGill, 2007; Lopez-Pastor et al., 2011; Schön, 1984). Action research is one method for the connection of theory, practice, and reflection. Research shows that action research supports an individual's development and reinforces the relationship between theory and practice (Fairclough, 2003; O'Grady, 2008). Osses (2008) found that action research cycles improved educators' professional capacity and autonomy. Action research is a rewarding form of SDPL for educators due to their ownership of the content and process (Craft, 2000).

One form of action research is systemic action research that engages stakeholders and processes across organizational systems. Lewin (1997) described a field of relationships within an organization that are interconnected. Changes in one part of the system create changes throughout the system. According to Coghlan and Brydon-Miller (2014), "It can be effective to create changes in parts of the system that do not initially seem to be the centre of concern" (p. 749). Systemic action research focuses on changing system dynamics within an organization by making small changes that lead to larger shifts. Systemic action research practitioners often focus on complex problems that have conflicts of interests of the participants (Coghlan & Brydon-Miller, 2014). Burns (2007) stated that to fully make changes within a system, it is essential to begin at multiple contacts within the organization.

Principals leading schoolwide professional learning, such as through action research or PLCs, are most successful with a democratic leading style (Gordon, 2008). Two-way communication, collaboration, and inquiry associated with successful professional learning cannot thrive under authoritarian leadership (Glickman et al., 2018). It is productive to allow all members of the school community to investigate potential benefits and commitments associated with the professional learning (Gordon, 2008). In moving from self-directed professional learning to creating a specific action research plan that focuses on gifted identification and representation, it is clear a change at some level will be needed, but is it a change through professional learning and training of teachers, or is it a change in the identification system itself?

Planning a Route for Success

There are multiple possible approaches to leading change in a school; action research is a common method taught in many principal preparation programs, as it creates change with people by people. There are varying methods to action research—this is a familiar concept to those in gifted education, which has several theoretical frameworks and definitions. Mertler (2020) described approaches by Stringer (looking, thinking, acting); Lewin (find facts, plan, take action, evaluate, amend, take second action); Bachman (gathering information, planning actions, observing and evaluating, reflecting and planning); and Riel (plan, take action, collect evidence, reflect). Each of these has similar threads woven through, as does Mertler's (2020) own cycle of "the planning stage, the acting stage, the developing stage, the reflecting stage" (p. 17).

Many administration programs use the plan, do, study, act approach, as initially mentioned in Figure 3.1, in the action research step. This action research cycle was first introduced by Walter Shewhart in 1939 as plan, do, check, and act. It was further refined by W. E. Deming as the Deming Wheel in 1950, then the Shewhart Cycle in 1986, and finally evolved into the Plan, Do, Study, Act (PDSA) cycle in 1993 (Moen & Norman, 2010). PDSA is an action research cycle, but it is also used a change model and project planning tool (Tague, 2005). In the PDSA model, the four steps are:

- **Plan:** Recognize the opportunity for change/action research; analyze data or research; establish steps: list concrete tasks, responsible individuals, timelines.
- **Do:** Carry out the plan/test the change; follow the list of tasks.
- **Study:** Review/analyze what happened based on the plan; describe what happened and collate data; be explicit about what was learned from the implementation.

- **Act:** Take action based on what was learned, in most cases this is used to change/adjust the next cycle of the action research project, but the results can be used to implement change.

The goal of action research is to work with stakeholders. In this scenario, Dr. Jackson realizes that she needs to not only focus on the systems in place in the school around the nomination and selection of students for the gifted program, but also work with people to change mindsets and culture. The action research plan (see Figure 3.3) will consist of multiple cycles of improvement, each influencing the next, as required in any action research cycle method.

Before establishing her action research plan, Dr. Jackson spent time learning the school environment and conducting self-directed professional learning on gifted education and professional development models to determine the framework of a people and systems focus (Dempster, 2001). Action research benefits from grounding in a frame or lens in order to have a theoretical framework or approach to the work (Mertler, 2020). Understanding that action research is cyclical and that one stage can inform the next is an important part of the action research process, and the iterative nature is essential to the work. Although Figure 3.3 outlines the full action research plan in order to paint a full picture of the action research process, this chapter only details the people focus, the first round of the cycle on professional learning for faculty. We have, however, provided some insight into the systems focus in Mile 26.2.

From the Administrator's Shoes

Dr. Jackson felt empowered by her self-directed professional learning, as she gained new knowledge in gifted education. She decided to meet with the gifted teacher in her building to discuss the trends that she noticed. Maria Hernandez has been working at Lafayette School for 10 years, first as a fifth-grade teacher, and has been in the gifted resource position for 3 years. Tears welled up in her eyes as Dr. Jackson gently approached her with the observations. "Yes, Dr. Jackson, this is a significant issue! But my hands are tied. It's the identification system. This is who I have to have in the program. But the system is missing so many students. It is not working well." Together, they decided that they will take action. During her summer meet-

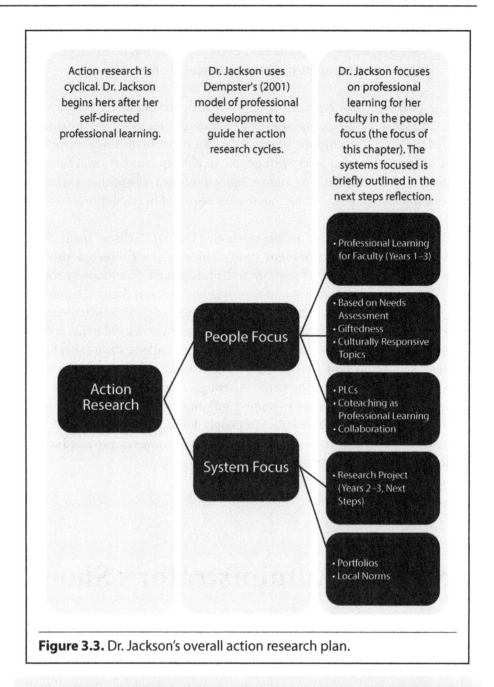

Figure 3.3. Dr. Jackson's overall action research plan.

ing with the superintendent, Dr. Jackson set her professional growth goal and determined that she will conduct a multiple yearlong systemic action research project so that she can report on the results of the implementation of the action research with the superintendent.

Dr. Jackson reflected on her studies from her principal preparation program and decided on a frame for her action research project that will best fit her goals for the school and herself. She wrote the following down

and posted it above her computer as a way to frame her thinking about her action plan:
- Prong 1: People Focus; professional learning on giftedness and culturally responsive practices
- Prong 2: Systems Focus; focused action research project on a specific strategy, using portfolios to increase representation

With a long-term plan in mind, she was ready to get started on the people focus, professional learning in her school.

Mile 13.2: People Focus

Socialization is the process by which individuals acquire the values and attitudes, interests and dispositions, skills, and knowledge in the group in which they are members (Merton, 1963). Because many new principals struggle with socialization into their new schools (Daresh, 1987), it is generally recommended in school administration programs that new principals make few, if any, large changes in their first year. Learn the culture and procedures of the school is important before making changes to the system. Often, it is in the second year and beyond that principals take on challenges of change to school culture, climate, and procedures. They want to find the appropriate learning plan for success.

From the Administrator's Shoes

Dr. Jackson waited until her second year to take on the challenge of disproportionality in the gifted program. Her first goal was the people focus; in order to create lasting change in the school, work must be done with teachers and staff to ensure a culturally responsive environment for all students. At the same time, she decided to implement ongoing professional learning for her faculty throughout the school year to meet the needs of diverse learners in the gifted program. Specifically, the professional learning will help develop the understandings of her teachers and staff around culturally responsive gifted identification.

Leadership and Professional Learning

Professional learning is an integral part of the school and is necessary for student growth and school improvement (Lieberman, 1995). School leaders can exert a direct impact on a teacher's professional learning (Pedder & Opfer, 2010). School-level factors can influence a teacher's professional learning, including a clear school vision on the part of the leader and teachers' participation in decision making (Mitchell, 2013). Although much of professional learning focuses on the deficits of teachers, Brown and McIntyre (1993) believed more benefit comes when building on present strengths and allowing for teacher self-analysis of their skills. When administrators facilitate the creation of a group vision or growth statement with faculty in which ideas and goals are identified and prioritized, they are bringing the teachers into the decision-making process and providing an element of self-direction and buy-in.

A needs assessment is a useful tool in the creation of a vision and/or in the planning of professional learning experiences, allowing a whole-staff approach to growth. As strengths, interests, and needs are identified, faculty are arranged into leaders and learners. These groups and placements can be flexibly arranged based on topic; as teachers differentiate learning for gifted students, so should professional learning meet the needs of teachers who work with gifted learners (Gilson, 2018).

Professional Learning Communities

Schoolwide professional learning can be complicated and too dependent on teacher involvement for school administrators to lead by themselves (Gordon, 2008). Teacher leadership is needed in various roles during the professional learning process. Teachers can be involved at different levels of the professional learning implementation throughout the school. Some may lead grade-level or department teams; others may work on a school improvement or professional learning team. Teacher input is necessary for buy-in at all stages of the professional learning process. PLCs reframe a school as a learning organization (MacBeth & Dempster, 2009; Senge et al., 2012). PLCs are often created by school leaders (principals) and build on the ideas of democratic social learning (Day & Sachs, 2004; Wenger, 1998). Through PLCs, a network of teacher leaders can develop. These nonsupervisory school leaders can present ongoing site-based professional development for teachers (Poekert, 2012). Unlike traditional, top-down professional development, PLCs can facilitate the balanced development of shared goals for school improvement (Mitchell, 2013). Principals can share the task of instructional leadership with teacher leaders to create a thriving learning organization.

Professional Learning Through Coteaching

A schoolwide, teacher-led approach to professional learning for gifted education that administrators can enact is coteaching. Fogarty and Tschida (2018) described several methods of coteaching that benefit both teachers involved. The strength in coteaching is the ability to learn from each other's specializations, so that by working together, a coaching relationship develops; coteachers engage each other in professional discourse and challenging ideas. A gifted and special education teacher may be paired to coteach differentiation strategies to the faculty or model a differentiated lesson in a classroom. The paired teachers are then providing professional learning to their peers while simultaneously learning from each other to establish combined knowledge of twice-exceptionality, an often-underrepresented population in gifted programs.

Culturally Responsive Professional Learning Through Coaching

Multicultural, culturally responsive, and *diversity* are terms specifically used in the majority of the seven NAGC-CEC Teacher Preparation Standards in Gifted and Talented Education, as is *collaboration* (NAGC & CEC-TAG, 2013). Culturally responsive teachers create classroom climates conducive to learning by members of different groups, using "cultural scaffolding" (Gay, 2002, p. 109), or using their own cultures and experiences to expand intellectual growth and achievement. Coaching also provides support in the process of culturally responsive learning for the teacher. Through targeted professional learning, teachers are coached first through the confrontation of their previously held beliefs and in the reflection on their own practices (von Glasserfeld, 2001). Ideally, coaching (1) supports the whole teacher in identifying how culture mediates one's cognitive engagement and how to honor these differing styles, and (2) facilitates teachers' reflection on and implementation of this knowledge (Farmer et al., 2005). The resources in Table 3.4 provide sources for teachers and administrators who wish to grow their own professional learning in the area of culturally responsive gifted education.

Table 3.4
Professional Learning Resources for Administrators on Culturally Responsive Gifted Topics and PLCs

Resources on Creating PLCs	• *Demystifying Professional Learning Communities: School Leadership at Its Best*, by K. Hipp and J. Bumpers Huffman (Rowman & Littlefield, 2010) • *Professional Learning Communities by Design: Putting the Learning Back into PLCs*, by L. B. Easton (Corwin, 2011) • *The School Leader's Guide to Professional Learning Communities at Work*, by R. DuFour and R. DuFour (Solution Tree Press, 2012) • *Learning by Doing: A Handbook for Professional Learning Communities at Work* (3rd ed.), by R. DuFour et al. (Solution Tree Press, 2016)
Gifted Professional Learning Resources	• *Best Practices in Professional Learning and Teacher Preparation* (Vols. 1 and 2), edited by A. M. Novak and C. L. Weber (Prufrock Press, 2018, 2019) • *Leading for Differentiation: Growing Teachers Who Grow Kids*, by C. A. Tomlinson and M. Murphy (ASCD, 2015) • *Exploring Critical Issues in Gifted Education: A Case Studies Approach*, by C. L. Weber, C. Boswell, and W. A. Behrens (Prufrock Press, 2014)
Culturally Responsive Resources	• *Culturally Responsive Teaching: Theory, Research, and Practice* (2nd ed.), by G. Gay (Teachers College Press, 2010) • *Strategies and Lessons for Culturally Responsive Teaching: A Primer for K–12*, by R. Chartrock (Pearson, 2009) • Teaching Tolerance (https://www.tolerance.org) • *Diversity in the Classroom: A Multicultural Approach to the Education of Young Children*, by F. E. Kendall (Teachers College Press, 1983)

Mile 26.2: The Reflective Focus

The race is over, but do not stop moving. Cool down, stretch, breathe . . . reflect. Action research is cyclical, and professional learning is ongoing, sustained, and recursive. Reflection mirrors this cyclical nature, and it is an essential element in gifted professional learning, both independent and collaborative (Slade, 2018). As the first cycle of action research and professional learning come to a close at the end of the year and Dr. Jackson writes up a report, reflection is a necessary step. If possible, the report would benefit from a survey of stakeholders (students, faculty, community) regarding their perceptions of changes made. Any applicable data can be collected for the report, such as nomination or referral rates, identification rates, and test scores. The final phase of the action research cycle, act, puts procedures into place based on the cycle that just finished and leaves the principal poised to reflect on next steps. Change is not just about people, but also about the systems in which they operate. Dr. Jackson knew that a people focus was not the only solution; even with new mindsets and a desire to push needed change, teachers were stuck in the systems and processes of the school and district, trying to enact the change they now know is necessary.

From the Administrator's Shoes

In planning for systems change in professional learning, Dr. Jackson considered the culture of the school, the level of change needed, and the pace by which that change could successfully be implemented. Dr. Jackson felt that one change per year would be a reasonable approach. In consultation with the action research team, a group of teachers that volunteered to be part of the project led by Dr. Jackson and the gifted resource teacher, she approached the district office for gifted programs with their ideas regarding new identification protocol: portfolios and local norms. The school board approved an action research project focus on portfolios over 2 years (from this point; in years 2 and 3 of Dr. Jackson's overall action research plan).

The team would begin studying information, reviewing related literature and developing a research plan over the summer, as well as attend targeted training on using portfolios. In the fall, the team should have a research plan ready to implement. They will collect and analyze the data over the course of the year in a portfolio-based action research plan. The selected teachers will gather portfolio samples on students and take part in the school-level identification team, so that they can evaluate the portfolios as part of the gifted identification system. As part of data analysis, the research team can then compare referral data and identification rates, to see if the portfolio system impacted the representation in the gifted program. The team will end the year with a summary of research questions, the findings, and recommended actions based on this information (Mertler, 2020). Dr. Jackson will round out the second year of her action research plan with reports that share the results of the systems research project and reflect on the process

> The action research plan continues through the summer; the second phase of the systems research project begins, following a similar process, focusing on local norms. Throughout the entire process, the people focus of the action research plan, professional learning for faculty, is ongoing.

Planning the Next Race: Action Research Resources for Equity in Gifted

Dr. Jackson has specific goals for her action research project; she has a focused interested in increasing the diversity of her gifted program and ensuring that it is representative of the school population. In developing an action research plan focused on this topic, the resources in Table 3.5 may be of value to administrators like Dr. Jackson.

Taking Another Lap: Professional Learning Is Ongoing

Dr. Jackson's story started with self-directed professional learning and when she moved on to the people focus and started implementing a professional learning plan, her personal self-directed professional learning continued. Eventually, as described in her overall action research plan, the people focus will transition to a system focus with yet another action research project; thus the professional learning will remain constant all 3 years, and ideally, the self-directed professional learning will continue. As the systems focus develops in more depth, action research ideas become plans, plans are implemented into classrooms, data are analyzed, and the cyclical process of action research begins again.

Summary

This chapter described an administrator, Dr. Jackson, who realized that there was disproportionality in her school's gifted program through observations and engaging with her students. Her thoughts were confirmed by

Table 3.5
Resources to Consider When Developing an Action Plan for Addressing Disproportionality

Action Research Resources	• *Action Research: Improving Schools and Empowering Educators* (6th ed.), by C. A. Mertler (SAGE, 2019) • *Collaborative Action Research: Developing Professional Learning Communities*, edited by S. P. Gordon (Teachers College Press, 2008) • *Action Research in Education* (2nd ed.), by E. Stringer (Pearson, 2007)
Local Norms Resources	• "Gifted and Talented: Finding and Calculating Representation Rates" (https://www.nagc.org/blog/gifted-and-talented-finding-and-calculating-representation-rates) • Office of Civil Rights Data Collection (https://ocrdata.ed.gov/DistrictSchoolSearch) • *Excellence Gaps in Education: Expanding Opportunities for Talented Students*, by J. A. Plucker and S. J. Peters (Harvard Education Press, 2016)
Portfolio Resources	• U-STARS PLUS and TOPS Folders (learn more on the CEC-TAG website, including webinar of the program) • Total Talent Portfolio (https://gifted.uconn.edu/schoolwide-enrichment-model/ttp) • "Portfolio: An Effective Way to Present your Child to the School," by C. N Neville-Garrison (https://www.davidson-gifted.org/search-database/entry/a10110)

reviewing data; thus, both quantitative and qualitative data supported the need for change and pushed her to act. Dr. Jackson's first step in making change was self-directed professional learning. This form of professional learning is common for school administrators who are often alone in their role on their campus or feel that they do not have the expertise to address a specific issue without additional information first. This professional learning led her to gather data and current research. She determined the need to approach both the people and the systems at work in her school's gifted program and referral process. Dr. Jackson used action research to meet both needs, creating a plan for self-directed professional learning and an action research project—both of which are recommended as best practices by administrative training and support associations in the field.

This exemplar, although not a perfect fit for all administrators, can be adapted to meet the needs of administrators in different settings. Resources provided, particular to this case, are examples of what can be found in similar settings on a variety of other topics that pertain to administrators facing challenges with regard to their gifted learners and programs. It is through self-directed professional learning, growth and change with a systems and/or people focus, and system action research that administrators can make a positive change in their "content areas," providing professional learning for their faculty and effecting systemic change in their schools.

References

Beatty, B. R. (2000). Teachers leading their own professional growth: Self-directed reflection and collaboration and changes in perception of self and work in secondary school teachers, *Journal of In-Service Education, 26*(1), 73–97. https://doi.org/10.1080/13674580000200102

Brockbank, A., & McGill, I. (2007). *Facilitating reflective learning in higher education* (2nd ed.). Open University Press.

Brown, S. A., & McIntyre, D. (1993). *Making sense of teaching.* Open University Press.

Brulles, D. (2019). School district and researcher collaboration: A school administrator's practice and perspective. *Gifted Child Today, 42*(2), 81–85. https://doi.org/10.1177/1076217518825372

Burns, D. (2007). *Systemic action research: A strategy for whole system change.* Bristol University Press.

Burrell, G., & Morgan, G. (1979). *Sociological paradigms and organisational analysis* (2nd ed.). Routledge. https://doi.org/10.4324/9781315609751

Coghlan, D., & Brydon-Miller, M. (Eds.). (2014). *The SAGE encyclopedia of action research.* SAGE.

Combs, E., & Silverman, S. (2016). *Bridging the gap: Paving the pathway from current practice to exemplary professional learning.* Frontline Research & Learning Institute. https://www.frontlineinstitute.com/uploads/2018/08/ESSA_Bridging_the_Gap_FINAL.pdf

Craft, A. (2000). *Continuing professional development.* Routledge/Falmer.

Croft, L. J. (2018). Professional learning in gifted education: Challenges for the sole practitioner. In A. M. Novak & C. L. Weber (Eds.), *Best practices in professional learning and teacher preparation: Methods and strategies for gifted professional development* (Vol. 1., pp. 137–150). Prufrock Press.

Daresh, J. C. (1987, April). *The highest hurdles for the first year principal* [Paper presentation]. Annual Meeting of the American Educational Research Association, Washington, DC, United States.

Day, C. (1999). Professional development and reflective practice: purposes, processes and partnerships. *Pedagogy, Culture & Society, 7*(2), 221–233.

Day, C., & Sachs, J. (2004). Professionalism, performativity and empowerment: Discourses in the politics, policies and purposes of continuing professional development. In C. Day & J. Sachs (Eds.), *International handbook on the continuing professional development of teachers* (pp. 3–32). Open University Press.

Dempster, N. (2001, May). *The professional development of school principals: A fine balance* [Paper presentation]. Griffith University Public Lecture Series, Queensland, Australia.

Dempster, N., Benfield, G., & Richard Francis, R. (2012). An academic development model for fostering innovation and sharing in curriculum design. *Innovations in Education and Teaching International, 49*(2), 135–147. https://doi.org/10.1080/14703297.2012.677595

Eraut, M. (2004). Informal learning in the workplace. *Studies in Continuing Education, 26*(2), 247–273. https://doi.org/10.1080/158037042000225245

Evans, L. (2011). The 'shape' of teacher professionalism in England: Professional standards, performance management, professional development and the changes proposed in the 2010 White paper. *British Educational Research Journal, 37*(5), 851–870. https://doi.org/10.1080/01411926.2011.607231

Fairclough, N. (2003). *Analysing discourse: Textual analysis for social research*. Routledge.

Farah, Y. N. (2019). Collaborative partnership: Opening doors between schools and universities. *Gifted Child Today, 42*(2), 74–80. https://doi.org/10.1177/1076217518822679

Farmer, J., Hauk, S., & Neumann, A. M. (2005). Negotiating reform: Implementing process standards in culturally responsive professional development. *The High School Journal, 88*(4), 59–71.

Fogarty, E. A., & Tschida, C. M. (2018). Using coteaching as a model of professional learning. In A. M. Novak & C. L. Weber (Eds.), *Best practices in professional learning and teacher preparation: Methods and strategies for gifted professional development* (Vol. 1, pp. 151–172). Prufrock Press.

Gay, G. (2002). Preparing for culturally responsive teaching. *Journal of Teacher Education, 53*(2), 106–116. https://doi.org/10.1177/0022487102053002003

Gilson, C. (2018). Moving toward differentiated professional learning for teachers learning to differentiate for gifted students. In A. M. Novak &

C. L. Weber (Eds.), *Best practices in professional learning and teacher preparation: Methods and strategies for gifted professional development* (Vol. 1, pp. 93–120). Prufrock Press.

Glickman, C. D., Gordon, S. P., & Ross-Gordon, J. M. (2018). *Supervision and instructional leadership: A development approach* (10th ed.). Pearson.

Gomez, A. I. P. (1997). Professional socialization of future teachers of the culture of the school: The myth of the practices. *Revista Interuniversitaria de Formación del Profesorado, 29,* 34–45.

Gordon, S. P. (2008). *Collaborative action research: Developing professional learning communities.* Teachers College Press.

Gravani, M. N. (2007). Unveiling professional learning: Shifting from the delivery of courses to an understanding of the process. *Teaching and Teacher Education, 23*(5), 688–704. https://doi.org/10.1016/j.tate.2006.03.011

Guskey, T. R. (2002). Professional development and teacher change. *Teachers and Teaching 8*(3), 381–391. https://doi.org/10.1080/135406002100000512

Haigh, N. (2005). Everyday conversation as a context for professional learning and development. *International Journal for Academic Development, 10*(1), 3–16. https://doi.org/10.1080/13601440500099969

Herbert, S., & Rainford, M. (2014). Developing a model for continuous professional development by action research. *Professional Development in Education, 40*(2), 243–264. https://doi.org/10.1080/19415257.2013.794748

Knowles, M. S. (1984). *Andragogy in action: Applying modern principles of adult learning.* Jossey-Bass.

Lewin, K. (1997). *Resolving social conflicts and field theory in social science.* American Psychological Association. https://doi.org/10.1037/10269-000

Lieberman, A. (1995). Practices that support teacher development: Transforming conceptions of professional learning. In F. Stevens (Ed.), *Innovating and Evaluating Science Education: NSF Evaluation Forums 1992–94* (pp. 67–78). National Science Foundation.

Lindsey, R. B., Nuri-Robins, K., Terrell, R. D., & Lindsey, D. R. (2018). *Cultural proficiency: A manual for school leaders* (4th ed.). Corwin.

Lopes, J. B., & Cunha, A. E. (2017, November). Self-directed professional development to improve effective teaching: Key points for a model. *Teaching and Teacher Education, 68,* 262–274. https://doi.org/10.1016/j.tate.2017.09.009

Lopez-Pastor, V. M., Monjas, R., & Manrique, J. C. (2011). Fifteen years of action research as professional development: Seeking more collaborative, useful and democratic systems for teachers. *Educational Action Research, 19*(2), 153–170. https://doi.org/10.1080/09650792.2011.569190

MacBeth, J., & Dempster, N. (Eds.). (2009). *Connecting leadership and learning: Principles for practice*. Routledge.

Meng, K. (2014). Research on self-directed professional development of a teacher of TESOL in Chinese context. In F. Zheng (Ed.), *Proceedings of the 2014 International Conference on Global Economy, Finance and Humanities Research* (Vol. 112, pp. 52–55). Atlantis Press. https://doi.org/10.2991/gefhr-14.2014.14

Mertler, C. A. (2020). *Action research: Improving schools and empowering educators* (6th ed.). SAGE.

Merton, R. K. (1963). Resistance to the systematic study of multiple discoveries in science. *European Journal of Sociology/Archives Européennes de Sociologie, 4*(2), 237–282. https://doi.org/10.1017/S0003975600000801

Mitchell, R. (2013). What is professional development, how does it occur in individuals, and how may it be used by educational leaders and manages for the purpose of school improvement? *Professional Development in Education, 39*(3), 387–400. https://doi.org/10.1080/19415257.2012.762721

Moen, R. D., & Norman, C. L. (2010). Circling back: Clearing up the myths about the Deming cycle and seeing how it keeps evolving. *Quality Progress, 43*(11), 22–28.

Mushayikwa, E., & Lubben, F. (2009). Self-directed professional development—Hope for teachers working in deprived environments? *Teaching and Teacher Education, 25*(3), 375–382. https://doi.org/10.1016/j.tate.2008.12.003

National Association for Gifted Children, & The Association for the Gifted, Council for Exceptional Children. (2013). *NAGC-CEC teacher preparation standards in gifted education*. http://www.nagc.org/sites/default/files/standards/NAGC-%20CEC%20CAEP%20standards%20%282013%20final%29.pdf

Novak, A. M. (2019). *Making a plan to learn: Self directed professional learning*. https://www.angelamnovak.com/blog/making-a-plan-to-learn-self-directed-professional-learning

O'Grady, K. (2008). How far can you go? Can you get reincarnated as a floorboard? Religious education pedagogy, pupil motivation and teacher intelligence. *Educational Action Research, 16*(3), 361–378. https://doi.org/10.1080/09650790802260315

Osses, S. (2008). Towards teachers' professional autonomy through action research. *Educational Action Research, 16*(3), 407–420. https://doi.org/10.1080/09650790802260398

Pedder, D., & Opfer, V. D. (2010). Planning and organisation of teachers' continuous professional development in schools in England. *The*

Curriculum Journal, 21(4), 433–452. https://doi.org/10.1080/09585176.2010.529652

Poekert, P. E. (2012). Teacher leadership and professional development: Examining links between two concepts central to school improvement. *Professional Development in Education, 38*(2), 169–188.

Schön, D. A. (1984). *The reflective practitioner: How professionals think in action.* Routledge.

Senge, P. M., Cambron-McCabe, N., Lucas, T., Smith, B., Dutton, J., & Kleiner, A. (2012). *Schools that learn: A fifth discipline fieldbook for educators, parents, and everyone who cares about education* (Updated ed.). Crown.

Slade, M. (2018). Reflection as an essential practice in professional learning for gifted education. In A. M. Novak & C. L. Weber (Eds.), *Best practices in professional learning and teacher preparation: Methods and strategies for gifted professional development* (Vol. 1, pp. 39–50). Prufrock Press.

Tague, N. R. (2005). *The quality toolbox* (2nd ed.). ASQ Quality Press.

Texas Association for the Gifted and Talented. (n.d.). *#GTCHAT*. https://www.txgifted.org/gtchat

Troxclair, D., Shaunessy-Dedrick, E., & Mursky, C. (2017). Designing professional development activities. In S. K. Johnsen & J. Clarenbach (Eds.), *Using the national gifted education standards for pre-k–grade 12 professional development* (2nd ed., pp. 109–126). Prufrock Press.

Van Eekelen, I. M., Vermunt, J. D., & Boshuizen, H. P. A. (2006). Exploring teachers' will to learn. *Teaching and Teacher Education, 22*(4), 408–423. https://doi.org/10.1016/j.tate.2005.12.001

van Veen, K., Zwart, R., & Meirink, J. (2012). What makes teacher professional development effective? A literature review. In M. Kooy & V. van Veen (Eds.), *Teacher learning that matters: International perspectives* (pp. 3–21). Routledge.

von Glasserfeld, E. (2001). Radical constructivism and teaching. *Prospects, 31*(2), 161–173. https://doi.org/10.1007/BF03220058

Vonk, H. (1991). Some trends in the development of curricula for the professional preparation of primary and secondary school teachers in Europe: A comparative study. *British Journal of Educational Studies, 39*(2), 117–137. https://doi.org/10.1080/00071005.1991.9973879

Wenger, E. (1998). Communities of practice: Learning as a social system. *The Systems Thinker, 9*(5), 2–3.

West Keur, R. A. (2019). Teacher expertise informing research and development in gifted education. *Gifted Child Today, 42*(2), 91–95.

Zepeda, S. J. (2019). *Professional development: What works* (3rd ed.). Routledge.

Zwart, R. C., Wubbels, T., Bergen, T. C. M., & Bolhuis, S. (2007). Experienced teacher learning within the context of reciprocal peer coaching. *Teachers and Teaching, 13*(2), 165–187. https://doi.org/10.1080/13540600601152520

Section 2

Curriculum Through a Content Lens

CHAPTER 4

Professional Learning Practices in Literacy Education for Gifted and Talented Students

Mary L. Slade and Tammy Burnham

Literacy education holds a place of prominence in Pre-K–grade 12 instruction, primarily with a focus on grade-level and below-grade-level students (Firmender et al., 2013; Latz et al., 2009; Marianetti, 2016). With increased emphasis on enhanced reading achievement in particular, students are spending significant amounts of time in the classroom receiving literacy instruction. Typically, the intended outcome of school-based literacy programs is grade-level achievement in reading, writing, and language development. As classroom teachers dedicate more extensive blocks of time to teaching literacy, advanced readers and writers endure learning experiences that are not aligned with their unique learning traits and needs (Adelson & Carpenter, 2015; Wood, 2008). However, there is little incentive for teachers to worry about students' learning once proficiency is established regarding grade-level curricula and instruction (Tomlinson, 2002), despite the fact best practice in literacy education calls for differentiation in teaching gifted and talented readers (Wood, 2008).

Classroom teachers responsible for teaching literacy struggle with providing quality differentiated curricula and instruction for gifted and talented readers (Levande, 1999). Professional learning in literacy education for regular classroom teachers is often specific to a school district's current literacy program adoption (Kennedy & Shiel, 2010). Seldom does the training reference the necessary differentiation of literacy education for gifted and talented students. In addition to classroom teachers, educators who focus on literacy in Pre-K–grade 12 education as their primary role in a school rarely are exposed to literacy education specific to gifted and talented students. Therefore, literacy educators such as literacy coaches and district-level literacy administrators would benefit from a text on professional learning that focuses on applying best practices in literacy education to gifted and talented students. Although these educators may be well-versed in the critical components of literacy education, they often do not know how to differentiate literacy training content to meet the needs of gifted students. Professional learning is most valuable when the impact of training results in enhanced student achievement, and in this instance, in gifted student achievement (Teaching Tolerance, n.d.).

This chapter focuses on professional learning for developing and implementing literacy education that addresses the unique needs of gifted and talented students. Specifically, professional learning content should include the necessary components of an effective literacy program, as well as effective pedagogical practices. The chapter includes three equally important components: (1) the relevant literacy content and pedagogical skills most likely to impact student achievement, (2) the necessary modifications to or adaptations of traditional literacy education programming to address the needs of gifted students, and (3) the unique aspects of literacy education for gifted and talented students.

Overview

Although most students may be placed in high, middle, or low reading groups during literacy instruction, this does not sufficiently meet the needs of gifted and talented readers (Catron & Wingenbach, 1986). Given their advanced reading ability, gifted and talented students' literacy needs are greater than what grade-level reading materials and activities offer (Levande, 1999). The higher the ability in reading, the greater the need for a differentiated literacy program (Tompkins, 2002). However, most schools are not readily engaged in making accommodations for gifted and talented students, and as much as half of the literacy curriculum is not challenging for these students (Reis et al., 2016).

Students proficient in reading are often left alone to read silently after completing standard reading assignments (Smith, 2009; Tomlinson, 2002; Wood, 2008). The traditional strategies of allowing gifted and talented readers to read more, read individually, and read more difficult books is no longer sufficient to meet their needs and, in fact, is a disservice to them (Reis, 2009). Because accelerated readers are often receiving minimal levels of appropriately differentiated instruction, their development in literacy skills is halted, and motivational issues arise. This can result in a cycle of stagnation, underachievement, and lack of interest for gifted readers (Smith, 2009; Wood, 2008). Moreover, a lack of differentiation in the reading curriculum causes gifted and talented students to lose interest in reading and creates lapses in their literacy development as they progress through upper elementary, middle, and high school (Wood, 2008). Thus, not differentiating for gifted and talented students is punitive (Levande, 1999).

Consensus does not exist regarding the definitive traits of gifted and talented readers, as not all gifted and talented students are advanced readers, and not all advanced readers are gifted and talented (Crammond, 2004; Reis et al., 2004). However, characteristics do exist that substantially differentiate gifted readers from other learners, including (1) reading early and at advanced levels, (2) using advanced processing skills in reading, (3) reading with enthusiasm and enjoyment, and (4) demonstrating advanced language skills (Reis et al., 2004). Many advanced readers are as much as 2 years above grade level in terms of achievement (Catron & Wingenbach, 1986; Kenney, 2013; Reis, 2009; Wood, 2008). Therefore, gifted and talented students often enter school as readers, possess an advanced understanding of a variety of texts, have expansive vocabularies, and can employ higher order thinking strategies often and appropriately (Catron & Wingenbach, 1986; Dooley, 1993; Reis, 2009). In addition to accelerated reading and language skills, gifted and talented students may demonstrate advanced aptitude in many areas of literacy, such as creative writing, literary analysis, oral communication, linguistic and vocabulary development, and critical and creative reading (VanTassel-Baska & Stambaugh, 2005). The unique characteristics of gifted and talented readers present a challenge to most literacy educators; thus, grade-level teaching needs to be adapted or modified to address their differentiated needs. Because of learner differences, gifted and talented readers need instruction that is challenging and includes opportunities to extend learning using complex texts (Wood, 2008).

Unfortunately, many of the teachers tasked with teaching literacy are well trained in the instruction of reading but not the process of aligning pedagogies with diverse student abilities and needs. Seldom do these individuals experience training specific to the needs of competent, advanced, or gifted readers (Wood, 2008). Thus, professional learning for educators responsible for teaching gifted and talented students in the area of literacy must address the lack of differentiation through exposing the teachers to a variety of strategies and methods that not only are appropriate for gifted and talented readers, but also allow for an easy planning and implementation process for the teacher. Emphasis on the teacher's pivotal role in providing quality instruction for gifted readers encourages them to address the differentiation, as research continues to suggest that the teacher is the most important factor for student achievement and success, including for gifted and talented students (Smith, 2009). A teacher's educational decisions and instructional practices will greatly affect students' learning and academic achievement (Darling-Hammond et al., 2017; Geake & Gross, 2008).

To facilitate professional learning for literacy relevant to gifted and talented students, teachers must possess the ability to organize the reading curriculum in a manner that allows for modifications that enhance the reading instruction, enabling growth and enrichment for students (Smith, 2009). A distinction must be made between presenting gifted and talented readers with access to reading materials at an advanced level and teaching advanced reading curricula (Wood, 2008).

Teachers must not only assign challenging texts and use instructional strategies to stimulate higher order thinking for gifted and talented students, but also teach advanced literacy curricula. Instead of participating in grade-level reading lessons, gifted and talented students need an altered, more challenging learning experience during the time that mastered skills are being taught to peers. Accordingly, gifted and talented students move through the curriculum at the correct level and pace when differentiation occurs (Dooley, 1993; Reis, 2009). This is the focus of the requisite professional learning that school districts must implement in order to provide the appropriate learning opportunities to students in order to positively impact students' literacy achievement.

Although appropriate content and book selection for the gifted and talented student lays the foundation for an effective differentiated curriculum, additional adaptations to traditional literacy programs are accomplished via instructional modifications. These adjustments to standard programs of study include higher order thinking and inquiry, which align with the advanced cognitive abilities of gifted and talented students (Catron & Wingenbach, 1986; Wood, 2008). Hence, all aspects of the grade-level literacy education program must be modified and adapted to meet the needs of gifted and talented students.

Literacy Programming Components

When contemplating the best professional learning strategies for the modification and adaptation of existing literacy education programs to include the needs of gifted and talented students, collaborative initiatives should be on the forefront of planning. Educators are trained in literacy curricula adopted by the school district. Simultaneously, the necessary professional learning related to gifted and talented students must be addressed, including necessary instructional modifications. Given the need to adapt and supplant adopted literacy materials for gifted and talented students, media specialists or literacy coaches and gifted and talented coordinators can provide information about the availability and selection of texts.

The foundation of an effective literacy program includes phonemic awareness, phonics instruction, vocabulary, fluency, and comprehension, along with writing (Birsh, 2011; Chall, 2000; National Reading Panel, 2000; Pressley, 2006). Addressing these program components in light of gifted and talented students' unique literacy characteristics and needs is the foundation of differentiated literacy education.

Phonemic Awareness

Phonemic awareness is the initial stage of beginning reading and is a solid predictor of reading success (McBride-Chang et al., 1996; Stainthorp & Hughes, 2004). The ability to hear and identify phonemes is a skill that gifted and talented readers find easy, and little instruction is required in this area. Phonics provides that important link between hearing the sounds and reading the words. Many children find learning phonics to be difficult, but this is not the case with gifted and talented students who intuitively recognize the sounds, patterns, and codes of learning to read. Entering kindergarten with these first two components mastered is common with gifted and talented students (Reis, 2009; Stainthorp & Hughes, 2004; Wood, 2008).

Professional learning for phonemic awareness should focus on how teachers can differentiate instructional time for young gifted and talented students when class time is being spent building awareness for other students. Given that the curriculum of literacy education does not require differentiation necessarily for all gifted and talented learners, the instructional time dedicated to phonemic awareness should be adapted and supplemented. Thus, for this type of professional learning activity, gifted and talented education coordinators can prepare training specific to curriculum compacting, ability grouping, and literacy acceleration. Curriculum compacting allows teachers to align the rate and pace of phonemic awareness instruction, as well as buy time for enrichment in other areas of literacy education. Similarly, the flexible grouping of students by ability and advanced needs allows for the differentiation of the instructional activities and engagement of gifted students. Finally, instructional strategies such as literacy acceleration would address the diverse, if not competing, needs of twice-exceptional gifted learners, as well as underrepresented gifted learners.

Phonemic Instruction

Whereas phonemic awareness focuses on the oral expression of letters as sound, phonemic instruction emphasizes the relationship between sound and spelling as applied to the written word. Although the early phonemic awareness exists as a common characteristic of gifted and talented readers, it is unclear as to whether this reading precociousness translates into long-term achievement in instruction regarding the written word (Stainthorp & Hughes, 2004). Phonemic instruction is a highly individualized process for gifted and talented students. Thus, diagnostic measures are required to assess mastery and deficits in reading skills.

Teachers must know how to assess current skill levels to determine entry points for phonemic instruction. Professional learning in this area must consist of a demonstration of the instruments available and assessment strategies required to determine gifted and talented students' skill strengths and deficits in phonics. District-level leaders in literacy, assessment, school psychology, and special education should consult on the content of related professional learning initiatives. The aforementioned educators have collective expertise in the practice of assessment relative to literacy education as well as the nature of instruments available across the school district. Instruction should focus on filling gaps while building on strengths. Gifted and talented education leaders should demonstrate the development and implementation of general education plans for spelling, reading, and writing endeavors involving phonics instruction.

Reading Fluency

Fluency refers to reading accurately with expression and allows the reader to comprehend the text more fully. Fluency results in students reading at higher degrees of satisfaction. Although this is often an overlooked area for gifted and talented readers, fluency needs to be explicitly taught to these readers. Oral fluency proficiency within a given heterogeneously grouped classroom ranges from the first to the 99th percentile (Firmender et al., 2013). Thus, professional learning in this area should focus on differentiation for all students, including gifted and talented students. Best practices that should be taught to educators include, but are not limited to, repeat reading with guided questions, choral reading, and reader's theater, as well as metacognition skills that promote awareness of comprehension during reading.

Vocabulary

Vocabulary instruction is crucial for thinking deeply as well as using different modes of expression in oral communication and writing. Gifted and talented students possess precociousness for understanding and using language (Piirto, 2002). Yet, advanced language learners are expected to increase their vocabulary through incidental reading of high-quality literature. However, the literature aligned with today's core curricula is not as high-quality as it was historically for gifted and talented students (Gallagher, 2017). Advanced programs of word or language study should be used in place of grade-level spelling and vocabulary curricula. The nature of the advanced programs and accompanying programs are discussed in detail later in this chapter.

Comprehension

Well-developed comprehension skills enable the reader to understand the text and apply this new learning to different situations. Research reveals that comprehension levels vary greatly within heterogeneous classrooms (Firmender et al., 2013; Shaunessy-Dedrick et al., 2015). The gifted and talented student needs specific strategies for comprehending texts that go beyond what is conventionally taught in a reading lesson (Kenney, 2013). In fact, inclusion of critical thinking enriches literacy education by advancing comprehension skills and supporting academic growth (McCollister & Sayler, 2010).

Critical literacy skills include inference, assumption, deduction, interpretation, prediction, and evaluation (Catron & Wingenbach, 1986). As an extension of basic comprehension skills, these six skills encourage deeper metacognition for the advanced student and will sustain motivation in reading tasks. Allowing the movement from skill development to interpretive reading addresses the necessity of higher order thinking for the gifted and talented student (Catron & Wingenbach, 1986; Dooley, 1993; Wood, 2008).

In addition to critical and analytical thinking, creative thought is considered the highest intellectual contribution to the gifted and talented student's literacy program, and is often the most neglected component for teaching the gifted reader (Catron & Wingenbach, 1986; Wood, 2008). Gifted and talented students are creative thinkers (Kenney, 2013). In creative reading, the gifted and talented student extends the understanding of the text to include applications and creations of new ideas and insights. Identifying unsolved problems, integrating new ideas, and synthesizing interpretations of events and themes allow the student to create and invent (Catron & Wingenbach, 1986; Dooley, 1993; Wood, 2008). Creative thinking can lead to the development of alternative interpretations of the characters, events, or current world issues as differentiated learning activities. Related creative thinking instructional approaches stimulate the gifted and talented student to become adept in asking prediction questions, finding gaps in knowledge, and determining alternative solutions to problems. Artistic outlets—including drawing, creating writing, and acting—strengthen skills and motivate students to continue the pursuit of reading to learn (Dooley, 1993; Reis, 2009; Wood, 2008).

Classroom teachers and other literacy educators need to understand the requisite curricular and instructional modifications for gifted and talented students who spend most of their time in literacy instruction designed for their same-age peers. Accordingly, significant professional learning is warranted when it comes to developing comprehension skills in gifted and talented readers. Related professional learning should be conducted by leaders in gifted education. Training activities must emphasize appropriate instructional practices for gifted and talented education accompanied by demonstrations of recommended curricular materials. For example, the Frayer Model could be used as a method for teaching advanced vocabulary. Leaders in gifted education on a local or state level are viable professional learning trainers on this topic.

Writing

Typically, writing is an area of literacy education that presents a challenge to most learners, and thus the instructional focus is on grade-level standards and outcomes. But advanced or gifted writers experience stagnant learning when only grade-level materials and expectations are presented to them (Olthouse & Miller, 2012). Undeniably, struggling students deserve literacy instruction and curricula to improve their writing performance. Equally, gifted and talented students merit challenging instruction, curricula, and assessment that lead to growth in writing performance (Olthouse & Miller, 2012). Therefore, differentiation for gifted and talented students must be implemented in order for these students to reach their full potential in this area of literacy. In order to provide the necessary differentiation of writing instruction, educators need to participate in professional learning specific to the nature and needs of gifted writers. Leaders in gifted education can provide training in writing education differentiation. Further, the introduction of specialized curricula and cocurricular writing programs should be presented to all classroom and literacy teachers. For example, a school may offer afterschool programs that challenge students' literacy skills, such as Future Problem Solving or Destination Imagination. In the classroom, teachers may be introduced to specialized curricula spotlighted by the National Association for Gifted Children's Curriculum Studies Network.

Literacy Education for Gifted and Talented Students

Gifted and talented students need curricular and instructional differentiation from traditional literacy education programs in order to make continuous progress (Reis, 2009). Specific recommendations exist for literacy education modifications that render curriculum and instruction in line with the unique needs of gifted and talented students. Additionally, guidelines for the selection of appropriately challenging literacy materials, the use of bibliotherapy, advanced word study approaches that replace grade-level spelling programs, and in-depth discussions around literature studies are discussed to demonstrate the need for literacy education components specifically for gifted and talented students.

Selection of Literacy Materials

Taking a comprehensive and thoughtful approach to the collection of reading material for the gifted and talented reader provides a solid foundation for an advanced literacy program. A differentiated reading curriculum contains books that close the reading gap as compared to traditional basal readers or grade-level reading lists. As books are being selected, attention to a variety of genres is also necessary. This may include fiction, such as historical fiction and fantasy, but also expository writings. For example, persuasive essays, news articles, and research pieces are often neglected in the selection of challenging texts. Once a reading list is comprised, the teacher can survey the gifted and talented readers on their interests and topics they wish to explore (Catron & Wingenbach, 1986; Dooley, 1993; Weber, 2010).

Foremost, literature for educating gifted and talented students should align with their advanced reading levels. Thus, the Lexile should be at least 1–2 years above grade level for younger children and as much as 4 years above for adolescents (VanTassel-Baska, 2017). However, reading level is not the sole criterion for text selection. The advanced levels of language and vocabulary contained within a text must also be considered. Reis et al. (2004) affirmed that gifted and talented students require complex texts for literacy education. In addition to selecting texts based on the level of challenge presented to gifted and talented students, the developmental appropriateness should also be considered in order to determine its utility in teaching about affective issues (Crammond, 2004).

It follows that related professional learning must include gifted and talented education teachers, media specialists, literacy coaches, and instructional leaders to plan and deliver training activities regarding appropriate text selection. Gifted education leaders should make reading lists for gifted and talented students available. Online book lists are maintained for teacher, parent, and student use. For example, the Center for Talented Youth at Johns Hopkins University posts a reading list by grade level for gifted and talented learners on their organization's website. Further, the gifted and talented educators can collaborate with school officials responsible for the purchase of texts in the classroom and school libraries.

Bibliotherapy

Using literature to address gifted and talented students' differentiated social-emotional needs is called bibliotherapy (Wood, 2008), which has been defined as a type of therapeutic reading that helps students work through adverse situations (Ford et al., 2019). In reading literature with gifted and talented characters, readers not only identify with characters, but also learn coping skills and solutions to problems through engaging with literature. Thus, gifted and talented students learn about themselves and their giftedness and talent through bibliotherapy. Rather than focusing on traditional reading skills, students engage with the literature in order to experience feelings as a reaction to the literature. Gifted and talented students often face challenges given their unique differences trying to live and learn in environments aligned more with their same-age peers (Schlichter & Burke, 1994).

Lists of age-appropriate texts and related bibliotherapy resources are available to share through professional learning activities. Gifted education leaders can work collaboratively with guidance counselors to train classroom teachers in using bibliotherapy as a process that promotes readers' identification with the characters and themes in targeted literature. Forgan (2002) recommended that educators are trained in the four essential components of using bibliotherapy for understanding in the classroom. Thus, professional learning content might include prereading, guided reading, post-reading discussion, and problem solving. Related training activities will focus on participants practicing these steps. A fishbowl activity would allow participants the opportunity to alternatively practice bibliotherapy as well as observe others engaged in the practice.

Language Study

Literacy programs for gifted students must include a strong language study component (Thompson, 2001; VanTassel-Baska & Stambaugh, 2005). Thompson (2001) advocated for direct vocabulary instruction, whether through the study of common words in great works of literature or learning the Latin and Greek heritage of the English language. The study of Greek and Latin stems offers advantages over traditional word study beyond an increased vocabulary. For example, students will gain comfort with unknown words that can be broken down into familiar stems. Similarly, students gain comfort in spelling words that are composed of recognizable stems. Learning the language of the disciplines is another aspect of rigorous vocabulary study for gifted and talented students (Job & Coleman, 2016). Further, the authors suggested that reading nonfiction literature can help build vocabulary in specific content areas such as science or math.

Leaders in gifted and talented education must provide professional learning in vocabulary studies. Experts can be consulted to share existing advanced vocabulary curricula and associated programs, such as *Word Within a Word* and *Caesar's English*. Training participants must include classroom teachers, gifted education teachers, and other educators engaged in literacy education within a school district. School administrators and curriculum specialists in the school district need training in the supplemental vocabulary programs available for advanced learning in preparation for curricular materials adoptions.

In-Depth Book Discussions

Gifted and talented students benefit from book discussion groups such as those outlined by the Great Books Foundation (Reis et al., 2004). Likewise, using the Socratic method in conjunction with the reading guides encourages gifted students to delve deeper into literacy content and skills (Kenney, 2013). Because gifted students move through material at a faster pace, additional discussion time can be spent to consider all aspects of the text being read. Irrespective of the type of discussion format employed, it is critical that gifted students engage in discussing quality literature, as it develops higher level thinking skills (Kenney, 2013).

Gifted education leaders in the district can provide training specifically for teaching how to facilitate in-depth discussions. The teachers and coordinator can provide professional learning regarding Socratic seminars. Gifted and talented teachers and classroom teachers can coteach lessons using the Socratic method in place of customary reading group discussions. Local gifted and talented leaders can provide training in instructional differentiation that can provide alternative learning activities for the discussion of appropriately challenging texts. Demonstration lessons can model best practices in the classroom for general education teachers.

Implications

Literacy education occupies a major portion of daily instruction in most pre-K–grade 8 classrooms. In grades 9–12, education edicts, as well as legislation at state and national levels, call for the inclusion of literacy instruction in core subject areas. Regardless of whether specific policies are put into place, students' academic achievement is dependent upon their reading ability. Therefore, all educators must possess literacy knowledge and the skills to support student academic success. Furthermore, educators must be aware of the need to differentiate literacy curricula and instruction for all students, including those who are gifted and talented. Because literacy education permeates the roles and responsibilities of most school personnel, the need to inform most educators about the specialized literacy needs of gifted and talented students is imperative.

As most initial licensure education preparation programs do not include formal training in teaching gifted and talented students, professional learning initiatives for practicing educators are crucial to preparing educators for their students' literacy success. As noted previously, professional learning for regular classroom teachers is often specific to a school district's current literacy program adoption (Kennedy & Shiel, 2010). Seldom does the training reference the necessary differentiation of literacy education for gifted learners. There are, however, critical elements of an effective literacy program that includes modifications and adaptations for advanced students. General classroom teachers need training that provides the necessary guidance. After all, gifted students spend a significant amount of time in general education throughout their elementary years. Literacy educators, such as literacy coaches and district-level literacy administrators, also need to understand the literacy development of gifted and talented students. Thus, those who direct and lead gifted and talented education programs must collaborate with school leaders to design and implement professional learning specific to literacy education that appropriately addresses students needs.'

Summary

Emphasis on literacy education for all students remains constant in schools. Teachers spend increasing amounts of time teaching literacy. Typically, literacy education programming is designed, delivered, and assessed considering low or grade-level achievement foremost. Without the necessary consideration of modifications and differentiation of the grade-level literacy program, gifted and talented students spend most of their time in literacy-based learning experiences that stagnate their growth and development.

Whether it be reading Lexile levels advanced for their age by as much as two grade levels, early reading, or advanced knowledge of language, gifted and talented students are different from their same-age peers when it comes to literacy education needs. Student differences exist when they enter school and remain throughout their precollegiate educational experience. Advanced literacy abilities may be demonstrated by an early reader, a creative writer, or a student with significant vocabularies. The equilibrium of any learning environment can be upset by the existence of misalignment of student needs and learning expectations. Students may be reading in kindergarten or first grade, other young readers may request that librarians assist them in finding books far above their grade level, and high school students may read an entire book in high school after being assigned only a few chapters.

Literacy education for gifted and talented students requires the intentional modification of grade-level curricula and instruction, as well as the inclusion of specific literacy education components that align with the unique needs of these students. The components of literacy education must be modified, adapted, or supplemented with specialized literacy education practices. Knowledge of differentiated materials, procedures, and assessment must be learned by all school staff and faculty who teach gifted and talented students. Educators require professional learning experiences that inform them of the changes warranted in their literacy curricula and instruction in order for gifted and talented students to reach their full potential and demonstrate continuous progress in reading, writing, and language development.

Resources

The following annotated resources are suggested for use in planning and implementing professional learning in literacy education for gifted and talented students.

Professional Learning in Gifted and Talented Education Support Materials

Creativity in Gifted Education. (n.d.). *Socratic seminars.* https://creativegiftededucation.weebly.com/socratic-seminars.html

National Association for Gifted Children. (2009). *Grouping* [Position statement]. https://www.nagc.org/sites/default/files/Position%20Statement/Grouping%20Position%20Statement.pdf

Redmond, S. (2013). *Expanding the vocabularies of gifted students.* Prufrock Press. https://www.prufrock.com/Expanding-the-Vocabularies-of-Gifted-Students.aspx

Reis, S. M., & Renzulli, J. S. (n.d.). *Curriculum compacting: A systematic procedure for modifying the curriculum for above average ability students.* University of Connecticut, Renzulli Center for Creativity, Gifted Education, and Talent Development. https://gifted.uconn.edu/schoolwide-enrichment-model/curriculum_compacting

Reading Lists for Gifted and Talented Students

Hoagies' Gifted Education Page. (2019). *Reading lists for your gifted child.* https://www.hoagiesgifted.org/reading_lists.htm

Luth, B. (2009). *Bibliotherapy with gifted students.* https://bibliotherapywithgiftedstudents.blogspot.com

Tolan, S. (2009). *Books and plays.* https://www.stephanietolan.com/books.htm

Vocabulary and Word Study Materials

Pearson Education. (2005). *Words their way literacy program.* Pearson.

Thompson, M. C. (1994). *The word within the word.* Royal Fireworks Press.

Thompson, M. C. (2000). *Caesar's English* (2nd ed.). Royal Fireworks Press.

Literacy Curricula for Gifted and Talented Learners

Center for Gifted Education. (n.d.). *Literature units.* https://education.wm.edu/centers/cfge/curriculum/languagearts/materials/literatureunits/index.php

Great Books Foundation. https://www.greatbooks.org

References

Adelson, J. L., & Carpenter, B. D. (2015). Grouping for achievement gains: For whom does achievement grouping increase kindergarten reading growth? *Gifted Child Quarterly, 55*(4), 265–278. https://doi.org/10.1177/0016986211417306

Birsh, J. R. (Ed.). (2011). *Multisensory teaching of basic language skills* (4th ed.). Brookes.

Catron, R. M., & Wingenbach, N. (1986). Developing the potential of the gifted reader. *Theory Into Practice, 25*(2), 134–140. https://doi.org/10.1080/00405848609543213

Chall, J. S. (2000). *The academic achievement challenge*. Guilford Press.

Crammond, B. (2004). Reading instruction for the gifted. *Illinois Reading Council Journal, 32*(4), 31–36.

Darling-Hammond, L., Hyler, M. E., & Gardner, M. (2017). *Effective teacher professional development*. Learning Policy Institute.

Dooley, C. (1993). The challenge: Meeting the needs of gifted readers. *The Reading Teacher, 46*(7), 546–551.

Firmender, J. M., Reis, S. M., & Sweeny, S. M. (2013). Reading comprehension and fluency levels ranges across diverse classrooms: The need for differentiated reading instruction and content. *Gifted Child Quarterly, 57*(1), 3–14. https://doi.org/10.1177/0016986212460084

Ford, D. Y., Walters, N. M., Byrd, J. A., & Harris, B. N. (2019). I want to read about me: Gifted Black girls reading using multicultural literature and bibliotherapy. *Gifted Child Today, 42*(1), 53–57. https://doi.org/10.1177/1076217518804851

Forgan, J. W. (2002). Using bibliotherapy to teach problem solving. *Intervention in School and Clinic, 38*(2), 75–82. https://doi.org/10.1177/10534512020380020201

Gallagher, S. A. (2017). Exploring the efficacy of Word Within the Word for the gifted and typically developed learner. *Roeper Review, 39*(2), 96–111. https://doi.org/10.1080/02783193.2017.1289486

Geake, J. G., & Gross, M. U. M. (2008). Teachers' negative affect toward academically gifted students: An evolutionary psychological study. *Gifted Child Quarterly, 52*(3), 217–231. https://doi.org/10.1177/0016986208319704

Job, J., & Coleman, M. R. (2016). The importance of reading in earnest: Nonfiction for young children. *Gifted Child Today, 39*(3), 154–163. https://doi.org/10.1177/1076217516644635

Kennedy, E., & Shiel, G. (2010). Raising literacy levels with collaborative on-site professional development in an urban disadvantaged school. *The Reading Teacher, 63*(5), 372–383. https://doi.org/10.1598/RT.63.5.3

Kenney, J. (2013). Fostering critical thinking skills: Strategies for use with intermediate gifted readers. *Illinois Reading Council Journal, 41*(2), 28–39.

Latz, A. O., Spiers Neumeister, K. L., Adams, C. M., & Pierce, R. L. (2009). Peer coaching to improve classroom differentiation: Perspectives from Project CLUE. *Roeper Review, 31*(1), 27–39.

Levande, D. (1999). Gifted readers and reading instruction. *CAG Communicator, 30*(1).

Marianetti, G. (2016). *Literacy strategies to challenge advanced readers* [Unpublished master's thesis]. The College at Brockport, State University of New York.

McBride-Chang, C., Manis, F. R., & Wagner, R. K. (1996). Correlates of phonological awareness: Implications for gifted education. *Roeper Review, 19*(1), 27–30. https://doi.org/10.1080/02783199609553779

McCollister, K., & Sayler, M. F. (2010). Lift the ceiling: Increase rigor with critical thinking skills. *Gifted Child Today, 33*(1), 41–47. https://doi.org/10.1177/107621751003300110

National Reading Panel. (2000). *Teaching children to read: An evidence-based assessment of the scientific research literature on reading and its implications for reading instruction*. National Institute of Child Health and Human Development.

Olthouse, J. M., & Miller, M. T. (2012). Teaching talented writers with Web 2.0 tools. *Teaching Exceptional Children, 45*(2), 6–14. https://doi.org/10.1177/004005991204500201

Piirto, J. (2002). *"My teeming brain": Understanding creative writers*. Hampton Press.

Pressley, M. (2006). *Reading instruction that works: The case for balanced teaching* (3rd ed.). Guilford Press.

Reis, S. M. (2009). *Research-based practices for talented readers*. Research into Practice Reading. https://assets.pearsonschool.com/asset_mgr/current/201216/ReaMonTalentedRdrsReis.pdf

Reis, S. M., Renzulli, J. S., & Burns, D. E. (2016). *Curriculum compacting: A guide to differentiating curriculum and instruction through enrichment and acceleration* (2nd ed.). Prufrock Press.

Reis, S. M., Gubbins, E. J., Briggs, C. J., Schreiber, F. J., Richards, S., Jacobs, J. K., Eckert, R. D., & Renzulli, J. S. (2004). Reading instruction for talented readers: Case studies documenting few opportunities for continuous progress. *Gifted Child Quarterly, 48*(4), 315–338. https://doi.org/10.1177/001698620404800406

Schlichter, C. L., & Burke, M. (1994). Using books to nurture the social and emotional development of gifted students. *Roeper Review, 16*(4), 280–283. https://doi.org/10.1080/02783199409553598

Shaunessy-Dedrick, E., Evans, L., Ferron, J., & Lindo, M. (2015). Effects of differentiated reading on elementary students' reading comprehension and attitudes toward reading. *Gifted Child Quarterly, 59*(2), 91–107. https://doi.org/10.1177/0016986214568718

Smith, S. R. (2009). A dynamic ecological framework for differentiating primary curriculum. *Gifted and Talented International, 24*(2), 9–20. https://doi.org/10.1080/15332276.2009.11673526

Stainthorp, R., & Hughes, D. (2004). An illustrative case study of precocious reading ability. *Gifted Child Quarterly, 48*(2), 107–120. https://doi.org/10.1177/001698620404800204

Teaching Tolerance. (n.d.). *Teaching teachers: PD to improve student achievement.* https://www.tolerance.org/professional-development/teaching-teachers-pd-to-improve-student-achievement

Thompson, M. C. (2001). Vocabulary and grammar: Critical content for critical thinking. *Journal of Secondary Gifted Education, 13*(2), 60–66. https://doi.org/10.4219/jsge-2002-367

Tomlinson, C. A. (2002). Proficiency is not enough. *Education Week, 22*(10), 36, 38.

Tompkins, G. E. (2002). *Language arts: Content and teaching strategies* (5th ed.). Merrill Prentice Hall.

VanTassel-Baska, J. (2017). Curriculum issues: The importance of selecting literature for gifted learners. *Gifted Child Today, 40*(3), 183–184. https://doi.org/10.1177/1076217517713783

VanTassel-Baska, J., & Stambaugh, T. (2005). *Comprehensive curriculum for gifted learners* (3rd ed.). Pearson.

Weber, C. L. (2010). Providing a challenging learning environment for middle school and secondary gifted and advanced readers. *Florida Reading Journal, 46*(2), 33–39.

Wood, P. F. (2008). Reading instruction with gifted and talented readers: A series of unfortunate events or a sequence of auspicious results? *Gifted Child Today, 31*(3), 16–25. https://doi.org/10.4219/gct-2008-783

CHAPTER 5

Research-Based Essentials in Professional Learning:
Social Studies

Kimberley L. Chandler

Introduction

Professional learning opportunities in gifted education span a wide variety of topics and methodologies. Often, conference workshop sessions and school-level presentations primarily emphasize ideas about the nature and needs of gifted students. This chapter focuses on professional learning for teachers in K–12 as it relates to social studies instruction. Included is information about the standards that drive such professional learning; key strategies with a focus on the College, Career, and Civic Life (C3) Framework for Social Studies State Standards (National Council for the Social Studies [NCSS], 2013); and sample professional learning plans for developing expertise in social studies for teachers of the gifted.

Overview

Professional learning options in gifted education are often limited within school districts. However, many professional learning opportunities can be found *outside* the school district setting in conferences, institutes, webinars, and other varied formats. Common topics include the characteristics of gifted students, the curricular needs of these children, and their social-emotional traits. Conference sessions often include information about classroom practices and strategies for meeting the needs of gifted students. Seldom, however, is there a focus on professional learning in the content areas of science and social studies; if discipline-specific information is covered, it is typically in mathematics or English language arts. This is because many gifted education programs employ an identification protocol that emphasizes testing with focuses on mathematics and English language arts.

Additionally, there is rarely any training available specifically on how to prepare teachers to work with their gifted students in developing expertise in social studies. In order to achieve this, there are numerous gifted student cognitive characteristics that can be addressed through curriculum and instruction, including how gifted students can:

- comprehend information at a deep level,
- learn new content easily,
- synthesize thoughts quickly,
- generalize across disciplines,
- develop and use conceptual frameworks,
- understand varied and atypical relationships, and
- think critically at an advanced level (Callahan, 2018).

Pairing advanced content with appropriate pedagogy has the potential to transform the discipline of social studies in such a way that gifted students' cognitive needs may be met at an optimal level.

Ultimately, curriculum and instruction in social studies should move students toward expertise. For the gifted students who possess cognitive strengths that are particularly applicable in social studies, teachers must capitalize on these characteristics as they plan student learning activities. This chapter provides information about the professional learning strategies specific to social studies that are important for teachers of gifted students, as well as those individuals responsible for planning such training, to know and understand.

Standards as a Backdrop

Standards tend to drive much of the work in education. These include both content area standards and those developed by professional organizations, such as the National Council for the Social Studies (NCSS), the National Association for Gifted Children (NAGC), and Learning Forward. Understanding the standards that relate to content and professional learning is essential in order to develop high-quality training programs for teachers of students in grades K–12.

Standards in Gifted Education

The NAGC (2019) Pre-K–Grade 12 Gifted Programming Standards provide guidance for using student outcomes as a basis for program development in six areas, including professional learning. The NAGC-CEC Teacher Preparation Standards in Gifted Education (NAGC & The Association for the Gifted, Council for Exceptional Children [CEC-TAG], 2013) specifically provide information about the knowledge and skills needed by professionals who are pursuing a program of studies in gifted education; they may also be used to design a professional learning program. These standards should be considered when developing any professional learning activity.

The six areas included in the NAGC (2019) Pre-K–Grade 12 Gifted Programming Standards are: Learning and Development, Assessment, Curriculum Planning and Instruction, Learning Environments, Programming, and Professional Learning. Each standard includes a framework in which a student outcome is supported by specific evidence-based practices. Student Outcome 6.1, which is related to talent development, includes Evidence-Based Practice 6.1.1:

> State agencies, institutions of higher education, schools and districts provide comprehensive, research-supported professional learning programs for all educators involved in gifted programming and services. This professional learning addresses the foundations of gifted education, characteristics of diverse students with gifts and talents, identification, assessment, curriculum planning and instruction, learning environments, and programming. High-quality professional learning is delivered by those with expertise in gifted education as guided by the NAGC-CEC Teacher Preparation Standards in Gifted and Talented Education. (p. 16)

Although other standards and other evidence-based practices relate to professional learning, 6.1.1 subsumes all of the components that need to be considered when planning activities in a specific content area. These standards are written in a generic way, not specific to any given subject; however, the emphases on student characteristics, assessment, and curriculum planning and instruction are particularly relevant to planning for professional learning in an area such as social studies.

The NAGC-CEC Teacher Preparation Standards in Gifted Education (NAGC & CEC-TAG, 2013) represent the foundational knowledge and skills needed by preservice and inservice teacher candidates in the field of gifted education. There are seven standards: Learner Development and Individual Learning Differences, Learning Environments, Curricular Content Knowledge, Assessment, Instructional Planning and Strategies, Professional Learning and Ethical Practice, and Collaboration. Curricular Content Knowledge, Assessment, and Instructional Planning and Strategies are the standards that would be most important to consider for professional learning planning. Curricular Content Knowledge relates to the need for strong content knowledge; this may not be covered in professional learning sessions specifically, as the assumption might be that the content would be covered in social studies coursework. Although many of the components of the assessment standard are related to assessment for identification purposes, one does focus on the assessment of learning; this is an element of instruction that should be covered in training for teachers. Within the Instructional Planning and Strategies standard, most relevant for professional learning is 5.1: "Beginning gifted education professionals know principles of evidence-based, differentiated, and accelerated practices and possess a repertoire of instructional strategies to enhance the critical and creative thinking, problem-solving, and performance skills of individuals with gifts and talents" (NAGC & CEC-TAG, 2013, p. 5).

Standards Related to Professional Learning

In 2011, Learning Forward (formerly known as the National Staff Development Council) released its updated Standards for Professional Learning. Using the term *professional learning* instead of "professional development" or "staff development" represents an emphasis on the learner being actively engaged with the training. There are seven Professional Learning Standards: Learning Communities, Leadership, Resources, Data, Learning Designs, Implementation, and Outcomes; these represent the characteristics of effective professional learning that must be considered when planning how to improve the knowledge and skills of educators. Although it is beyond the scope of this chapter to address specifics about the Learning Forward standards (see Volume 1 of this series), those designing and delivering professional learning experiences should consider them when working within any discipline.

The Implementation Standard does warrant an emphasis, however: "Professional learning that increases educator effectiveness and results for all students applies research on change and sustains support for implementation of professional learning for long term change" (Learning Forward, 2011, Implementation, para. 1). The Implementation Standard emphasizes the ways in which pedagogical change must be supported over time. Most important in this standard is the idea that substantive change can only occur when professional learning is supported systematically and over an extended period of time; the single workshop model is inadequate for supporting change. Another element of this standard is the emphasis on establishing and maintaining a feedback loop. In the section of this chapter in which sample professional learning plans are presented, trainers should prepare an ongoing program related to the prescribed content, keeping in mind best practices related to the implementation standard.

Standards in Social Studies

According to the NCSS (n.d.)., the National Curriculum Standards for Social Studies "provide a framework for professional deliberation and planning about what should occur in a social studies program in grades Pre-K through 12. The framework provides ten themes that represent a way of organizing knowledge about the human experience in the world" (para. 8). There are also national history standards from the National Center for History in the Schools (NCHS), national geography standards from the Geography Education Standards Project, and economics standards from the Council for Economic Education. The NCSS social studies standards relate to comprehensive student learning and overall curriculum design. The state standards and the national content standards for the individual disciplines provide the scope of specific content through which student learning outcomes can be developed. All of these standards can serve as the basis for professional learning experiences that are content and expertise driven for gifted educators.

Additionally, in 2010, 14 professional organizations worked with the NCSS to produce the *College, Career, and Civic Life (C3) Framework for Social Studies State Standards: Guidance for Enhancing the Rigor of K–12 Civics, Economics, Geography, and History*. The C3 Framework's "objectives are to: a) enhance the rigor of the social studies disciplines; b) build critical thinking, problem solving, and participatory skills to become engaged citizens; and c) align academic programs to the Common Core State Standards for English Language Arts and Literacy in History/Social Studies" (NCSS, 2013, para. 1). The C3 Framework includes four dimensions: developing questions and inquiries, applying disciplinary tools and concepts, evaluating sources and using evidence, and communicating conclusions and taking informed action. Collectively, the four dimensions compose the Inquiry Arc; they serve as "a set of interlocking and mutually reinforcing elements" that address "the intersection of ideas and learners" (Grant, 2013, p. 322). As the Inquiry Arc emphasizes inquiry-based learning, it is especially engaging for gifted learners.

The C3 Framework, in particular, is an important way to view social studies instruction and the areas of need for professional learning for teachers of all students. Thus, the four dimensions should be used as the framework for designing professional learning experiences for gifted education teachers of social studies. Modifications and additions based on best practices in gifted education will ensure that trainers bridge the gap between general education and gifted education.

A Framework for Professional Learning Through a C3 Lens

The three types of standards previously discussed should serve as the backdrop for the work in professional learning in social studies. All of these standards must be considered in developing professional learning plans in order to compose the most robust program for participants. For the specific professional learning plans delineated in this chapter, the C3 Framework is used as the organizer because the social studies emphasis should be in the forefront.

In gifted education, both practitioners and university personnel have tended to operate within a silo confined to the ideals and theories of that field; the research and resources of general education have been ignored despite the fact that most teachers who interact with gifted students are regular classroom teachers. Often, this has resulted in a disconnect between actual disciplinary practice, district assessment requirements, and the needs of gifted students. The use of the C3 Framework as a guiding document for developing professional learning experiences should ensure that the basic premises of social studies education will serve as the foundation for all that is done to train the teachers who will work with gifted students.

Developing Questions and Inquiries

Dimension 1 of the C3 Framework "features the development of questions and the planning of inquiries. With the entire scope of human experience as its backdrop, the content of social studies consists of a rich array of facts, concepts, and generalizations. The way to tie all of this content together is through the use of compelling and supporting questions" (NCSS, 2013, p. 17). Questioning for critical and creative thinking is often considered a hallmark of gifted education; in almost any workshop about strategies for use with gifted students, questioning will likely be discussed. Unfortunately, the training relative to questioning is often superficial in nature.

An important aspect of developing professional learning experiences about questioning is to develop a practice activity that is directly related to social studies content; often discussions about questioning are done in the abstract, with teachers developing questions that are general in nature. Additionally, even if the specific content area is addressed in some way, the focus on questioning often does not address the disciplinary skills of the social sciences. According to Sandling (2017):

> In order to develop the habits of mind of the social sciences and to achieve significant outcomes, students must move beyond memorization and repetition of facts to active analysis and higher order thinking. In the social sciences, each discipline addresses various questions that students should attempt to answer as they begin developing disciplinary skills and habits of mind. (p. 245)

Therefore, prior to planning the professional learning activities, trainers should solicit information from the teachers about the specific content they teach, such as government, American history, or another course. This will help in finding resources that are directly applicable to the participants' contexts.

The next step is to determine which questioning model will be used. Bloom's revised taxonomy (Anderson & Krathwohl, 2001) is a common one, as is Webb's (2002) Depth of Knowledge. For creative thinking, many heuristics could be used, such as the Creative Problem Solving Model developed by Osborn and Parnes (Creative Education Foundation, n.d.) and de Bono's (1992) Thinking Hats. Regardless of the questioning model employed, the trainer must understand the conceptual basis of the model and how the elements can be connected with social studies as a discipline. Trainers need to not only help teachers understand which types of questions to ask, but also move them beyond simply focusing on facts and toward the concepts and generalizations that are important in the social sciences. This should include an emphasis on inquiries, as "Central to a rich social studies experience is the capability for developing questions that can frame and advance an inquiry. Those questions come in two forms: compelling and supporting questions" (NCSS, 2013, p. 24).

The development of compelling questions should include the following types of considerations: understanding why compelling questions are important to students and others, identifying disciplinary ideas, explaining how questions are representative of key ideas in the field, delineating the various points of view associated with a compelling question, and describing how a question relates to an enduring issue in the field. The construction of supporting questions should include the following types of considerations: identifying the facts and concepts related to a supporting question, making connections between compelling questions and supporting questions, explaining the relationship between supporting and compelling questions in an inquiry, delineating the various points of view associated with a supporting question, and explaining how supporting questions relate to inquiry and can lead to new questions through using engaging sources (NCSS, 2013). Trainers should note that "a compelling question frames an inquiry and a supporting question helps make the compelling question actionable" (Grant et al., 2017, p. 200). Compelling questions must be intellectually rigorous, but also relevant to students. The skills emphasized in the C3 Framework "represent the academic intentions of the disciplines that make up social studies and the special purposes of social studies as preparation for civic life" (NCSS, 2013, p. 27). Table 5.1 illustrates examples of questions that are based on the C3 Framework and are appropriate for meeting the cognitive needs of gifted students.

The C3 Framework's emphasis on developing questions and inquiries requires all students to participate in the challenging process of developing compelling and supporting questions. Therefore, teachers need to understand the nature of these questions and be able to pose such questions themselves. In addition, they must be able to pitch the questions at an even higher level for gifted students so that they are working at appropriate levels of depth and complexity. In a professional learning experience, trainers will have to help teachers choose the best questioning model, determine how to implement it in concert with a specific focus on developing questions and

Table 5.1
Sample Questions Based on the C3 Framework and
Geared to the Cognitive Needs of Gifted Students

Social Studies Content:
Ancient Civilizations, Grade 3, Virginia Standards of Learning

Type of Question	Example
Factual Versus Conceptual	
Factual	What were two contributions of the ancient Greeks?
Conceptual	How did the contributions of the ancient Greeks lead to change throughout the world?
Compelling Versus Supporting	
Compelling	How do contributions from ancient civilizations matter today?
Supporting	• How did the ancient Greeks contribute to ideas about democracy? • What are the important features of ancient Greek and Roman architecture? • Why did the location of the ancient _____ civilization change over time?

inquiries, and prepare illustrative questions that are sufficiently rigorous for gifted students.

A sample professional learning plan with an emphasis on developing questions and inquiries should include the following:

1. Trainer preparation:
   - Administer a needs assessment to determine teachers' areas of content expertise and experience with developing questions.
   - Select a questioning model. Review the conceptual basis of the model and how its elements can be connected with social studies as a discipline.
   - Prepare examples of compelling and supporting questions that can be posed within the selected questioning model.

2. Professional learning outline:
   - Discuss the C3 Framework and the use of Dimension 1, Developing Questions and Inquiries, as a basis for the professional learning experience.
   - Introduce the questioning model, its conceptual framework, and how its elements can be connected with social studies as a discipline.

- Introduce the C3 Framework's emphasis on students developing compelling and supporting questions.
- Demonstrate how to implement the questioning model in concert with a specific focus on developing questions and inquiries, and with an emphasis on students creating compelling and supporting questions.
- Collaboratively develop illustrative questions that are sufficiently rigorous for gifted students.
- Have teachers develop sample questions for their content areas.
- Have teachers critique each other's questions.
- Debrief.

Applying Disciplinary Tools and Concepts

Dimension 2, Applying Disciplinary Concepts and Tools, provides the backbone for the Inquiry Arc. Working with a robust compelling question and a set of discrete supporting questions, teachers and students determine the kind of content they need in order to develop their inquiries (NCSS, 2013, p. 17). In describing this dimension, the authors noted that a framework offers conceptual content, while curricular standards specify content standards. The content standards specify the big ideas to be taught in courses at given grade levels. The conceptual content indicates the big ideas that form the basis of the curricular content (NCSS, 2013). This emphasis on conceptual content is the area in which professional learning activities for this dimension should be focused. Conceptual content in social studies can relate to theories, such as those associated with land use, economics, or political behavior. It can also connect to overarching concepts, such as change, cause and effect, or systems.

As with Dimension 1 of the C3 Framework, trainers should develop a practice activity that is directly related to social studies content. Trainers should administer a needs assessment to determine which specific content the participants teach and what knowledge and experience they have with concept-based instruction.

Most teachers were not taught with an emphasis on concept-based instruction, nor were they oriented to related pedagogical methods. Thus, this tends to be an area where a great deal of professional learning should be conducted. Commonly used models for concept-based instruction in gifted education are: Taba's (1966) Model of Concept Development and Erickson's (2008) ideas about concept-based curriculum and instruction. In the Taba Model of Concept Development, participants work through four steps to come to an understanding of a concept: listing examples of the concept, categorizing, listing nonexamples, and determining generalizations about the concept. Erickson focused on concepts through a content-specific lens. Although the models differ slightly in their orientations, they both focus on a concept as a universal idea that is timeless and has applicability across disciplines. The C3 Framework's emphasis on applying disciplinary tools and concepts requires teachers to have a solid grasp of their subject matter, including advanced content, so that they can frame their curriculum within an overarching concept. This use of an overarching concept addresses the needs of gifted students to work at high levels of abstraction (VanTassel-Baska, 1986). Teachers should use advanced content framed through a conceptual lens in order to provide optimal opportunities for intellectual challenge. In a professional learning experience, the trainer will have to help teachers select a model for concept-based instruction, determine how to implement the model within the disciplinary context, and develop instructional tasks that are appropriate for gifted students.

A sample professional learning plan with an emphasis on applying disciplinary tools and concepts should include the following:

1. Trainer preparation:
    - Administer a needs assessment to determine teachers' knowledge of concept-based instruction.
    - Select a model for concept-based instruction. Review the conceptual basis of the model and how its elements can be connected with social studies as a discipline.
    - Prepare examples of using concepts as frames for social studies curricular content.

2. Professional learning outline:
    - Discuss the C3 Framework and the use of Dimension 2, Applying Disciplinary Tools and Concepts, as a basis for the professional learning experience.
    - Introduce the model to be used for concept-based learning, its conceptual framework, and how its elements can be connected with social studies as a discipline.
    - Introduce the C3 Framework's emphasis on using disciplinary tools and concepts within specific components of the social studies discipline.
    - Demonstrate how to implement the concept-based model of instruction as a frame for the social studies content the participants teach.
    - Collaboratively develop an example of a concept-based framework for one strand/course in social studies.

- Have teachers develop concept-based curriculum frameworks for their social studies content.
- Have teachers critique each other's questions.
- Debrief.

Evaluating Sources and Using Evidence

A central feature of Dimension 3, Evaluating Sources and Using Evidence, is "helping students develop a capacity for gathering and evaluating sources and then using evidence in disciplinary ways" (NCSS, 2013, p. 18). This dimension focuses on helping students learn to analyze information and develop a conclusion to an inquiry by gathering and evaluating sources, developing claims, and using evidence to support the claims. This is a sophisticated set of skills that is an expectation for all students. For gifted students, then, educators must consider how to add increasing levels of rigor to the skills work.

Paul's (1993) elements of reasoning is one critical thinking model that has been incorporated in various curriculum materials in gifted education. The eight elements of thought that he included in his model provide an excellent basis for helping students to evaluate sources and make evidence-based claims: question at issue, purpose, point of view, information, interpretations and inferences, concepts, assumptions, and implications and consequences. In a professional learning experience, trainers will have to help teachers understand the model, determine how to implement it within the disciplinary context, and develop instructional tasks that are sufficiently rigorous for gifted students.

Dimension 3 requires students to analyze information and develop a conclusion to an inquiry by gathering and evaluating sources, developing claims, and using evidence to support the claims. Using Paul's (1993) elements of reasoning, an example in social studies might look like this:

- **Question at issue:** Should the monuments of Civil War generals in Richmond, VA, be moved from Monument Avenue to a museum?
- **Purpose:** The purpose of examining this issue is to develop a viable solution for the city of Richmond that will provide historical documentation of the Civil War in a manner that is sensitive to all constituents.
- **Point of view:** The points of view of many stakeholders must be considered: city council members, the mayor, residents, descendants of slaves, descendants of the Civil War generals, historians, etc. When examining points of view, this is when students will have to gather and evaluate sources.

- **Information:** Information can be gathered from many different sources, such as through interviews of various stakeholders, historical documents, surveys of stakeholders, and public opinion polls. Students will also have to gather and evaluate sources to find data about the issue.
- **Interpretations and inferences:** The interpretations and inferences will come after the information is gathered and reviewed. When an individual makes interpretations and inferences, this is when they can begin to develop claims. They will use all of the evidence gathered to support the claims.
- **Concepts:** Some concepts or ideas that we can use to make sense of this information might include personal freedom, freedom of expression, historical significance, and historical context.
- **Assumptions:** Assumptions are the beliefs that people take for granted. The beliefs of all of the stakeholders must be examined and considered.
- **Implications and consequences:** The implications are related to one's thoughts about an issue. The consequences follow one's actions related to an issue. Once an individual has reviewed information related to all of the other elements and takes a stance, what will the implications and consequences be? In this example about the Civil War monuments, if city leaders examine the evidence and take the stance that the monuments should not be removed, what will be the implications and consequences?

Paul's elements of reasoning provide a framework for evaluating sources and using evidence. The information gathered can be used in debates, oral presentations, and research papers. This model moves students from simply stating that they agree or disagree with something to providing claims that are based on evidence.

A sample professional learning plan with an emphasis on evaluating sources and using evidence should include:

1. Trainer preparation:
   - Administer a needs assessment to determine teachers' knowledge of models relating to evaluating sources and using evidence (e.g., Paul's elements of reasoning).
   - Review the conceptual basis of the model and how its elements can be connected with social studies as a discipline.
   - Prepare examples of using the model with social studies-specific content.

2. Professional learning outline:
   - Discuss the C3 Framework and the use of Dimension 3, Evaluating Sources and Using Evidence, as a basis for the professional learning experience.
   - Introduce Paul's elements of reasoning model, its conceptual framework, and how its elements can be connected with social studies as a discipline.
   - Introduce the C3 Framework's emphasis on evaluating sources and using evidence within specific components of the social studies discipline.
   - Demonstrate how to implement Paul's elements of reasoning with a strand of social studies content that the participants teach.
   - Collaboratively develop an example of a lesson plan incorporating Paul's elements of reasoning, focusing on how to evaluate sources and use evidence.
   - Have teachers develop lesson plans incorporating Paul's elements of reasoning, focusing on how to evaluate sources and use evidence.
   - Have teachers critique each other's lesson plans.
   - Debrief.

Communicating Conclusions and Taking Informed Action

Dimension 4, Communicating Conclusions and Taking Informed Action, "advocates expanding the means by which students communicate their preliminary and final conclusions" (NCSS, 2013, p. 19). This dimension goes beyond Dimension 3 to include expectations for students to collaborate with others, communicate their findings from evaluating sources and using evidence, and critique their conclusions publicly. A common instructional strategy recommended for use with gifted students that provides such an opportunity is problem-based learning (PBL). Problem-based learning is an instructional strategy in which students work in teams to solve an open-ended real-world problem. It is particularly appropriate for use with gifted students because of its focus on advanced content, complex concepts, interdisciplinary connections, and ethical discussions. PBL aligns well to the four dimensions of the C3 Framework because of the emphasis on inquiry in both. According to Gallagher (2009), "Part of the relevance [of PBL] comes from the match between gifted students' learning characteristics and the PBL structure, part from the opportunity PBL presents to transform gifted students' unique characteristics into more mature skills, attitudes, and dispositions" (p. 203). After students have worked through the PBL scenario, a presentation to a real-world audience is considered an important culminating activity.

In social studies, a teacher could develop a problem statement, which is the starting point for every PBL scenario, related to some component of the content being studied. A sample problem statement related to the debate about Civil War monuments could be:

> You are the mayor of a small southern city. A monument of a Civil War general occupies a prominent place in your city. You are charged with leading a task force to determine whether the monument should stay in its current location or be moved to a museum. The city council has requested that your task force complete the task and make a recommendation within 2 months.

This real-world sample problem requires students to take on the role of a stakeholder, involves considering the viewpoints of various stakeholders, and has a time limit for resolution.

A sample professional learning plan with an emphasis on problem-based learning as a route to help students communicate conclusions and take informed actions should include the following:

1. Trainer preparation:
   - Administer a needs assessment to determine teachers' knowledge of PBL.
   - Review the conceptual basis of the model and how its elements can be connected with social studies as a discipline.
   - Prepare examples of using the model with social studies-specific content.

2. Professional learning outline:
   - Discuss the C3 Framework and the use of Dimension 4, Communicating Conclusions and Taking Informed Action, as a basis for the professional learning experience.
   - Introduce PBL to participants.
   - Introduce the C3 Framework's emphasis on communicating conclusions and taking informed actions within specific components of the social studies discipline.
   - Demonstrate how to implement PBL with a social studies topic that the participants teach.

- Collaboratively develop an example of a PBL ill-structured problem based on the participants' content, focusing on communicating conclusions and taking informed actions.
- Have teachers develop PBL ill-structured problems based on the participants' content, focusing on communicating conclusions and taking informed actions.
- Have teachers critique each other's ill-structured problems.
- Debrief.

Summary

Social studies is a content area that is rarely emphasized in training sessions for teachers of the gifted. Yet, the curriculum and pedagogy associated with social studies are both well-suited for the cognitive needs of gifted students. Through nesting the professional learning for teachers and trainers within the context of the C3 Framework and its focus on the four dimensions of the Inquiry Arc, a rich experience for students can be developed.

In this chapter, the focus was on professional learning for teachers in K–12, relative to social studies education. Standards in gifted education, standards that undergird professional learning, and the C3 Framework served as the backdrop. Key instructional strategies that connect well to the C3 Framework and important approaches for developing expertise in social studies were delineated. Information about the professional learning ideas specific to social studies that would be important for teachers of gifted students to know and understand was provided.

Resources

The following resources are websites that could be used when conducting professional learning activities for social studies teachers. These sites feature information about social studies content.

- 100 primary source documents from the National Archives: https://www.ourdocuments.gov
- Information about Paul's Elements of Reasoning: https://www.criticalthinking.org/pages/learn-the-elements-and-standards/861
- Digital Classroom, the National Archives' gateway for resources about primary sources: https://www.archives.gov/education
- The Gilder Lehrman Institute of American History: https://www.gilderlehrman.org
- Historical Thinking Matters: http://historicalthinkingmatters.org
- iCivics: https://www.icivics.org
- Library of Congress: https://www.loc.gov
- National Council for the Social Studies: https://www.socialstudies.org
- Teaching History: https://teachinghistory.org
- Teaching Tolerance: https://www.tolerance.org
- World History Matters: http://worldhistorymatters.org

References

Anderson, L., & Krathwohl, D. R. (Eds.). (2001). *A taxonomy for learning, teaching, and assessing: A revision of Bloom's taxonomy of educational objectives* (Complete ed.). Longman.

Callahan, C. M. (2018). The characteristics of gifted and talented students. In C. M. Callahan & H. L. Hertberg-Davis (Eds.), *Fundamentals of gifted education: Considering multiple perspectives* (2nd ed., pp. 153–166). Routledge.

Creative Education Foundation. (n.d.). *The CPS process*. http://www.creativeeducationfoundation.org/creative-problem-solving/the-cps-process

de Bono, E. (1992). *Six thinking hats for schools: Book 3*. Hawker Brownlow Education.

Erickson, H. L. (2008). *Stirring the head, heart, and soul: Redefining curriculum and instruction* (3rd ed.). Corwin.

Gallagher, S. A. (2009). Problem-based learning. In J. S. Renzulli, E. J. Gubbins, K. S. McMillen, R. D. Eckert, & C. A. Little (Eds.), *Systems and models for developing programs for the gifted and talented* (2nd ed., pp. 193–210). Prufrock Press.

Grant, S. G. (2013). From inquiry arc to instructional practice: The potential of the C3 Framework. *Social Education, 77*(6), 322–326.

Grant, S. G., Swan, K., & Lee, J. (2017). Questions that compel and support. *Social Education, 81*(4), 200–203.

Learning Forward. (2011). *Standards for professional learning.* https://learningforward.org/standards

National Association for Gifted Children. (2019). *2019 Pre-K–Grade 12 Gifted Programming Standards.* http://www.nagc.org/sites/default/files/standards/Intro%202019%20Programming%20Standards.pdf

National Association for Gifted Children, & The Association for the Gifted, Council for Exceptional Children. (2013). *NAGC-CEC teacher preparation standards in gifted education.* http://www.nagc.org/sites/default/files/standards/NAGC-%20CEC%20CAEP%20standards%20%282013%20final%29.pdf

National Council for the Social Studies. (n.d.). *National Curriculum Standards for Social Studies: Introduction.* https://www.socialstudies.org/standards/introduction

National Council for the Social Studies. (2013). *College, Career, and Civic Life (C3) Framework for Social Studies State Standards: Guidance for enhancing the rigor of K–12 civics, economics, geography, and history.* https://www.socialstudies.org/c3

Paul, R. W. (1993). *Critical thinking: What every person needs to survive in a rapidly changing world* (2nd ed.). Foundation for Critical Thinking.

Sandling, M. M. (2017). Social studies curricular considerations for advanced learners. In J. VanTassel-Baska & C. A. Little (Eds.), *Content-based curriculum for high-ability learners* (3rd ed., pp. 303–331). Prufrock Press.

Taba, H. (1966). *Teaching strategies and cognitive functioning in elementary school children.* San Francisco State College.

VanTassel-Baska, J. (1986). Effective curriculum and instructional models for talented students. *Gifted Child Quarterly, 30*(4), 164–169. https://doi.org/10.1177/001698628603000404

Webb, N. L. (2002). *Depth-of-knowledge levels for four content areas.* Wisconsin Center for Education Research.

CHAPTER 6

Foreign Language Education and Professional Learning for Teachers of Advanced Language Learners

Bronwyn MacFarlane

As a second-year teacher, I was charged with leading the districtwide gifted education program. As I pondered what to teach in a curriculum for elementary and secondary gifted students, my mother advised me with wise words, "Whatever you do, don't waste their time." As a veteran teacher and mother, she understood how important instructional time was and that the wasting of limited class minutes would result in the loss of valuable instructional time, productivity, and opportunity. All learners, whether in childhood, adolescence, or adulthood, desire engaging learning experiences that enable them to increase understanding and complete tasks successfully. Professional learning should incorporate all of the best practices and tenets of quality education. The time spent in exchange for the learning outcomes should be worthwhile.

In educational settings for students or adult learners, time is of the essence in order for valuable learning to occur. How instructional time is structured for learning to happen is paramount in designing quality educational experiences. In education, good teaching is generally operationalized by the interconnected planning of curriculum, instruction, and assessment (C-I-A). In meaningful professional learning, teachers must also experience good teaching that meets their professional learning needs across these three areas of C-I-A. In planning professional learning experiences for educators, typical learning goals and desired outcomes include increasing content expertise and pedagogical skill among teachers. With foreign language education, professional learning goals cover a wide range of relevant content in foreign language instruction. The American Council on the Teaching of Foreign Languages (ACTFL, 2006) developed five national standards, interdisciplinary in nature, that have been identified as the five C's for communication in a global world. These five standards can be used to guide the development of learning goals in the following areas of world language education:

1. **Communication:** Communicate in languages other than English.
2. **Cultures:** Gain knowledge and understanding of other cultures.
3. **Connections:** Connect with other disciplines and acquire information.
4. **Comparisons:** Gain insight into the nature of language and culture.
5. **Communities:** Participate in multilingual communities at home and around the world.

There has been a consistent call in national reports dating back to the 1960s for the American educational system to cultivate a greater number of fluent foreign language speakers (Arrow & Capron, 1959; National Academy of Sciences et al., 2007; National Research Council, 2007). But limitations in program funding and support, in addition to limited instructional time and decreasing enrollments have not resulted in attainment of the U.S. Department of Education's national goal of students' demonstrated competency in foreign languages (Goals 2000: Educate America Act, 1994). Curricular elimination has impacted foreign language instruction. There was a decrease in the percentage of public and private elementary schools offering foreign language instruction from 31% in 1997 to 25% in 2008 (Skorton & Altschuler, 2012). Foreign language instruction in public elementary schools dropped from 24% to 15%, with rural districts hit the hardest, and the percentage of all middle schools offering foreign language instruction decreased from 75% to 58% (Skorton & Altschuler, 2012).

Learning a second language exposes children to new language systems, cultures, and helps them understand English better (VanTassel-Baska, 1987; VanTassel-Baska et al., 2017b). Communication in a global world involves proficiency in language syntax, usage, and cultural literacy, which allow recognizing and participating in multilingual communities around the world (VanTassel-Baska et al., 2017a). The case for the importance of studying a foreign language and beginning language study early has been made repeatedly by foreign language education associations (ACTFL, 2006, 2015). As Stevens and Marsh (2005) pointed out:

> The learning of a foreign language exposes individuals to a range of new experiences. It touches not only upon social interaction, but also personal development and creative exploration, as well as intellectual and skills development. At its best, language learning opens up new worlds to learners within which self-discovery is a positive consequence. Individuals develop skills and acquire new dimensions of social interaction which, even at their simplest, open up new areas of communicative potential. (p. 113)

Skilled world language teachers are at a premium with a shortage of qualified foreign language teachers reported by about 25% of elementary schools and 30% of middle schools. Relatedly, by 2009–2010, only 50.7% of higher education institutions required foreign language study for a baccalaureate across degree programs, down from 67.5% in 1994–1995 (Skorton & Altschuler, 2012). Although the study of world languages has long been a valued component of a rich liberal arts education and the founders of American democracy were steeped in the study of classic Latin and Greek, as well as various romance languages as they forged diplomatic alliances internationally (MacFarlane, 2009), without well-trained teachers in foreign language programs, advanced language proficiency outcomes may be just a lucky coincidence. To achieve student advanced competency in foreign language, teachers must be well trained with meaningful professional learning experiences.

In planning professional learning to coalesce foreign language and gifted education, considering what to include is important so as to not regret the price of the time paid for it. In this chapter, the assumed educational outcome for the professional learning experiences is for language teachers to more effectively differentiate for advanced language learners.

Learning and Training Needs of Foreign Language Teachers

The foreign language teaching profession has endured fluctuating enrollments and a shortage of qualified teachers. In order to be effective, foreign language teachers need a critical combination of competencies

(Curtain & Pesola, 1994). In addition to the general areas of educational competencies needed (Met, 1999), specific skills and knowledge needed by foreign language teachers, as listed in Table 6.1, include a high level of language proficiency in all modalities, cultural understanding, communicative competence and applied use, deep understanding of the interconnected social realities associated with the target language, and proficiency with specific pedagogical knowledge and skills with a repertoire of strategies for developing proficiency and cultural understanding in all students (Guntermann, 1992; Peyton, 1997). These competencies lend themselves to teaching in a variety of programs. Strong language skills are essential for teachers to use the target language exclusively in foreign language classrooms. With educational emphases on designing thematic curriculum, working as a collaborative team member with other content area teachers, developing self-directed learning experiences for different students' cognitive needs, increasing classroom use of technology, and more, foreign language teachers face a variety of skills and knowledge needed in their professional learning. Furthermore, variance in enrollments at different grade levels may call upon a language teacher to teach at a wider range of grade levels than they have in the past. Understanding cultural, socio-economic, linguistic, and academic diversity among the student population enables foreign language teachers in working with different learners (Tedick & Walker, 1996). The interdisciplinary teaching of foreign language syntax, grammar, vocabulary, and culture integrated across an academic curriculum also calls upon a range of skills and knowledge, as detailed in Table 6.1.

Foreign language teachers must maintain and improve proficiency in the target language and stay current on issues related to the target culture as an ongoing process (MacFarlane, 2012a; Peyton, 1997). Among foreign language educators, a range of professional development options are well established, from language coursework, summer seminars, lectures, or workshops at universities, to participation in study and travel abroad programs, summer institutes and seminars, and both formal and informal opportunities for immersion weekends and regular conversation groups where the target language is used to discuss current events and other ideas. With online professional development and learning options, learning experiences for teachers should be (a) research-based, (b) infused with technology, (c) job-embedded, (d) team-based with coaching to enhance target language communication, and (d) tailored for local impact, and should (e) include a global component for worldwide connections. Rural and urban schools may face special challenges in ensuring highly qualified language faculty, and professional learning needs should be designed to provide learning options in multiple ways and formats.

Table 6.1
Specific Professional Skills and Knowledge
Needed by Foreign Language Teachers

1.	General education competencies and interpersonal skills (Met, 1999).
2.	A high level of world language proficiency in all modalities of the target language—speaking, listening, reading, and writing.
3.	The ability to use the target language in real-life contexts for both social and professional purposes.
4.	The ability to comprehend contemporary media in the foreign language, both oral and written, and interact successfully with native speakers in varying locations.
5.	A strong background in the liberal arts and content areas.
6.	Understanding of the social, political, historical, and economic realities of the regions where the language is spoken.
7.	Pedagogical knowledge and skills, including knowledge about human growth and development, learning theory and second-language acquisition theory, and a repertoire of strategies for developing proficiency and cultural understanding in all students.
8.	Knowledge of technologies and how to integrate them into instruction (Guntermann, 1992; Peyton, 1997).

Peyton (1997) suggested that instead of separating language teacher preparation into different departments specializing in English as a second language (ESL), foreign language, bilingual, and immersion, teachers should be prepared to teach in more than one second-language context. With preparation and continued training to teach in multiple areas, language teachers are better equipped for the range of assignments that may come their way among various program changes. For example, historically foreign language education certification has covered K–12, but may or may not have included training in both elementary and secondary education. Understanding cognitive processes associated with language acquisition, better prepares these teachers for both ESL and foreign language classes. Theory and practice should be integrated throughout continuing education.

Research in second-language acquisition and pedagogy almost always yields findings that are subject to interpretation rather than giving conclusive evidence (Brown, 2002), and so it may be clear that "enlightened" language teachers take an eclectic approach to pedagogy with the use of dynamic classroom tasks and activities (MacFarlane, 2012b). At least eight language teaching methods, or a combination thereof, may be in practice today, including (a) the grammar translation method, (b) the direct method, (c) the audiolingual method, (d) the silent way, (e) suggestopedia, (f) community language learning, (g) the total physical response method, and (h) the communicative approach (Met, 1999), as well as content-based language instruction and computer technologies. See Table 6.2 for a description of each pedagogical approach. But no comparative study has consistently demonstrated the superiority of one method over another for all teachers, all students, and all settings (College Board, 1986; Snow, 1994). How a particular method is manifested in a foreign language classroom depends heavily on the individual teacher's interpretation of the method's principles.

Integrating foreign language study with other content areas has also been encouraged, especially in the areas of social studies, the arts, and STEM (science, technology, engineering, and mathematics) for making global connections (Baska, 2018; MacFarlane, 2015b). STEM programs integrating world language study should integrate target language vocabulary into the curriculum with the language instructor playing a role in the STEM training, and not treat language development as a separate skill with a separate teacher (MacFarlane, 2016). STEAM programs that integrate the arts content in concert with STEM content should also introduce and regularly use key terms and vocabulary from the target language with the development of global awareness and the production of artistic products, such as important artistic terms in French that originated from the French Academy of Fine Arts (Academie des Beaux-Arts). In addition to content areas, students should learn the following skills to organize specific content knowledge: literacy, patterns, systems, design, citizenship, data, research, and philosophy (Heick, 2016). To achieve these educational goals, professional learning should include specific adult instruction about teaching to differentiate for advanced learners (MacFarlane, 2017a).

Training in Gifted Education for Foreign Language Teachers

Professional learning experiences for foreign language teachers need to include a specialized focus on meeting the educational needs of high-ability and gifted students. Although some Advanced Placement (AP) teachers and school administrators believe that AP courses are sufficiently advanced to meet the differentiated educational needs of gifted learners, it has been found that there is a lack of differentiated pedagogy in AP classrooms for

Table 6.2
Foreign Language Teaching Methods

Method	Description
Grammar Translation Method	This method originated in teaching classical languages and focuses upon students learning grammar rules and relevant vocabulary to acquire skills in reading and writing; less attention is paid to speaking and listening. The teacher corrects student errors.
Direct Method	The primary goal of this method is for students to communicate in the target language directly in the target language as opposed to translating from their native language to the second language. This method emphasizes communication processes, such as requesting, apologizing, narrating, commanding, and expressing an opinion. The focus is on oral communication through the study of everyday speech. Grammar is taught with examples in the target language and writing through dictation exercises. In contrast to the grammar translation method, no translation in the student's native language is permitted.
Audiolingual Method (ALM)	ALM was developed in the U.S. during World War II to quickly train people to use foreign languages for military purposes, with the goal for students to learn to communicate automatically, without translation. Language learning was viewed as a process of habit formation derived from learning language in context. By attempting to follow the "natural order" of language learning of listening, speaking, reading, and writing (the sequence in which children learn their first language), grammar was not taught explicitly, but errors were corrected immediately to avoid bad habit formation. ALM teaching techniques include repetition and substitution drills directed by the teacher, as well as imitation and repetition of dialogues.
The Silent Way	The goal of the silent way is for students to be able to use the target language to express their thoughts, perspectives, and feelings. The name of the method was derived from the idea that as students learn more of the target language, the teacher says less. Beginning with the sounds of the target language and moving on to linguistic structures, the teacher does not model the new sounds but rather uses gestures, sound-color charts, and instructional manipulatives to direct students. The teacher sets up situations that focus students on the structures of the target languages. All four skills are taught from the beginning but follow in the order of listening, speaking, reading, and writing. Peer correction is encouraged with student errors.

Table 6.2, continued.

Suggestopedia	Based on the idea that environmental, social, and psychological variables positively and negatively influence a student's ability to learn a target language, this method emphasizes the importance of relaxation during the language learning process and removing the feature of failure. Techniques include listening to music, a comfortable learning environment, and the use of dialogues that contain language that students can use immediately.
Community Language Learning (CLL)	CLL techniques were derived from group counseling with a focus on the "whole person" and their desire to learn the target language with considerations of the learner's feelings, physical reactions, and instinctive defense mechanisms to assist and support learning. Elements of this approach include providing a sense of security, allowing students to assert themselves, focus on one task at a time, reflect on what has been learned, integrate new material with what was previously learned, and distinguish differences among target language forms. Cooperation among students is emphasized to build a sense of community in the classroom and students are permitted to express feelings in native language, which are then translated in the target language.
Total Physical Response Method (TPR)	TPR uses teacher commands to direct student behavior. Student responses involve physical movements or actions in which students indicate that a word, phrase, or concept has been understood. For example beginning commands could include, "Stand up. Sit down. You will need a piece of paper and pencil, etc." After learning to respond to oral commands, students learn to read and write them. The approach is based on observing early language learning by listening, observing, attempting to use the form heard, and eventually combining forms in different ways. Students are allowed to use their native language at the beginning to respond to teachers to concentrate on listening comprehension.
Communicative Approach	The goal of this method is for students to use "authentic language" in a social setting. Students need knowledge of the linguistic structure and forms, meaning, and functions in the target language. The skills of listening, speaking, comprehension, reading, and writing, are developed from the beginning, but typically the lessons emphasize language function and usage over correct grammatical form.

Table 6.2, continued.

Content-Based Language Instruction (CBI)	CBI is the concurrent teaching of academic subject matter and second-language skills. At the heart of the language practice is the study of a subject-matter core, with the integrated use of authentic language, texts, and assignments, with adaptations of materials and approaches to meet the needs of the language learner. The CBI method may vary in practice with different variations and implementation models.
Computer Technologies	Language listening and learning labs evolved with technology over the years, and many instructors use different computer software and programs in classrooms as a supplementary tool for language teaching.

Note. These pedagogical approaches are often combined in an eclectic approach. Adapted from Reppy and Adames (2000).

secondary gifted students (Hertberg-Davis et al., 2006) and AP teachers are not required to be trained in gifted education instructional practices. By integrating specific instructional strategies to enhance the learning of gifted students, foreign language teachers can become skilled at adding rigor at all levels of language proficiency. When working with advanced language learners, foreign language teachers need to recognize and understand the unique characteristics of high-ability students, as well as be able to individualize and differentiate instruction for gifted language learners (MacFarlane, 2009). In a study of AP world language teacher perceptions of gifted students, teachers reported somewhat positive attitudes toward providing support to advanced learner needs, but also reported ambivalent attitudes toward ability grouping and actively advocating for these learners. Moreover, they reported somewhat negative attitudes toward acceleration and limited use of differentiated strategies in the AP classroom. They also reported limited teacher training in gifted pedagogy (MacFarlane, 2009). These findings illustrate the specific training needs for meeting the needs of gifted language learners. Professional learning experiences for teachers should address differentiating curriculum, instruction, and assessment with the use of advanced instructional practices.

Characteristics of advanced learners that match the second-language educational experience include advanced vocabularies, wordplay, creative and curious interdisciplinary connections, opportunities for linguistic comparative analysis for adding depth and complexity, and divergent and convergent thinking processes (VanTassel-Baska et al., 2017a). By understanding the educational needs of advanced learners, language teachers can be attuned to making curriculum and instructional modifications for high-ability language learners. Specific skills and knowledge needed by foreign language teachers who work with advanced learners are listed in Table 6.3.

To collaborate across curriculum content areas, foreign language teachers need guidance on connecting to various units of study and specific planning time to work with content area teachers. Second-language instruction embedded in STEM instruction offers an advanced interdisciplinary curriculum for talented learners to integrate understanding of the social customs, politics, arts, literature, and philosophy of a foreign culture through world language study. Thus, it enhances crosscultural competence and communication skills for the 21st century (MacFarlane, 2018). As with mathematics, gifted learners can begin a second language early and accelerate that learning at a rate comfortable for them, often taking two second languages during their K–12 years (VanTassel-Baska et al., 2017b).

Table 6.3
Specific Professional Skills and Knowledge Needed by Foreign Language Teachers When Working With Advanced Learners

> In addition to the skills and knowledge listed in Table 6.1, foreign language teachers working with advanced learners should also have the following professional skills and understanding specific to high ability learners:
> 1. proficiency with and depth of foreign language content knowledge,
> 2. opportunities to collaborate with other advanced language teachers,
> 3. skill in designing and leading differentiated instruction,
> 4. knowledge of advanced instructional strategies, and
> 5. knowledge of advanced learner characteristics.

Examples of Designing Foreign Language Professional Learning

In order for educators to have a greater appreciation for meeting the learning needs of advanced gifted students, professional learning experiences should be designed to integrate complexity into the training for teacher participants and model how to integrate complexity into foreign language classroom teaching to differentiate for ready learners. Foreign language education may be offered in a variety of settings from across K–12 and ranging from separate classes to immersion experiences. Just as foreign language education should be pitched to the learner's readiness level, so too, should professional learning for teachers be designed to match proficiency levels among teachers. The conundrum for professional learning providers and facilitating administrators can be how to serve the varying needs of foreign language teachers with varying levels of proficiency. Some states have developed lists of the competencies that foreign language teachers should have, and the experiences recommended for developing the competencies with resources to aid teacher professional learning and development. For example, the North Carolina World Language Essential Standards (WLES) can be downloaded from the North Carolina Department of Public Instruction's website (https://www.dpi.nc.gov/documents/curriculum/worldlanguages/scos/world-language-essential-standards), which provides a link to a website with many resources, including an "Instructional Toolkit" (see https://europe.unc.edu/toolkits for classroom teaching materials and professional learning materials).

For teachers of the gifted who wish to integrate foreign language study into the gifted class curriculum, the scope of what is possible is dependent upon the teacher's foreign language training. Language integration will be more comfortable for teachers of the gifted who have had language courses and achieved proficiency level. For teachers who have not achieved proficiency or are at the novice level, it may be possible to begin with a culture, history, and geography unit, followed with the integration of key terms. There are limited curricular resources available targeted at differentiated language learning but there are some resources focused upon the study of Latin and listed below.

- Baska, A., & VanTassel-Baska, J. (2014). *Ancient roots and ruins: A guide to understanding the Romans, their world, and their language.* Prufrock Press.
- Spielhagen, F. (2018). *Ecce Caeciliae et Verus set.* Royal Fireworks Press.

For teachers in foreign language classrooms, a needs assessment should be conducted prior to designing professional learning activities to understand their proficiency level and what they view to be their greatest areas of professional learning needs to differentiate their teaching. A needs assessment should be aligned with ACTFL's 5 C's. In reference to the skills and understandings listed in Table 6.3 for foreign language teachers working with advanced learners, consider the following training scenarios in which teachers could learn greater depth for classroom application and educational leaders can apply the ideas in professional learning activities. Professional learning outcomes from Table 6.3 follow with ideas for professional learning training formats:

- **Proficiency with and depth of foreign language content knowledge:** Make arrangements for advanced language coursework. Schools should plan to make advanced language courses accessible online, or to partner with a nearby university or with a language consultant to provide targeted training sessions with educators to build their language capacity.
- **Opportunities to collaborate with other advanced language teachers:** Conference with other foreign language teachers. Professional learning is an important part of the annual school budget. School leaders should plan to provide resources for annual professional conferences for teachers to meet and share ideas.
- **Skill in designing and leading differentiated instruction:** Provide differentiation workshops and curriculum writing labs. For teachers to practice revising curriculum using differentiated instruction, workshops should offer examples and opportunities to revise existing curriculum plans with specific methods from gifted education literature.

- **Knowledge of advanced instructional strategies:** Provide training in advanced instructional strategies and application. Professional learning experiences that provide for both the study of and application of instructional strategies incorporate practice opportunities to operationalize the focus of the training in classrooms with observation and feedback from colleagues within a supportive professional learning group.
- **Knowledge of advanced learner characteristics:** Provide identification case studies and talent spotting checklists. Opportunities to review diverse gifted student cases provide teachers with additional insight about advanced learner characteristics to look for and talent indicators to recognize.

Professional learning for improved teaching and learning in the classroom should include a focus on designing curriculum and instruction pitched to varying learner levels and needs (MacFarlane, 2012b; 2015a). Using examples of curriculum prompts that are pitched to different levels ranging from novice to advanced should be included in teacher training and include specific information about acceleration. When designing professional learning experiences around curriculum and instruction learning outcomes, facilitators should plan to use a variety of prompts to illustrate how the quality of differing prompts may stimulate the quality of learning outcomes. Demonstrating how rigor varies with a range of curricular examples may be used in workshop trainings or in professional learning communities (PLCs) as a participant exercise for analysis and discussion, and subsequently lead to a teacher-based task of evaluating the rigor levels in the existing classroom curriculum. Consider how the curriculum writing example of integrating complexity in Table 6.4 could be used in professional development sessions for foreign language teachers to increase rigor in classroom curriculum. The activity in Table 6.4 demonstrates a sample tiered activity for a typical middle school world language curriculum and how it may be designed to move from simple to complex in order to meet the needs of diverse learners, including gifted students, in the world language classroom.

Similar pedagogical exercises should be developed and practiced with foreign language teachers to advance the rigor level in foreign language classroom curriculum, instruction, and assessment (MacFarlane, 2017b). Professional learning experiences for world language teachers should not only cover the basics of gifted education, but also be demonstrated through the use of gifted pedagogical learning experiences that require sophisticated thinking and reasoning with multiple sources and complex questions

Table 6.4
Sample Tiered Activity for a Middle School World Language Curriculum

Middle School—World Language	
Objective—The student engages in the written exchange of information, opinions, and ideas in a variety of time frames in formal and informal situations (College Board, 2011, p. 12).	
Simple (typical learner)—Write a letter to a pen pal. Describe something that is important to you and why. Use correct verb conjugations and at least three different tense forms.	Complex (gifted language learner)—Write a letter to the editor of the local bilingual newspaper to support K–12 world language education programs in the schools. Clearly state your case and argue your point of view, using at least three reliable sources.

Note. From *Curricular Considerations in World Languages for Advanced Learners*, by B. MacFarlane, in J. VanTassel-Baska and C. A. Little (Eds.), *Content-Based Curriculum for High-Ability Learners* (3rd ed., p. 346), 2017, Prufrock Press. Copyright 2017 by Prufrock Press. Reprinted with permission.

to solve. Teachers should experience good teaching that meets their professional learning needs across the three areas of C-I-A.

Similarly, training for teachers of the gifted and talented should also focus on how their gifted program curriculum can be differentiated to stimulate sophisticated critical thinking and global understanding. The activity in Table 6.5 demonstrates a sample problem-solving activity for a gifted classroom curriculum integrating a world language study and how a curricular task may be designed to move from simple to complex in order to meet the accelerated needs of advanced learners in a gifted program.

By aligning the five C's (ACTFL, 2006) for communication with the best practices in gifted education, professional development learning goals can be designed to increase content expertise and pedagogical skill among world language teachers. Integrating advanced thinking processes with advanced language content will increase the rigor of professional learning for language teachers and provide a model for increasing classroom rigor and differentiation needed in order to meet the needs of gifted learners.

To reflect upon previous valuable professional learning experiences and create a plan for future professional learning, faculty leaders may use a table of specifications to guide the development of learning goals in the different areas of world language education. Table 6.6 illustrates how a table of specifications may be used to guide professional learning reflection and as a needs assessment for planning PLCs in alignment with the five C's (ACTFL, 2006). To further elaborate upon student tasks in a table

Table 6.5
Sample Tiered Activity For A Middle School
Gifted Curriculum World Language Study

Middle School—Gifted Classroom Integrated Unit With World Language	
Learning Outcome: Students should be able to integrate multiple sources to communicate a global understanding about a foreign culture using key terms from the target language and culture of study to creatively identify and offer solutions to a global problem.	
Learning Activity: Simple Using the scientific method, identify and solve a global problem that impacts a specific foreign country. Present your conclusions using relevant terminology and findings.	**Learning Activity: Complex** Research and identify a global problem. Using two creative thinking methods (one must be Creative Problem Solving [CPS] and one your choice), create two sustainable solutions. Present your rationale, recommendations, and conclusions using data.
Professional Learning Prompts for Teachers: 1. Analyze the differences between the two prompts. How do the prompts vary in complexity? 2. Discuss possibilities that would adjust the prompts to a simpler level and to a more advanced level. 3. Using a table of specifications, evaluate the rigor levels in the existing classroom curriculum prompts, activities, and performance tasks. 4. Identify and revise five student learning experiences in the existing classroom curriculum that would be possible to increase the rigor level for what students are asked to do and understand.	

of specifications, reference the ACTFL (2015) Performance Descriptors for Language Learners document.

Summary

The skillful development of understanding and application of differentiated instruction in teaching foreign language is an important component in planning meaningful professional learning experiences to impact diverse gifted students. As discussed, many foreign language teachers have reported limited to no training about gifted education and how to differentiate for advanced language learners. By considering appropriately accel-

Table 6.6
Table of Specifications

Directions: Rate the following standards on a scale of 1 (no, low) to 4 (yes, high).			
ACTFL's (2006) Five C's	As a teacher, rate your comfort level with teaching this foreign language standard.	To what degree is this standard included in the current curriculum and instruction?	Is this an area in which you would benefit from additional professional learning?
Communication: Communicate in languages other than English.			
Cultures: Gain knowledge and understanding of other cultures.			
Connections: Connect with other disciplines and acquire information.			
Comparisons: Gain insight into the nature of language and culture.			
Communities: Participate in multilingual communities at home and around the world.			

erated content and the use of complex pedagogical methods, the learning experiences for gifted students can be raised in sophistication and beyond advanced proficiency. Professional learning leaders need to conceptualize and identify the needs in a local setting and create a plan using the ideas and recommendations presented in this chapter as starting points for increasing the quality of rigor in foreign language teaching and learning experiences. Teachers of gifted foreign language learners need professional learning experiences to deepen their language skills and cultural understanding with embedded opportunities to build upon and revise the curriculum and instruction for use with advanced students.

Resources

Books

MacFarlane, B. (Ed.). (2016). *STEM education for high-ability learners: Designing and implementing programming.* Prufrock Press.

Suggested Chapter: "International STEM Education and the Integrated Role of Second Language Study," by B. MacFarlane (pp. 187–206)

MacFarlane, B. (Ed.). (2018). *Specialized schools for high-ability learners: Designing and implementing programs in specialized school settings.* Prufrock Press.

Suggested Chapter: "Specialized Second Language Academies: Optimizing Advancement for Gifted Learners," by A. Baska (pp. 135–148)

MacFarlane, B., & Stambaugh, T. (Eds.) (2009). *Leading change in gifted education: The festschrift of Dr. Joyce Vantassel-Baska.* Prufrock Press.

Suggested Chapter: "Global Learning: Teaching World Language to Gifted Learners," by B. MacFarlane (pp. 299–310)

VanTassel-Baska, J., & Little, C. A. (Eds.) (2017). *Content-based curriculum for high-ability learners* (3rd ed.). Prufrock Press.

Suggested Chapter: "Curricular Considerations in World Languages for Advanced Learners," by B. MacFarlane (pp. 337–359)

VanTassel-Baska, J., MacFarlane, B., & Baska, A. (2017). *Second language learning for the gifted: Connection and communication for the 21st century.* National Association for Gifted Children.

Websites

American Council on the Teaching of Foreign Languages. (n.d.). https://www.actfl.org

American Council on the Teaching of Foreign Languages. (n.d.). *Assessment & professional development.* https://www.actfl.org/assessment-professional-development

North Carolina Department of Public Instruction. (2016). *World Language Essential Standards.* https://www.dpi.nc.gov/documents/curriculum/worldlanguages/scos/world-language-essential-standards

Office of Postsecondary Education. (1996). *Improving elementary school foreign language teacher education.* https://www2.ed.gov/notclamped/about/offices/list/ope/fipse/lessons3/center.html

References

American Council on the Teaching of Foreign Languages. (2006). *World-readiness standards for learning languages.* https://www.actfl.org/sites/default/files/publications/standards/World-ReadinessStandardsforLearningLanguages.pdf

American Council on the Teaching of Foreign Languages. (2015). *Performance descriptors for language learners.* https://www.actfl.org/sites/default/files/pdfs/ACTFLPerformance-Descriptors.pdf

Arrow, K. J., & Capron, W. M. (1959, May). Dynamic shortages and price rises: The engineer-scientist case. *The Quarterly Journal of Economics, 73*(2), 292–308.

Baska, A. (2018). Foreign language programs. In B. MacFarlane (Ed.), *Specialized schools for high-ability learners: Designing and implementing programs in specialized school settings* (pp. 135–148). Prufrock Press.

Brown, H. D. (2002). English language teaching in the "post-method" era: Toward better diagnosis, treatment, and assessment. In J. C. Richards & W. A. Renandya (Eds.), *Methodology in language teaching: An anthology of current practice* (pp. 9–18). Cambridge University Press.

College Board. (1986). Speech delivered by Hanford, G. The SAT and Statewide Assessment. *Vital Speeches of the Day, 52*(24), 765.

Curtain, H., & Pesola, C. (1994). *Languages and children: Making the match* (2nd ed.). Longman.

Goals 2000: Educate America Act, H.R. 1804 § 102 (1994). https://www2.ed.gov/legislation/GOALS2000/TheAct/sec102.html

Guntermann, G. (1992). An analysis of interlanguage development over time: Part II, ser and estar. *Hispania, 75*(5), 1294–1303.

Heick, T. (2016). *What students will learn in the future.* TeachThought. https://www.teachthought.com/the-future-of-learning/what-students-will-learn-in-the-future

Hertberg-Davis, H., Callahan, C. M., & Kyburg, R. M. (2006). *Advanced Placement and International Baccalaureate Programs: A "fit" for gifted learners?* (RM06222). University of Connecticut, The National Research Center on the Gifted and Talented.

MacFarlane, B. (2009). Global learning: Teaching world languages to gifted learners. In B. MacFarlane & T. Stambaugh (Eds.), *Leading change in gifted education: The festschrift of Dr. Joyce VanTassel-Baska* (pp. 299–310). Prufrock Press.

MacFarlane, B. (2012a). Differentiating teacher professional development with design. *Understanding Our Gifted, 24*(2), 9–14. http://www.our-gifted.com/UOG24-2.pdf

MacFarlane, B. (2012b). Perspective from the periphery: Teaching gifted foreign language students. *TEMPO, 33*(2), 26–30.

MacFarlane, B. (2015a, January). Teaching what is essential. *Teaching for High Potential.*

MacFarlane, B. (2015b, June). The case for integrating social studies education and world languages for gifted learners. *Teaching for High Potential*, 4–5.

MacFarlane, B. (2016). International STEM education and the integrated role of second language study. In B. MacFarlane (Ed.), *STEM education for high-ability learners: Designing and implementing programming* (pp. 187–206). Prufrock Press.

MacFarlane, B. (2017a, November). Translating PD into high-powered classroom curriculum. *Teaching for High Potential*, 5, 11.

MacFarlane, B. (2017b, February). Using regular review for improving lesson planning. *Teaching for High Potential*, 4.

MacFarlane, B. (2018, February). High-level questioning and cognition in advanced curriculum. *Teaching for High Potential*, 11, 19.

Met, M. K. (1999). Research in foreign language curriculum. In G. Cawelti (Ed.), *Handbook of research on improving student achievement* (2nd ed., pp. 86–111). Educational Research Service.

National Academy of Sciences, National Academy of Engineering, & Institute of Medicine. (2007). *Rising above the gathering storm:*

Energizing and employing America for a brighter economic future. The National Academies Press. https://doi.org/10.17226/11463

National Research Council. (2007). *International education and foreign languages: Keys to securing America's future.* The National Academies Press. https://doi.org/10.17226/11841.

Peyton, J. (1997). *Professional development of foreign language teachers* (ED414768). ERIC. https://files.eric.ed.gov/fulltext/ED414768.pdf

Reppy, J. & Adames, J. (2000). Pedagogical Approaches in English as a Second Language. In J. Rosenthal (Ed.), *Handbook of undergraduate second language education* (pp. 77–82). Erlbaum.

Skorton, D., & Altschuler, G. (2012). *American's foreign language deficit.* Forbes. https://www.forbes.com/sites/collegeprose/2012/08/27/americas-foreign-language-deficit

Snow, R. (1994). Abilities in academic tasks. In R. J. Sternberg & R. K. Wagner (Eds.), *Mind in context: Interactionist perspectives on human intelligence* (pp. 3–37). Cambridge University Press.

Stevens, A., & Marsh, D. (2005). Foreign language teaching within special needs education: Learning from Europe-wide experience. *Support for Learning, 20*(3), 109–114. https://doi.org/10.1111/j.0268-2141.2005.00373.x

Tedick, D. J., & Walker, C. L. (1996). R(T)eaching all students: Necessary changes in teacher education. In B. H. Wing (Ed.), *Foreign languages for all: Challenges and choices* (pp. 187–220). National Textbook Company.

VanTassel-Baska, J. (1987). A case for the teaching of Latin to the verbally talented. *Roeper Review, 9*(3), 159–161. https://doi.org/10.1080/02783198709553036

VanTassel-Baska, J., MacFarlane, B., & Baska, A. (2017a). *Second language learning for the gifted: Connection and communication for the 21st century.* National Association for Gifted Children.

VanTassel-Baska, J., MacFarlane, B., & Baska, A. (2017b). The need for second language learning. *Parenting for High Potential, 6*(5), 4–9.

CHAPTER 7

Research-Based Essentials in Professional Learning in the Arts

Hope E. Wilson

Arts educators, including teachers of the visual and performing arts, face unique challenges in pursuing professional learning opportunities. However, the importance of the arts to develop critical and creative thinking skills, academic achievement, motivation, and areas of talent (e.g., Catterall, 2009) make it imperative that teachers of the arts receive high-quality professional learning opportunities (Sabol, 2006). This professional learning should include active engagement with the discipline, arts-specific pedagogy, opportunities for collaboration, and reflective practice. As arts educators who teach gifted learners, these experiences can provide the necessary foundations for the development of talent of advanced learners and artistically talented students.

Types of Arts Educators for Gifted Learners

Arts educators of gifted learners may fall into three groups that serve different types of learners in different contexts. These three types of arts educators are: educators who integrate the arts, general arts educators, and specialized arts educators (Wilson, 2017). These educators also serve various types of gifted and talented learners: intellectually/academically talented learners (those who are traditionally identified for gifted programs), artistically talented learners (those who exhibit specific talents in the arts), those who are both intellectually and artistically gifted, and those who may have academic challenges but have artistic talents (sometimes thought of as prodigies or having a learning disability that may or may not be diagnosed; Wilson 2009, 2017). This chapter discusses these types of gifted learners in detail, as well as the types of arts educators that benefit from professional learning.

Educators Who Integrate the Arts

The first group of arts educators may not even consider themselves teachers of the arts, but teachers of another content area who work actively to integrate the arts into their students' learning. These teachers might be using the arts to enhance math or science as part of a STEAM (science, technology, engineering, arts, and mathematics) initiative, incorporate art history into social studies, or use music to enrich literature or reading lessons. Intellectually gifted learners will benefit from this approach because it allows them to synthesize ideas and make deep connections across disciplines. Artistically gifted learners benefit from this approach as it provides additional opportunities to develop their areas of talent and can provide motivation and engagement in content areas. Teachers in this group benefit from specific professional learning opportunities that provide pedagogical content knowledge and disciplinary content knowledge that can develop deep understandings of the arts and effective strategies for integration.

General Arts Educators

The next group of arts educators provides arts instruction to a wide variety of students, including a range of both academic and artistic abilities.

These teachers teach primarily arts-based classes (e.g., visual arts, vocal or instrumental music, theater, or creative writing) to a general education population in elementary, middle levels, and secondary schools. These teachers may be the only teacher in their discipline in their school building, or may travel between several schools, providing arts education intermittently to students. Their classes may be classified as a resource, special, or elective class and not necessarily part of the core curriculum in the school system. Nevertheless, arts educators in this group are in need of high-quality professional learning opportunities that are specific to their discipline and help them to develop the artistic talents of the gifted students in their classroom. They are also in need of professional learning to learn how best to meet the unique needs of intellectually and academically gifted learners through their content-specific instruction, using the arts to promote advanced critical and creative thinking and synthesis of ideas across content areas.

Specialized Arts Educators

The final group of arts educators are teaching courses dedicated to the advanced development of talent among artistically talented students. These teachers may be at specialized arts schools (e.g., public magnets or private conservatories) or teaching advanced classes (e.g., Advanced Placement [AP] or International Baccalaureate [IB]) at a comprehensive school. Although these teachers may be offered more instructional support for the development of talent areas and have more advanced and dedicated students, they are still in need of effective professional learning opportunities to develop their content expertise and skill with individualizing instruction to maximize development for advanced students. Many educators will find that they may fit into more than one of these groups, and that the professional learning needs of each of these groups often overlap.

Qualities and Challenges of Professional Learning

Professional learning for arts educators should encompass the diverse needs of arts educators of gifted learners. It should be active, involving participation in the discipline (Combs & Silverman, 2016); individualized, focused on specific arts areas (Conway, 2008; Lind, 2007); collaborative, allowing for a community of practice (Conway, 2008; Lind, 2007; Stanley, 2011); and reflective, encouraging individual development and personal professional goals (Bautista et al., 2017; Conway, 2008). These practices will help arts educators tailor their teaching for both academically and artistically gifted and talented learners.

Arts educators of gifted learners, however, face unique challenges for professional learning within the current school system. Given their distinct role, arts educators have specific circumstances, including isolation, lack of relevant content, marginalization, and value only in support of other disciplines in regard to traditional professional learning offered in schools (Sabol, 2006), which are directly related to the four areas of focus for high-quality professional learning for arts educators of gifted learners.

Professional Learning Should Be Active

The arts are often marginalized in comparison to the other disciplines, primarily those assessed by state accountability measures. Although this is not the experience of all arts educators, it is a common occurrence among many (e.g., Nompula, 2013). This marginalization may be subtle, as in ignoring the needs of arts educators in schoolwide professional learning, or more overt, as in direct comments regarding the unimportance of the discipline. This pervasive attitude within school systems leaves arts educators with lower levels of support for continued professional growth, particularly in disciplinary content knowledge and pedagogical content knowledge (Conway, 2008). Due to this marginalization, arts educators are often not afforded the resources to participate in high-quality professional learning that engages them with their own disciplines.

Professional learning for arts educators should actively engage educators in the arts discipline, which may require additional resources, time, and materials. Content knowledge and pedagogy in the arts disciplines require the development of skill, which occurs through practice and hands-on learning. Arts educators must have the opportunity to actively engage in these types of learning opportunities to further develop their practice, learn new skills, and participate in experiential learning. For educators of disciplines outside of the arts who are exploring opportunities to integrate the arts in meaningful ways, professional learning must include active learning that provides scaffolding for teachers to gain comfort levels with the new content and skill areas. This type of leaning typically requires greater resources, in terms of space, materials, and time, than traditional professional development activities, but follows the trend of professional learning in all disciplines to include greater engagement of teachers over longer periods of time (Combs & Silverman, 2016).

Specific strategies to engage arts educators in their disciplines can include providing opportunities for workshops with professional artists to learn new techniques, such as photography, printmaking, or sculpture. Attending national and state conferences specifically for arts disciplines, such as the National Association for Music Educators or the International Thespian Festival, provides another opportunity for arts educators to develop their craft. Finally, many schools have formed alliances with and written grants to receive funding for artists in residence, which have brought community artists into classrooms to teach students and educators about their crafts. In such partnerships, these artists in residence have been able to provide professional learning opportunities for all the educators in the schools that they visit.

Professional Learning Should Be Individualized

Relatedly, when teachers of the arts participate in professional learning at the school or district level, these activities are often not content-specific for the arts. Much of the professional learning at schools focuses on data and assessment as they pertain to state accountability requirements (e.g., Hochberg & Desimone, 2010). This leads to an emphasis on reading and mathematics skill development, along with other tested subject areas, which is less relevant to the content taught outside of language arts, mathematics, science, and social studies classrooms. Even when professional learning is not directly related to state assessments, it focuses on topics (such as content standards, classroom management, or special education accommodations), which are framed around traditional classrooms. Although these topics are applicable to teachers of the arts, the context of arts classrooms often makes the implementation of strategies unique. For example, although many teachers may develop classroom management techniques to help students maintain quiet, individual work time, a theater teacher will need strategies to organize the cooperative movement of students and encourage the projection of voice. Similarly, accommodations for students with exceptionalities will vary by art discipline and may require differentiated strategies from typical classrooms. Art standards vary greatly as compared to math, language arts, social studies, or science standards, and ways to teach and assess those standards are also quite different. Thus, professional learning that is offered at the school, and often the district level, is often less relevant to the needs of the teachers of the arts (Conway, 2008; Lind, 2007), and should be tailored to the specific arts areas for the educators' content.

Given the unique needs of arts educators, professional learning opportunities must be individualized. This will allow educators to have relevant experiences to their contexts. Even when arts educators have the opportunity to come together for professional learning, individualization allows teachers to adapt the experience for their own classrooms. For example, music teachers may all benefit from an opportunity to experience and practice with steel drums; however, elementary and secondary teachers will need space to consider how to incorporate the learning into their classrooms in very different ways. Additionally, a secondary instrumental teacher at a comprehensive high school will use this learning experience differently than an educator at a magnet school that specializes in the arts. Professional learning must be adaptable and provide opportunities for educators to individualize the experience for their unique classrooms and students.

This can be accomplished simply by not taking a one-size-fits-all approach to professional learning. Specifically, facilitators should allow time for educators to apply concepts and techniques to their own unique classrooms and contexts. This may be made explicit through brainstorming and sharing exercises in which teachers are encouraged to discuss how they will implement the new learnings into their classrooms and the challenges that their contexts will present.

Additionally, districts and schools should provide frequent opportunities for arts educators to come together by discipline for professional learning that can focus on specific pedagogical content knowledge and the development of the craft of their discipline. In large districts, professional learning days can be devoted to specific art disciplines, providing studio space for educators to practice and learn new skills, such as printmaking, improvisational theater, or vocal technique. In smaller districts, in which there may only be one or two teachers of a specific discipline (e.g., theater or instrumental music), there must be funds available for educators to attend conferences at the regional, state, or national level to learn from discipline experts.

Collaborative

In many schools, the teachers of the arts may be the only professionals in their building with their content area expertise (Scheib, 2006). This may happen in elementary schools in which there is one visual art teacher and one music teacher to teach all of the students in kindergarten through fifth or sixth grade. In many systems, these teachers may travel between several schools, weakening their connection to any one community of professionals. It is also common to only have a few teachers of the arts in middle and high schools, especially in rural areas or in smaller schools. This presents challenges to professional learning, in that communities of practice are often unavailable and content-specific learning for teachers is limited (Maher et al., 2010). The isolation of arts educators leads to fewer opportunities for students to benefit from the professional collaboration of teachers (Maher et al., 2010).

Although arts educators often work in relative isolation, they benefit when they can learn in collaborative communities of practice (Doğan & Adams, 2018). The rise of professional learning communities (PLCs) within school systems has benefitted educators and students, but arts educators are often without a significant community of practice in which to engage. Sometimes schools have arts educators across disciplines participate in PLCs together, but this can result in less meaningful learning, as the pedagogical content in visual arts, music, and theater can be quite diverse. An art teacher struggling with materials management is not likely to have significant pedagogical discourse with their music teacher colleague who is concerned with how to select appropriate musical selections for the range of developing voices. Better practice would be for school systems to coordinate PLCs to allow collaboration for similar arts disciplines to work together, for example, elementary visual art educators in their own PLC across several school buildings within a school system. Although this arrangement faces some structural barriers (e.g., travel time between campuses), it can produce more meaningful learning for all involved. Another promising model is virtual PLCs, in which educators connect through digital means to discuss and contextualize their problems of practice (Maher et al., 2010).

These PLCs should begin with a common issue or problem that the educators would like to explore during the length of the PLC, typically over the course of a semester or year. Some successful topics have been: assessment, pedagogy, or exploration of a skill or craft. For example, during a PLC on assessment, educators each brought in rubrics that they use in their classrooms, and together they created ways to incorporate formative assessments and student reflections into their assessment plans. Although no resources that directly relate to arts assessments were found, the group relied on general education books, such as *Understanding by Design* (Wiggins & McTighe, 2005) and *How to Create and Use Rubrics for Formative Assessment and Grading* (Brookhart, 2013), and then, as a group, applied what they learned to the arts contexts. Even though the materials selected did not specifically relate to the arts, by working together in their discipline, they were able to make meaningful connections and applications that would not have been possible in isolation.

Reflective

Finally, arts educators, and those educators who are integrating the arts into other content areas, face the challenge of the idea that the arts should be used primarily in support of other disciplines. One argument used to support arts education is that it promotes achievement in reading and mathematics (Catterall, 2009), and although this may be a powerful way to secure additional support and funding for programs, it can be detrimental when it indicates that the arts are not an important discipline in and of themselves (e.g., Hetland & Winner, 2001). For example, studies show that studying music may increase students' capacity to achieve in mathematics (Southgate & Roscigno, 2009); however, studying music is also important to develop skill and engage students in this area of creative thought. When educators are encouraged to integrate the arts into content area disciplines, such as language arts and mathematics, to increase engagement and achievement in the content area, rather than as an equal exploration of both topics, the arts areas are often relegated to a lower level of importance within the curriculum. This has profound implications for professional learning for educators, in that the opportunities to develop content knowledge in the arts are often superficial or focused on how the arts can develop skills outside of the target area of the arts. Therefore, professional learning should allow opportunities for educators to be reflective on their practice outside of the academic pressures of the school administration.

With the emphasis in traditional arts professional development on creation and hands-on activities, often focusing on how it may promote learning in other content areas, providing time for reflection and metacognitive processes is often limited or absent. Ideally, professional learning for educators should be aligned to the professional goals of each educator, allowing for reflection on experiences as they work toward these goals. More generally, professional learning opportunities should provide ample time and space for educators to synthesize the content of the learning and contextualize it for their own classroom contexts. These learning experiences should have time for educators to reflect and collaborate together on ways in which the understandings can be implemented in their classrooms, how they relate to the standards and goals set forth for their curriculum and student learning, and how they relate to overall school curricular goals.

Specifically, incorporating a model of professional learning that is individualized and goal-oriented generally benefits arts educators, in that they can build personal goals that are reflective of their own disciplines, rather than goals set forth by state or district achievement scores. For example, as part of their annual evaluation, teachers were asked to put forth two to three measurable goals for their classroom. One elementary art teacher set one of her goals to incorporate rubrics to assess her students' artwork and demonstrate improvement in their critical thinking through reflective statements measured on the rubrics. Thus, her professional learning during the school year was centered around reflective practice linked to specific professional goals that were individualized to her specific context. This freed her from being tied to performance standards based upon metrics connected to teaching reading or mathematics standards, and allowed her to focus on her specific discipline.

These qualities (active, individualized, collaborative, and reflective) are important for effective professional learning for arts educators of the gifted. Although they face significant challenges in the current climate of education, these qualities can help maintain high-quality professional learning for this group of educators.

Types of Gifted Learners in Art Contexts

In reflecting on the professional learning needs for arts educators, accounting for the gifted learners in arts classrooms is particularly important. First, educators must consider the types of gifted and talented learners that they may encounter: academically/intellectually gifted, artistically talented, artistically and academically talented, and academically challenged/artistically talented (Wilson, 2009, 2017).

Academically/Intellectually Gifted Learners

Academically/intellectually gifted learners are the types of learners that are typically identified through gifted programs. They think at high levels, learn quickly, and have the potential to be successful at school-related tasks. Many of these students, but not all, are high achievers in school. However, this does not necessarily translate to ability in artistic domains. In art classrooms, academically and intellectually gifted learners may be able to analyze works of art at deeper levels, make connections between art disciplines more easily, and process abstract and complex topics at greater depths as compared to typical students (Wilson, 2009, 2017).

Artistically Talented Learners

Artistically gifted learners are those students who possess advanced skill in specific art domains. This could be skill at creating art, such as painting or matching pitch. It may also be in seeing or hearing artistic pieces and processing that information. Finally, this skill could be in composing a piece of artwork, music, dance, or theater piece (Wilson, 2009, 2017). This talent may lie outside of academic domains, as a set of psychomotor skills, or may be more closely related to intelligence and creativity (Wilson, 2009, 2017). In the art classroom, educators must work to provide advanced materials and curricula to develop these students' talents.

Artistically and Academically Talented Learners

Many artistically talented learners may also be academically and intellectually gifted. These students have advanced academic and intellectual potential that allows their artistic talents to flourish. Often these students feel pressures to pursue many areas of talent, outside of the arts, and care must be taken that they are not overwhelmed. On the other hand, the abundance of talent allows for greater growth as intellectual and artistic areas of talent build from each other (Wilson, 2009, 2017).

Academically Challenged/ Artistically Talented Learners

Finally, the last group of learners are students who demonstrate advanced talent in art areas, but struggle academically. The struggle may be due to a learning disability or other exceptionality. Sometimes, when this exceptionality occurs with high levels of intelligence, the disability can go undiagnosed. In either case, diagnosed or undiagnosed, students who struggle academically, but excel in the arts areas, often find the art classroom as an oasis—a place in which they feel welcome and safe. It is imperative that arts educators use these talents to build the motivation and self-concepts of these students.

Strategies for Arts Educators of Gifted Learners

This section considers that, across the arts areas (e.g., visual arts, music, theater, creative writing, etc.), gifted and talented students may be intellectually and academically gifted and/or artistically gifted and talented within the arts domain (and may or may not have academic difficulties). Thus, professional learning must be planned carefully. In addition to the general goals of professional learning, such as the development of professional goals, pedagogical and disciplinary content knowledge, and specific curricular or content area initiatives, professional learning for arts educators of gifted learners may have additional goals. These goals may include the development of thinking skills, talent, and motivation of gifted learners. These goals can benefit each of the four types of gifted learners outlined in the previous section.

Develop Thinking of Intellectually and Academically Gifted Learners

When considering the intellectually and academically gifted learners in arts classrooms, arts educators are in need of specific professional learning to meet the needs of advanced students. Professional learning regarding the nature and needs, identification, and curriculum for gifted learners will benefit arts educators. However, this professional learning must be individualized, differentiated, collaborative, and reflective to meet the needs of arts educators as previously suggested.

Professional Learning Needs. The ways in which arts educators meet the needs of academically and intellectually gifted learners in their classrooms will be different from strategies for meeting the needs of gifted students' more traditional content area peers. On one hand, educators' strategies may rely less on the types of skills traditionally valued by schools (and which many gifted students excel at), such as reading and mathematics, but on the other hand, they may provide greater opportunities for creativity and expression. This emphasizes the need for the professional learning to allow for individualization and opportunities for arts educators to collaborate on ways in which the concepts explored can be applied to the arts classroom. Finally, time for reflection within the ongoing professional learning should be allocated for teachers to align the learning to their professional goals and curricula in their specific contexts.

Benefits for Gifted Learners: Art Classrooms. The arts can be a powerful vehicle for the development of critical and creative thinking. Artistic production can be developed to encourage creative expression through the synthesis of ideas. This type of thinking is particularly relevant for gifted learners, who benefit from the development of creative thinking skills, and is a key component to many gifted education programs. Note that not all arts programs are inherently creative, and it takes professional learning and intention on the part of educators to infuse creative thinking into the curriculum.

In addition to creative thinking, the arts can be valuable in the development of critical thinking skills. Whether this involves the visual analysis of a painting in art class or the dissection of a monologue in theater, gifted learners benefit from the development of these skills throughout their curriculum. Professional learning for arts educators can focus on how these deep critical thinking skills can be developed throughout the arts curriculum and across arts disciplines. Through reflective practice and ongoing, collaborative experiences, arts educators can work to develop critical and creative thinking in their arts classrooms.

Specific resources for arts educators can be adapted from the resources used for general classroom teachers. For example, the classic *Developing Minds: A Resource Book for Teaching Thinking* (Costa, 2001) discusses general ideas for teachers to develop thinking skills in students, but art educators can easily adapt these ideas to their classrooms. Elementary art teachers can engage students in flexible thinking by asking them to consider different perspectives when examining a piece of artwork (e.g., "What do you think a grandmother would say about this piece of modern art?").

Benefits to Gifted Learners: General Classroom. Finally, when general classroom teachers work to integrate the arts into their curriculum, across disciplines, this can provide unique benefits to academically and intellectually gifted learners (Wilson, 2009). The opportunity to synthesize diverse content areas and make conceptual connections develops the critical and creative thinking of gifted learners. However, in order to do this effectively, and to put equal value on all content areas, including the arts, educators must have opportunities to participate in high-quality professional learning. This must allow the educators opportunities for active engagement with the arts disciplines and reflection to apply the concepts to the unique classroom contexts represented. Collaboration between educators across disciplines can also help to ensure that deep conceptual understandings of multiple content areas are achieved, resulting in high-quality critical thinking opportunities for gifted learners. Specifically, providing opportunities for art educators to plan with educators in other content areas leads to meaningful integration of content areas, without sacrificing either.

In addition, if general education teachers are interested in incorporating more arts experiences into their content areas, professional learning opportunities around art experiences must be provided. Most local art museums, symphonies, and theaters offer educational programs with specific learning opportunities for teachers throughout the year. Sometimes these are held in the evenings and can include a nice spread of food and beverages, free of charge to interested educators. In addition, they offer free or discounted rates to visit the exhibits and guided tours on an ongoing basis. School administrators and coordinators can facilitate this process for educators by organizing group visits for educators. As part of a professional learning experience, general education teachers should gain a level of comfort with content areas that are outside of their typical areas so that they can more easily incorporate them into their curricula.

In considering professional learning for arts educators, the inclusion of experiences directly related to academically and intellectually gifted learners can provide opportunities to enrich both art and general classrooms to meet the needs of the learners. With careful consideration of active engagement, individualization, collaboration, and reflection, these professional learning opportunities can benefit arts educators and other content area educators who wish to integrate the arts, and, ultimately, benefit gifted learners.

Develop Talent of Artistically Gifted Learners

Another key aspect of professional learning for arts educators is the development of talent for artistically gifted learners. Although most art educators have training and background in arts areas and the development of curricula for general classroom populations, there is often little direct professional learning opportunities, either for preservice or inservice educators, regarding the development of talent for artistically gifted learners. This type of knowledge is typically learned on the job, anecdotally, or through past experiences as a student themselves.

Strategies for Educators: Arts Classrooms. There is little research into the efficacy of differentiation or acceleration options for artistically talented students, especially at the elementary levels. And although in traditional subjects, such as math, a talented student may need less time to complete a task, a talented artist may require more time to complete a project in an art classroom, so research studies in other disciplines may not directly apply. In general, particularly at the early ages, a combination of enrichment (exploration of a variety of artistic media) and acceleration (development of specific areas of talent) is warranted. As students progress through the development of their talent, there tends to be a greater focus on their area of specific talent and concentration in that arts area.

Although relatively less research and resources have been devoted to the development of talent in the arts in the field of gifted education (Oreck et al., 2000), the need for professional learning in this area remains. This type of professional learning should be specific to each arts area, individualized by level (e.g., elementary, middle, and high school), and collaborative. Arts educators should work together to discuss local resources for enrichment opportunities for the development of talent (e.g., local artists, galleries, or museums) and continuing development of talent (e.g., schools of the arts, out-of-school lessons, and postsecondary institutions). Specific topics for this professional learning might include the development of portfolios (visual arts) or audition pieces (performing arts) and how to provide sustained time for talent development of gifted individuals (e.g., after school or additional time within school schedules).

For example, a group of elementary art educators could read *The Differentiated Classroom: Responding to the Needs of All Learners* (Tomlinson, 2014). Although this book does not discuss art classroom specifically, art educators could take the principles outlined in the book and work as a PLC to apply them to the elementary art classroom. By setting up a studio model in the art classroom, they could incorporate more student choice and differentiate content and product. This would benefit the artistically talented artists in their classrooms by providing opportunities to express their talents and exposure to advanced art materials.

Strategies for Educators: General Classrooms. General classroom teachers can also benefit from specific professional learning regarding the development of talent for artistically gifted students. Although they may not be responsible for the direct development of artistic talent within their language arts, mathematics, or science classrooms, they may be able to use the strengths of these gifted students in their instruction. Through professional learning that is individualized and collaborative, general classroom teachers could have the opportunity to gain understandings of artistically gifted learners. This type of opportunity would allow them to reflect on their current practices and adapt instruction to better differentiate for the gifted learners in their classroom. By incorporating activities that appeal to artistically gifted students' strengths, they can better educate the students (Baldus & Wilson, 2016). This professional learning could be incorporated into the general professional learning about gifted education for educators, specifically mentioning learners with talents in the arts and strategies that would benefit them.

In developing professional learning activities for both general and arts educators, including opportunities to better understand artistically gifted learners greatly benefits educators. This helps arts educators better develop the talents of these students, ultimately providing greater opportunities for the students and the schools. It also helps general classroom teachers to differentiate lessons to draw upon the strengths of each student.

Develop Motivation and Utility Value for Academically Challenged/ Artistically Talented Learners

Finally, professional learning for arts educators can help teachers to better meet the social-emotional needs of gifted learners. Arts can be a motivating factor for underachieving gifted learners, and participation in the arts is a protective factor in the prevention of dropping out of school (Brown, 2017). Arts can provide both a creative outlet of expression and a reason to continue to attend school for many students, including gifted individuals.

Through professional learning regarding the social-emotional needs of gifted learners, arts educators, in art classrooms and in general classrooms, can tailor lessons and curricula to better meet their needs, specifically those needs of underachieving students. Through ongoing and collaborative professional learning around these needs, educators of gifted learners can work together to develop supportive classroom structures that can nurture the talents of these learners. By incorporating engaging lessons, safe environments, and strategies understood through professional learning, underachieving students can see the value of the curricula, and teachers can provide more motivation for learners.

A PLC could easily be formed with educators within arts disciplines to strategize on how to increase utility value of their arts programs for talented artists. The group might do a book study using Siegle's (2013) *The Underachieving Gifted Child: Recognizing, Understanding, and Reversing Underachievement*, focusing on ways in which they could adapt lessons and curricula to further meet the needs of their artistically talented students. Conversely, a group across disciplines, but including the same underachieving students, could be formed to work on creating a safety net for those students and work together to create strategies that work across disciplines and teachers to ensure success.

Each of these types of professional learning, focusing on both academically and artistically gifted learners, for arts educators in general and arts classrooms, can benefit the professional growth and the students of the teachers. These professional learning opportunities should be built upon the principles of active, individualized, collaborative, and reflective practices.

New Insights

Although there is much research to support professional learning in general, professional learning for gifted educators, and professional learning for arts educators, there is little research regarding the professional learning for arts educators of gifted learners. The new insights of this chapter are the synthesis of ideas from arts education and gifted education to professional learning for educators. Although little is known or researched about the intersection of these areas, this chapter has drawn conclusions from the existing research across the fields. As professional learning for arts educators and educators of the gifted is strengthened, these principles may provide a foundation for future studies and practical applications.

Final Thoughts

Although both arts education and gifted education are often neglected by school systems (National Association for Gifted Children, 2015; Sabol, 2006), the needs of professional learning for educators at the intersections of these topics should not be ignored. Through careful consideration of the challenges facing this population, school systems can design effective professional learning based upon the principles of active engagement, relevant individualization, meaningful collaboration, and deep reflection. This type of experience, when engaged in thoughtful and systematic ways, will enrich and enhance school systems, the professional growth of educators, and, ultimately, the gifted learners in the classrooms.

Summary

This chapter describes how professional learning for arts educators (including both teachers who integrate the arts into general instruction and those who teach primarily arts content) should include specific understandings regarding gifted learners (both academically and intellectually gifted students and artistically talented students). These professional learning opportunities should include active engagement in the arts, individualized and relevant content, meaningful collaboration within arts areas, and time for deep reflection. Professional learning at the intersection of arts and gifted education can enhance the critical and creative thinking of academically gifted learners, nurture the talent of artistically gifted learners, and develop the motivation of underachieving gifted students.

Resources

Professional Learning in the Arts

Americans for the Arts. (n.d.). *ArtsU: For arts professionals in the know.* http://artsu.americansforthearts.org

California County Superintendents Educational Services Association. (2008). *A guidebook for high quality professional development in arts education.* http://ccsesaarts.org/wp-content/uploads/2015/07/ProfDevToolkit.pdf

National Art Education Association. (n.d.). *Virtual art educators.* https://virtual.arteducators.org

Educating Artistically Talented Students

Arts Schools Network. (n.d.). https://www.artsschoolsnetwork.org

National Association for Gifted Children. (2014). *Arts education and gifted and talented students* [Position statement]. https://www.nagc.org/sites/default/files/Position%20Statement/Arts%20Education%20and%20Gifted%20and%20Talented%20Students.pdf

Arts Education

Dallas Symphony Orchestra. (n.d.). *Resources and lesson plans.* https://www.mydso.com/dso-kids/for-teachers/resources-and-lesson-plans

Louvre Museum. (n.d.). *Learning about art.* https://www.louvre.fr/en/oal

New York Philharmonic. (n.d.). *Teacher resources.* https://nyphil.org/education/learning-communities/teacherresources

The Metropolitan Museum of Art. (n.d.). *Educators.* https://www.metmuseum.org/learn/educators

The Solomon R. Guggenheim Foundation. (n.d). *Teaching materials.* https://www.guggenheim.org/for-educators/arts-curriculum

General Education

Brookhart, S. M. (2013). *How to create and use rubrics for formative assessment and grading.* ASCD.

Costa, A. L. (2001). *Developing minds: A resource book for teaching thinking* (3rd ed.). ASCD.

Siegle, D. (2012). *The underachieving gifted child: Recognizing, understanding, and reversing underachievement.* Prufrock Press.

Tomlinson, C. A. (2014). *The differentiated classroom: Responding to the needs of all learners* (2nd ed.). ASCD.

Wiggins, G., & McTighe, J. (2005). *Understanding by design* (2nd ed.). ASCD.

References

Baldus, C. M., & Wilson, H. E. (2016). Beyond recitals and refrigerator art: Encouraging your young artist. *Parenting for High Potential, 6*(1), 2–4.

Bautista, A., Yau, X., & Wong, J. (2017). High-quality music teacher professional development: A review of the literature. *Music Education Research, 19*(4), 455–469. https://doi.org/10.1080/14613808.2016.1249357

Brookhart, S. M. (2013). *How to create and use rubrics for formative assessment and grading.* ASCD.

Brown, K. (2017). *The arts and dropout prevention: The power of art to engage.* National Dropout Prevention Center/Network.

Catterall, J. S. (2009). *Doing well and doing good by doing art: The effects of education in the visual and performing arts on the achievements and values of young adults.* iGroup.

Combs, E., & Silverman, S. (2016). *Bridging the gap: Paving the pathway from current practice to exemplary professional learning.* Frontline Research and Learning Institute.

Conway, C. M. (2008). Experienced music teacher perceptions of professional development throughout their careers. *Bulletin of the Council for Research in Music Education, 176,* 7–18.

Costa, A. L. (Ed.). (2001). *Developing minds: A resource book for teaching thinking* (3rd ed.). ASCD.

Doğan, S., & Adams, A. (2018). Effect of professional learning communities on teachers and students: Reporting updated results and raising questions about research design. *School Effectiveness and School Improvement, 29*(4), 634–659. https://doi.org/10.1080/09243453.2018.1500921

Hetland, L., & Winner, E. (2001) The arts and academic achievement: What the evidence shows. *Arts Education Policy Review, 102*(5), 3–6. https://doi.org/10.1080/10632910109600008

Hochberg, E. D., & Desimone, L. M. (2010). Professional development in the accountability context: Building capacity to achieve standards. *Educational Psychologist, 45*(2), 89–106. https://doi.org/10.1080/00461521003703052

Lind, V. R. (2007). High quality professional development: An investigation of the supports for and barriers to professional development in arts education. *International Journal of Education & the Arts, 8*(2), 1–18.

Maher, J., Burroughs, C., Dietz, L., & Karnbach, A. (2010). From solo to ensemble: Fine arts teachers find a harmonious solution to their isolation. *Journal of Staff Development, 31*(1), 24–29.

National Association for Gifted Children. (2015). *2014–2015 state of the states in gifted education: Policy and practice data.* https://www.nagc.org/sites/default/files/key%20reports/2014-2015%20State%20of%20the%20States%20(final).pdf

Nompula, Y. (2013). The marginalization of arts education: Optimization of teaching time limitation. *International Journal of Arts and Commerce, 2*(2), 102–108.

Oreck, B., Baum, S., & McCartney, H. (2000). *Artistic talent development for urban youth: The promise and the challenge.* The National Research Center on the Gifted and Talented.

Sabol, F. R. (2006). *Professional development in art education: A study of needs, issues, and concerns of art educators.* National Art Education Foundation.

Scheib, J. W. (2006). Policy implications for teacher retention: Meeting the needs of the dual identities of arts educators. *Arts Education Policy Review, 107*(6), 5–10.

Siegle, D. (2013). *The underachieving gifted child: Recognizing, understanding, and reversing underachievement.* Prufrock Press.

Southgate, D. E., & Roscigno, V. J. (2009). The impact of music on childhood and adolescent achievement. *Social Science Quarterly, 90*(1), 4–21. https://doi.org/10.1111/j.1540-6237.2009.00598.x

Stanley, A. M. (2011). Professional development within collaborative teacher study groups: Pitfalls and promises. *Arts Education Policy Review, 112*(2), 71–78. https://doi.org/10.1080/10632913.2011.546692

Tomlinson, C. A. (2014). *The differentiated classroom: Responding to the needs of all learners* (2nd ed.). ASCD.

Wiggins, G., & McTighe, J. (2005). *Understanding by design* (2nd ed.). ASCD.

Wilson, H. E. (2009). The Picasso in your classroom: How to meet the needs of talented artists in elementary school. *Gifted Child Today, 32*(1), 36–45.

Wilson, H. E. (2017). Curricular considerations for advanced learners in the arts. In J. VanTassel-Baska & C. A. Little (Eds.), *Content-based curriculum for high-ability learners* (3rd ed., pp. 361–381). Prufrock Press.

CHAPTER 8

Professional Learning in Science for Teachers of the Gifted:
A Focus on Science and Engineering Practices and Crosscutting Concepts

Kim A. Cheek

All learners, including the gifted, benefit from curriculum and instruction that is organized around key disciplinary concepts and principles and that enable them to learn content by engaging in open-ended problem solving (Robbins, 2011). This requires educators who understand key constructs, as well as the structures and tools of inquiry, of the discipline they teach (National Association for Gifted Children [NAGC] & The Association for the Gifted, Council for Exceptional Children [CEC-TAG], 2013). Although this statement has implications for professional learning for all science teachers, it is especially important for science teachers of the gifted due to the degree of rigor that should characterize their lessons. Science teachers of the gifted must understand how science works and the tools of inquiry the sciences employ. This will enable them to design learning experiences that enhance creativity, depth and complexity in subject-matter knowledge, and the development of learning progressions for core ideas across K–12 learning. Professional learning targeted specifically to science teachers of high-ability learners is needed to accomplish these goals.

Overview

Currently, resources for someone interested in professional learning for science teachers of gifted students originate either from a science education perspective or from a gifted education perspective. Resources developed by science educators (e.g., Loucks-Horsley et al., 2010) provide many suggestions for professional learning activities to meet two science education goals. The first is to increase teachers' science content knowledge. The second is to improve what is known as pedagogical content knowledge, or PCK (Shulman, 1986). PCK refers to the ability to integrate what teachers know about learners and the teaching/learning process with their knowledge of the subject matter they teach. Because professional learning for science educators focuses on improving the quality of instruction for all learners, it rarely provides information specific to the professional learning needs of science teachers of gifted students. Conversely, resources written by gifted education experts, such as Johnsen and Clarenbach (2017), provide general guidance for designing professional learning for teachers of gifted students, but are not domain specific and do not directly address the structures and tools of inquiry that characterize best practices in science education. Several authors have addressed the needs of gifted students in science (Adams, 2003; Johnsen & Kendrick, 2005; Robbins, 2011; VanTassel-Baska, 2017; VanTassel-Baska & MacFarlane, 2008), but much of their work predates the most recent reform efforts in science education that culminated with the development of the Next Generation Science Standards (NGSS Lead States, 2013).

This chapter bridges the gap between the two perspectives and provides guidance for designers and implementers of professional learning for science teachers of the gifted that will address the unique needs of gifted learners in science. To that end, I first briefly describe the NGSS, their structure, and why they can serve as a framework in which to design professional learning for science teachers of the gifted. Next, I discuss science professional learning and highlight two strategies that developers of professional learning for science teachers of the gifted may find useful. Finally, I sketch out a hypothetical plan for what such professional learning might include.

Three-Dimensional Learning in the Next Generation Science Standards

Science, in the real world, is an integrated enterprise. One cannot separate science content knowledge from the experience of doing science. A long-standing goal of K–12 science instruction has been a scientifically literate citizenry who understand the nature of science—how science works, the types of questions it answers, and its limits. Overarching themes or constructs that can be applied across the sciences enable humans to better understand the natural world. Several decades of research into teaching and learning in science, as well as students' conceptions of scientific phenomena, led to the creation of the NGSS (NGSS Lead States, 2013). The NGSS are based on an earlier volume, *A Framework for K–12 Science Education: Practices, Crosscutting Concepts, and Core Ideas* (National Research Council [NRC], 2012). The Framework laid out a vision for science education in the 21st century that would enable all high school graduates to become scientifically literate and possess the skills to pursue careers in science, technology, or engineering, if they chose. Both the Framework and the NGSS were the results of multiyear processes in which stakeholders from K–12 education, higher education, the sciences, and industry provided multiple rounds of feedback to the writing team, composed of K–12 and higher education science professionals. The NGSS employ a three-dimensional approach to instruction in which students learn core science concepts by engaging in the practices used by scientists and engineers, while attending to important themes, or crosscutting concepts, that impact the sciences more broadly. Performance expectations at each grade level (K–5) or grade band (middle or high school) within the NGSS require students to integrate at least one core idea, practice, and crosscutting concept.

Prior to the development of the NGSS, most state and district standards separated the three dimensions for the purposes of both instruction and assessment. The result was that students did not adequately grasp their connectedness. The equal emphasis upon disciplinary core ideas (DCIs), science and engineering practices (SEPs), and crosscutting concepts (CCCs) represents a significant conceptual shift in what science instruction should look like and distinguishes the NGSS from previous reform efforts in science education. The three-dimensional approach to instruction is designed to lead to a more holistic and powerful understanding of science (NGSS Lead States, 2013), one that is especially suited for gifted learners due to the complex thinking and problem-solving strategies learners will need to meet performance expectations. The following sections provide a brief introduction to each dimension of the NGSS.

Disciplinary Core Ideas

A consistent problem in American K–12 science education that has kept it from achieving the goals laid out in the Framework has been the prevalence of "a mile wide and inch deep" curricular approach. U.S. students traditionally study many science topics each year (the mile wide) at a superficial level (the inch deep). The emphasis has been on memorizing facts, as opposed to sense-making, which has served no one well, but especially not gifted learners. To address this, the Framework identified a finite number of disciplinary core ideas (DCIs) in the physical, life, and Earth and space sciences that students revisit across the K–12 span at increasingly greater depth and complexity (NRC, 2012). Each DCI has several subideas that contribute to an understanding of the core idea. The core ideas are an important feature of the NGSS, as they enable students to develop increasingly sophisticated, as opposed to merely shallow, understanding of science concepts (NGSS Lead States, 2013). Table 8.1 lists the disciplinary core ideas and their subideas for the physical, life, and Earth and space sciences.

Many gifted students will grasp DCIs earlier than their age-peers, so the identified core ideas and their development across K–12 learning should not be used to limit instructional rigor for high-ability learners. Descriptions in the Framework (NRC, 2012) and the NGSS (NGSS Lead States, 2013) of possible learning progressions for DCIs can provide guidance for science teachers of the gifted when designing appropriate instruction for students who have already mastered grade-level expectations.

The other two dimensions of the NGSS, the science and engineering practices (SEPs) and the crosscutting concepts (CCCs), may be less familiar to science teachers of the gifted than the disciplinary core ideas. Individuals who are scientifically literate possess sufficient understanding of scientific practices and broad concepts or themes to be able to make informed decisions regarding scientific issues, yet it can be argued that science education in the U.S. has fallen far short of providing instruction that can lead to scientific literacy. Placing the SEPs and the CCCs on an equal footing with DCIs can help learners and their teachers better understand the structures and tools of inquiry of the sciences, which, in turn, can improve scientific literacy.

Table 8.1

Disciplinary Core Ideas and Component Ideas from the Next Generation Science Standards

Physical Sciences	Life Sciences	Earth and Space Sciences
PS1: Matter and Its Interactions • PS1.A: Structure and Properties of Matter • PS1.B: Chemical Reactions • PS1.C: Nuclear Processes PS2: Motion and Stability: Forces and Interactions • PS2.A: Forces and Motion • PS2.B: Types of Interactions • PS2.C: Stability and Instability in Physical Systems	LS1: From Molecules to Organisms: Structures and Processes • LS1.A: Structure and Function • LS1.B: Growth and Development of Organisms • LS1.C: Organization for Matter and Energy Flow in Organisms • LS1.D: Information Processing LS2: Ecosystems: Interactions, Energy, and Dynamics • LS2.A: Interdependent Relationships in Ecosystems • LS2.B: Cycles of Matter and Energy Transfer in Ecosystems • LS2.C: Ecosystem Dynamics, Functioning, and Resilience • LS2.D: Social Interactions and Group Behavior	ESS1: Earth's Place in the Universe • ESS1.A: The Universe and Its Stars • ESS1.B: Earth and the Solar System • ESS1.C: The History of Planet Earth ESS2: Earth's Systems • ESS2.A: Earth Materials and Systems • ESS2.B: Plate Tectonics and Large-Scale System Interactions • ESS2.C: The Roles of Water in Earth's Surface Processes • ESS2.D: Weather and Climate • ESS2.E: Biogeology

Table 8.1, continued.

Physical Sciences	Life Sciences	Earth and Space Sciences
PS3: Energy • PS3.A: Definitions of Energy • PS3.B: Conservation of Energy and Energy Transfer • PS3.C: Relationship Between Energy and Forces • PS3.D: Energy in Chemical Processes and Everyday Life	LS3: Heredity: Inheritance and Variation of Traits • LS3.A: Inheritance of Traits • LS3.B: Variation of Traits	ESS3: Earth and Human Activity • ESS3.A: Natural Resources • ESS3.B: Natural Hazards • ESS3.C: Human Impacts on Earth Systems • ESS3.D: Global Climate Change
PS4: Waves and Their Applications in Technologies for Information Transfer • PS4.A: Wave Properties • PS4.B: Electromagnetic Radiation • PS4.C: Information Technologies and Instrumentation	LS4: Biological Evolution: Unity and Diversity • LS4.A: Evidence of Common Ancestry and Diversity • LS4.B: Natural Selection • LS4.C: Adaptation • LS4.D: Biodiversity and Humans	

Science and Engineering Practices

Inquiry is central to scientific investigation and developing solutions to engineering problems. Science educators have been advocating for the use of inquiry in K–12 science classrooms for decades. Too often, inquiry has been viewed merely as the process of completing science investigations, rather than as an attempt to engage in sense-making about the natural world (Schwarz et al., 2017). Sense-making is essential in both science and engineering. In classrooms, sense-making is "a dynamic process of building or revising an explanation in order to 'figure something out'—to ascertain the mechanism underlying a phenomenon in order to resolve a gap or inconsistency in one's understanding," (Odden & Russ, 2019). The SEPs are the means by which students engage in sense-making in science.

Earlier science reform efforts highlighted "science process skills" (i.e., observing, inferring, measuring; American Association for the Advancement of Science, 1993), rather than practices. Unfortunately, these "skills" were often taught in isolation and devoid of context at the beginning of the school year, never to be referred to again. The NGSS adopted the term *practices* to underscore the point that they are not merely the ability to execute a specific action. They also involve an understanding of the practice and how its use contributes to scientific sense-making. *Practice* is a richer term than *skills* because practices often integrate multiple skills (i.e., observing, inferring, and measuring are all part of designing and carrying out investigations). The NGSS call them science and engineering practices to emphasize the interconnectedness between the two fields and because some are used by both scientists and engineers (NGSS Lead States, 2013). In a few cases, scientists and engineers engage in similar, although not identical, practices (e.g., SEPs 1 and 6). Table 8.2 lists the eight science and engineering practices identified in the NGSS, along with a brief explanation of each one.

SEPs do not exist in isolation. They are not merely the scientific method renamed. Although it is common to begin the sense-making process by asking a question or defining a problem, the practices do not always occur in sequential order, and practices may overlap. K–12 students should have multiple opportunities to engage in all eight practices each school year; however, they will probably not engage in all of them within a single lesson. A focus on the SEPs is important for high-ability learners because students use them to engage in authentic problem-based learning, and their use over time can foster critical thinking (Taber, 2007a). Appendix F of the NGSS describes how each practice might develop across the K–12 grade span (NGSS Lead States, 2013). As is true for disciplinary core ideas, the

Table 8.2
Science and Engineering Practices from the Next Generation Science Standards

Science and Engineering Practice	Explanation of the Practice
1. Asking questions (science) and defining problems (engineering)	Scientists ask questions they can investigate. Engineers ask questions to determine problems that need to be solved.
2. Developing and using models	Scientists and engineers construct and use models to represent systems and their parts
3. Planning and carrying out investigations	Investigations are systematic ways scientists and engineers collect and analyze data to construct explanations or design solutions.
4. Analyzing and interpreting data	The data collected during investigations must be analyzed and interpreted to serve as evidence to support a conclusion.
5. Using mathematics and computational thinking	Scientists and engineers use numbers and mathematical symbols to represent physical variables and analyze relationships among them quantitatively. They use digital tools to perform mathematical operations.
6. Constructing explanations (science) and designing solutions (engineering)	Scientists construct cause-and-effect explanations based upon evidence they collect during investigations. Engineers use data collected during investigations to design solutions to human problems.
7. Engaging in argument from evidence	Scientists and engineers use reasoning to support claims based upon evidence collected during investigations. They also evaluate the strength of colleagues' arguments.
8. Obtaining, evaluating, and communicating information	Scientists and engineers communicate information through a variety of visual and oral means. They learn about the work of other scientists and engineers and evaluate the merit and validity of others' work based upon the strength of the evidence.

progression is useful for science teachers of the gifted but is not meant to limit instructional rigor for them.

Crosscutting Concepts

The third dimension of the NGSS are the crosscutting concepts (CCCs). Certain central concepts permeate the sciences and can be applied across multiple scientific disciplines. They function as coherence-makers or connectors among science disciplines that can be used to organize knowledge, facilitate analogical reasoning, and provide the depth and complexity that should characterize science learning for the gifted (Taber, 2007b). Analogical reasoning is an important problem-solving heuristic. When learners engage in analogical reasoning, they use their knowledge in a familiar domain to understand something in an unfamiliar domain. Because the CCCs span science disciplinary boundaries, they facilitate analogical reasoning and are as important for sense-making as the SEPs. Of the three dimensions, they are arguably the most challenging for teachers to meaningfully integrate into science instruction because it is likely that teachers' own science learning did not emphasize those connections. The seven CCCs named in the NGSS (NGSS Lead States, 2013), along with brief explanations of each one, can be found in Table 8.3.

Like the DCIs and SEPs, student understanding of CCCs should become more sophisticated through K–12 education. The CCCs can help students better grasp both DCIs and SEPs. They are not studied in isolation. Instead, students should be challenged to engage in analogical reasoning that considers how their application in one object or organism is similar to or different from that of another. For example, Systems and System Models is one of the CCCs. Complex systems have parts that work together and enable the entire object or organism to perform functions that none of the parts could do alone. A plant is a system containing specific parts that enable it to carry out its basic functions. Individual parts do not exist in isolation and are dependent upon other parts for the materials and energy they need to perform their specific task within the organism. A car is also a complex system that is designed using knowledge of forces, energy, and the properties of its materials. Like a plant, it needs a set of basic parts in order to function as a car. Thus, there are common features shared by systems whether considering a plant or a car. Tracking the inputs and outputs, as well as the flows of matter and energy, within and between systems can be used to make predictions and design systems for specific functions. Appendix G of the NGSS includes matrices for each CCC that describe how the concept develops across grades K–12 (NGSS Lead States, 2013). As students develop deeper understanding of CCCs and their applicability across science disciplines, they use analogical reasoning and consider differences in the two phenomena as well as their similarities. Employing that sort of analogical reasoning is important for all learners, but especially for gifted students.

Table 8.3
Crosscutting Concepts from the Next Generation Science Standards

Crosscutting Concept	Explanation of the Crosscutting Concept
Patterns	Scientists ask questions about patterns in the natural world and look for ways to explain them. Engineers analyze patterns to design and improve solutions.
Cause and effect	Explaining cause-and-effect relationships is an important goal of scientific investigation.
Scale, proportion, and quantity	Processes and systems in the natural world vary with scale. Proportional relationships can be described qualitatively or quantitatively.
Systems and system models	We live in a complex world made up of systems with parts that work together. Because systems are complex, scientists often construct simplified models that enable them to better understand the system.
Energy and matter	Energy and matter are neither created nor destroyed. By tracking the flow of energy and matter into, within, and out of a system, scientists can better understand the system.
Structure and function	An object's structure and its function(s) are related. Properties of components of a system and the relationships among those components determine the system's function.
Stability and change	Within systems, some aspects of the system remain stable while others change. Feedback loops either facilitate or inhibit change.

Reading the NGSS

The NGSS can be accessed at https://www.nextgenscience.org/search-standards. The organizational structure of the standards can seem daunting initially, as they are laid out differently than many previous national or state standards documents. This section of the chapter is designed to help familiarize readers with their layout. Readers who are regular users of the NGSS may want to skip to the next section. For those who are new to the standards, looking at a page from the standards while reading this section of the chapter will be helpful. Teachers accessing them for the first time will notice that the standards are organized by grade level for kindergarten through fifth grade, and by grade band for middle and high school. The latter is because students might take specific courses at different points within those grade bands. At the top of the page, the reader will see a title that corresponds to one of the four physical, four life, or three Earth and space science core ideas. In front of the title is the grade level or grade band (e.g., 2 or MS) and letters that indicate the domain of the core idea (e.g., PS, LF, or ESS).

Unlike previous standards that were often statements regarding content knowledge, the NGSS have performance expectations (PEs) that state what students should be able to do as well as what they should know by the end of a grade level or grade band. One or more PEs can be found below the title. Meeting the PEs requires students to integrate the three dimensions of the NGSS. PEs often contain clarification statements that provide either examples or further explicate the meaning of the PE. Assessment boundaries are included to provide guidance to developers of large-scale assessments regarding the level at which the PE should be assessed at a specific grade level or grade band. This was done to ensure that students are not being assessed at a level of depth or complexity incommensurate with the level of the PE. Alpha-numeric coding for the PEs links them to the core ideas in the physical, life, and Earth and space sciences, and identifies the grade level or grade band. For example, the code PE 1-PS4-1 means first grade (1), the fourth physical sciences core idea (PS4 Waves and Their Applications in Technologies for Information Transfer), and the first PE within the core idea for first graders (1).

Beneath the PEs are three color-coded columns called foundations boxes. This is where the reader will find which specific SEPs, CCCs, or DCI subideas or component ideas associated with each of the PEs. Again, the purposeful and explicit integration of the three dimensions is the major way in which the NGSS differ from other standards documents in K–12 science education. The SEPs are on the left in blue, DCIs are in the center in orange, and CCCs can be found on the right in green. The decision was made to associate one SEP, one CCC, and one DCI subidea with each PE. Other SEPs and CCCs may be applicable, but those that the writers deemed were most relevant are listed as ones to emphasize. This decision was not intended to limit teachers' ability to choose to emphasize other SEPs or CCCs. It was merely done to make the integration of the three dimensions more manageable. Included are verbal descriptions of what each of the applicable SEPs or CCCs looks like at a specific grade level or grade band. The component or subideas that apply to specific PEs are listed along with language that can help teachers determine the level of depth and complexity at which those ideas need to be addressed for students at a specific grade level to meet the PEs. Of course, they may not indicate the depth and complexity appropriate for gifted learners at those grade levels. Specific connections to characteristics of the nature of science can be found either at the bottom of the SEP or CCC column. Finally, beneath the foundations boxes is a section called connections boxes. These indicate possible connections between the PEs and:

- other disciplinary core ideas at this grade level or grade band,
- other grade levels or grade bands at which the same DCI is addressed, and
- relevant Common Core State Standards for English Language Arts and Mathematics that can be integrated into instruction.

Why Should Professional Learning for Teachers of the Gifted Emphasize SEPs and CCCs?

Science education for high-ability learners needs to be characterized by student-centered, open-ended inquiry (Adams, 2003). The Integrated Curriculum Model (ICM; VanTassel-Baska, 2017), which predates the NGSS, provides a framework for the development of coherent, challenging curriculum for the gifted. The model includes three dimensions essential for any curriculum for high-ability learners: advanced content knowledge, higher order thinking and processing, and learning experiences focused on complex issues or themes that enable learners to connect concepts within and across disciplines. The overlaps between the ICM and the three-dimensional approach to learning in the NGSS are striking. CCCs in the NGSS serve as themes that enable learners to make connections within and across science disciplines. The SEPs are authentic practices used by real scientists and engineers as they make sense of the natural and designed world. Sense-making (Odden & Russ, 2019) is central to three-dimensional science instruction and fosters deep, rather than superficial, content knowledge, as well as higher order thinking and the application of learning to complex issues. Those practices nurture scientific curiosity and students' cognitive and metacognitive abilities (Taber, 2007b), which are important for all learners, but especially high-ability learners. The use of questioning, models and analogical reasoning, constructing explanations, engaging in scientific argumentation, mathematical reasoning, and creativity in designing investigations in the SEPs address a number of the characteristics of learners who are gifted in science (Gilbert & Newberry, 2007). The goals of the NGSS's three-dimensional approach to instruction also dovetail with a number of key curriculum design elements in the ICM (VanTassel-Baska, 2017).

The NGSS are rigorous. They set high expectations for all learners, but gifted students will still need differentiated instruction that will enable them to make learning progress (NAGC & CEC-TAG, 2013). A shift to a three-dimensional approach to science instruction will be challenging for all teachers, including gifted education professionals. As of May 2019, more than three-fourths of U.S. schoolchildren resided in states that have either adopted the NGSS as is or have created standards that are based on the Framework for K–12 Science Education (NGSS Lead States, 2013). Many of the latter are very similar to the NGSS but include state-specific examples. (Readers can determine whether their state has adopted the NGSS or created similar standards by consulting their state department of education or the NGSS website.) Some readers of this volume reside in states that have not adopted the NGSS. Instead, they use state-created science standards, often ones that predate the NGSS. Why should gifted educators and those who provide professional learning for them feature the SEPs and the CCCs from the NGSS? As noted earlier, the NGSS's approach to learning and instruction has much in common with approaches advocated by gifted educators. Science process skills are often found in state-created science standards. They rarely combine practices with content in the way the NGSS does, yet high-ability learners benefit from their fusion (Robbins, 2011). The notion of crosscutting concepts or overarching themes in the sciences did not originate with the NGSS, but their purposeful integration is what distinguishes the NGSS from other standards documents. Gifted educators in states that do not use the NGSS or NGSS-aligned science standards will still find them useful for all of the reasons outlined above.

Professional Learning in Science

Professional learning for teachers of science should be generative (Melville, 2010), such that it leads to greater professional expertise, both in terms of teachers' science content knowledge and their PCK. That has not always been the case due to the all-too-common practice of the one-half-day or one-day workshop model that is disconnected from teacher practice. Fortunately, there is a significant body of research on the characteristics necessary for generative teacher professional learning. The first volume in this series highlights a range of methods and strategies for professional learning in gifted education. In the opening chapter in that book, Novak (2018) synthesized research on best practices in professional learning and

identified five themes from the research literature that characterize effective professional learning for teachers across subject areas. They are:
- goal-aligned and data driven;
- sustained;
- collaborative with opportunity for reflection;
- coherent, embedded, and immediately transferrable; and
- characterized by active learning that uses a variety of models and methods.

Little and Ayers Paul (2017) noted that professional learning for teachers of the gifted must emphasize rigor in terms of disciplinary content, the practices by which students learn the content, and the ability to integrate conceptual themes within the discipline. Said another way, professional learning for teachers of the gifted must focus on the two goals shared by developers of professional learning in science, namely the development of teacher content knowledge and PCK.

The science education community has its own set of attributes for professional learning developed by the Council of State Science Supervisors (2015), which largely dovetail with the characteristics cited by Novak (2018), undoubtedly because both lists are grounded in similar research literature. The science education attributes also reflect current understanding regarding how students construct explanations about phenomena in the natural world and the types of instruction that facilitate sense-making in science. Because they are science-specific, they include several additional attributes not specifically mentioned previously. All are important considerations when designing professional learning for science teachers of the gifted. They are:
- eliciting, interpreting and using students' reasoning to make instructional decisions;
- connecting science with learners' interests and experiences;
- designing and implementing a progression for coherent teaching across grade levels; and
- using instructional strategies that promote all learners' equitable participation in science (Council of State Science Supervisors, 2015).

Teachers who participate in professional learning opportunities are not a monolithic group. They have different professional learning needs and goals—sometimes multiple ones. A challenge for developers of professional learning experiences is being able to meet the needs of such a heterogeneous group. Loucks-Horsley et al. (2010) described 16 methods and strategies commonly used as part of professional learning in science and mathematics education, each of which is best suited to meeting particular professional learning needs and goals. Space does not permit discussion of all 16 in this chapter. Here I highlight two that seem especially promising for gifted educators' professional learning in science. Refer to Loucks-Horsley et al. (2010) for a discussion of the entire group.

Immersion

There is widespread agreement that professional learning programs need to be sustained (Learning Forward, 2011). There is some disagreement within the research literature regarding precisely how much time is necessary for science teacher professional learning programs to be considered sustained, with figures ranging from as few as 20 hours to as many as 160 hours to elicit a significant change in teaching behavior (Loucks-Horsley et al., 2010; National Academies of Sciences, Engineering, and Medicine, 2015). The important point for this discussion is that 3-hour or even full-day workshop models are simply inadequate to result in generative outcomes.

Immersion is one professional learning strategy often used in science education specifically to address the need for a sustained experience. In immersion programs teachers participate in an extended opportunity to engage in authentic science inquiry just as K–12 learners would do. Historically, immersion programs in science professional learning have emphasized specific science content—often topics that are difficult to teach or that have societal implications. At various points during the sessions, teachers are given the opportunity to reflect upon their own learning and to raise questions, both about the content and about how to teach it. There are two goals for immersion. The first is for teachers to learn how students learn the subject. The second goal is to deepen teachers' own understanding about a topic and how to teach it. In other words, immersion addresses the two goals for professional learning identified at the beginning of this chapter: improving teachers' content knowledge and pedagogical content knowledge, which are both essential for teachers of the gifted (Gubbins, 2008; Little & Ayers Paul, 2017). As part of their experience, teachers are asked to reflect on questions such as, "What types of educative experiences facilitate learning? How does student thinking develop as the class engages in those experiences?" Teachers often leave the immersion experiences with curricular materials so they can replicate the activities in their own classrooms.

Immersion programs are aligned with at least four of the five characteristics of effective professional learning outlined by Novak (2018). In addition to being sustained, they have definite goals for teacher learning, which are often driven by data regarding topics that are problematic or timely for students. Facilitators model collaborative active learning strategies teachers can use with their students when they return to the classroom. There is ample opportunity for teacher reflection throughout the experience. They are valuable for teachers of the gifted because they model the types of instructional practices that are appropriate for high-ability learners (Gilbert & Newberry, 2007; Taber, 2007b).

A professional development team, often comprised of content experts and teacher educators, collaboratively design and model the use of research-based curriculum materials and teaching strategies that can be implemented in a K–12 science classroom. Teachers who attend the programs work in teams to actively learn science content by engaging in the same practices their students will use (Little & Ayers Paul, 2017). Immersion professional learning experiences for science teachers often take place during the summer. They are generally day-long programs that run for one or more weeks. Depending upon the source of program funding, participants might all come from the same district or from several. If they are from a single district, they may be from the same school or come from multiple schools in the district serving the same grade levels. Immersion programs could be day programs at a K–12 school, a local university, or museum. Some are residential programs held at a university, museum, or a field site appropriate to the discipline. Immersion programs held at universities or museums often give teachers access to materials and scientific equipment that would not be available in a K–12 school. Many immersion professional learning experiences in K–12 science education are multiyear, grant-funded programs. The initial cohort of teachers return in one or more subsequent summers to both deepen their own content knowledge and PCK. Additional cohorts may be added during those subsequent years. Multiyear programs are beneficial because sustained change in teacher behavior typically requires several years of contact (Learning Forward, 2011).

One challenge with an immersion strategy is the time required, especially for multiyear events. Teacher attrition in the second or third years is common. Participants usually self-select for these programs, which can mean that teachers who would most benefit from the experience do not participate, perhaps due to worries that they will be unable to keep up with the others. It can be difficult to scale the instructional changes if only some teachers within a school or grade level participate. Providers of these experiences must ensure that what is done during the experience has a strong classroom focus. This can be challenging for program developers if teachers from different grade bands or from different states participate in the same experience. Whether or not participant teachers know each other ahead of time has implications for group dynamics during the program.

Immersion occurs outside the regular school year, so what is learned is not immediately transferrable. Thus, if used alone it rarely results in substantive changes in teacher practice. Immersion is often combined with one or more additional strategies that can either be part of the immersion experience or provide support to teachers during the academic year (Loucks-Horsley et al., 2010). One way to leverage the strength of immersion programs for science teachers of the gifted is to combine immersion with a more embedded, immediately transferrable professional learning strategy to better facilitate a change in teacher practice. Although there are many possibilities, one, examining student work, is provided here by way of illustration. For a fuller discussion of the range of professional learning strategies along with strengths and weaknesses of each, see Novak and Lewis (2018), in the first volume in this series.

Examining Student Work

Within the last decade, having teachers work in groups to examine student work has become an increasingly popular professional learning strategy (Loucks-Horsley et al., 2010). Small groups of teachers collectively scrutinize examples of several students' responses on the same assignment. Many state education departments and professional associations have developed protocols that can be used to guide teachers through the process. The strategy is both data and goal driven. It is collaborative. Obviously, teachers can individually analyze their students' work to improve the quality of their instruction; however, when teachers do so collaboratively, they begin to develop shared understanding about teaching and learning within a discipline. Examining student work is embedded because examples come from students in participants' classrooms. It is also immediately transferrable. The analysis protocol can be used to analyze other work samples from a teacher's own classroom. The work samples analyzed can serve as exemplars of student thinking against which other student work samples can be compared.

Participants are often grade-level teaching partners in a single school, but if using the strategy with teachers of the gifted, that may not be possible. When using the strategy for professional learning, it is useful to have the process be facilitated by a domain expert. Individual sessions typically last for 1–2 hours. There is a preidentified focus for the session, which in the present example would relate to one of the SEPs or CCCs. Prior to examining student work, participants can cocreate a rubric for evaluating the work products or use/adapt one that is available online to guide discourse. When the group meets, a teacher brings several (probably no more than three) samples of student work related to the focus and provides information on the learning outcomes for the lesson and a brief description of the lesson itself. Teachers can take turns bringing work samples, which means the group could remain focused on a single theme for the entire school year. The goal of the session is to identify trends or patterns in students' responses and thinking and to connect those to instructional practices. A good facilitator can ensure that the focus remains on building upon students' current understanding rather than merely identifying deficiencies in their responses (Loucks-Horsley et al., 2010). When examining student work related to a CCC or SEP across instructional units, teachers can develop a deeper understanding of how learning develops over time and how to help students engage in the complex thinking needed to understand core ideas and overarching themes across the sciences.

One reason the strategy has become widespread is because it focuses on the impact of teaching on learning as demonstrated by student work samples. It can be quite powerful but has the potential to be anxiety-producing if teachers feel that they are being judged based upon their students' work. Building a collaborative culture of trust is essential. The facilitator and the domain expert (who might be the same individual) have key roles to play in the process. The facilitator guides participants through difficult conversations and helps surface teacher biases. For example, when examining the work of a student who is twice-exceptional, a teacher may discount what can be learned from the work product. The domain expert helps teachers refine their own understanding of the construct being analyzed in the work samples and ways to modify instruction to improve student learning.

Professional Learning for Gifted Educators Around the SEPS and CCCs: An Example

What might professional learning for science teachers of high-ability learners based on a three-dimensional approach to science teaching look like? I present one possible design for professional learning that combines immersion and examining student work around one SEP and one CCC from the NGSS. Both strategies are commonly used in science education professional learning, often individually. They do not have to be used in tandem, but when combined, they address the essential characteristics of effective professional learning in general (Novak, 2018), professional learning for teachers of the gifted (Johnsen & Kendrick, 2005), and professional learning for science teachers (Council of State Science Supervisors, 2015). Combining immersion with examining student work can help science teachers of the gifted integrate what they know about high-ability learners with their own knowledge of science content and how to teach it (PCK).

Summer Immersion

In this scenario, the professional learning cycle begins with a one- or 2-week-long summer immersion experience. Professional learning providers may want to seek grant funding for the experience as, admittedly, the strategy can be costly. Partnerships between K–12 educators and higher education are attractive to funders as are ones with informal science education institutions, such as museums.

During the immersion, teachers engage in authentic science experiences around a DCI, while emphasizing one SEP and one CCC that are most relevant to it. Professional learning developers need to make the SEP and CCC explicit, or teachers may focus solely on the disciplinary content. Participants need to experience what the SEP and CCC look and feel like. They also need to reflect on how to facilitate student growth in them over time. This kind of focus on learning progressions for the SEP and CCC is useful for science teachers of high-ability learners because it enables them to adjust pacing and depth and complexity for their students. Before determining what DCI to use as the backdrop for the professional learning, it is useful to decide which SEP and CCC to focus on throughout the upcoming school year. I suggest beginning with a DCI that has multiple PEs, at least one of which is associated with Developing and Using Models (SEP 2) and/ or one that is associated with Constructing Explanations and Designing Solutions (SEP 6). The choice of CCC could vary, but Systems and System Models, Patterns, or Cause and Effect are all reasonable options.

Consider an immersion experience based around ESS2.C—The roles of water in Earth's surface processes (NGSS Lead States, 2013). Several CCCs could be highlighted when learning about the roles of water in Earth's surface processes, but Systems and System Models is a logical choice. The movement of water at Earth's surface is part of a larger system or cycle in which Earth's water circulates among the atmosphere, hydrosphere, biosphere, and solid Earth. Developing and Using Models is an appropriate SEP that relates both to the DCI and the CCC. Diagrams, drawings, physical models, and computer simulations are all possible ways to model how running water changes landscapes over time. The use of models enables learners to construct explanations and engage in sense-making about concepts, such as weathering, erosion, deposition, and mass wasting, to name a few. They can vary components, such as the volume or speed of running water, the gradient of a slope, or the composition of the Earth material to determine the impact on the system.

If the previous example was the focus of a typical science education immersion experience, participants would spend a significant portion of each day engaging in authentic inquiry designed to improve teachers' understanding of water's role in shaping Earth's surface, with daily debriefing about the science content. In professional learning focused more on developing understanding of Systems and System Models and Developing and Using Models, facilitators will still model best practices for authentic three-dimensional science teaching. Debriefing each day can include some discussion regarding water's role in surface processes, but the emphasis should be on how running water at Earth's surface is part of a larger system that involves transfer of matter and energy through the system. Multiple models for representing how water sculpts Earth's surface should be used. Teachers should have the opportunity to create their own models, evaluate their strengths and limitations, and revise them to test hypotheses about how a change in one component of the system impacts the rest of the system. Teachers can use these same activities with their high-ability students because of the complex thinking and analogical reasoning they require. Activities such as these also provide opportunities for learners to engage in authentic hypothesis-testing. The debrief can include an introduction to what the NGSS says about Systems and System Models and Developing and Using Models and how they progress throughout K–12 learning. If teachers are unfamiliar with the NGSS and their layout, a portion of the time can be spent exploring the standards and learning how to read them, although this does not need to occur the first day of the immersion. (The section of this chapter entitled Reading the NGSS could be helpful here.) If providing professional learning opportunities for teachers teaching in a state that has not adopted the NGSS, facilitators will need to discuss why emphasizing the SEPs and CCCs with high-ability learners is still a worthwhile enterprise, a point discussed earlier in this chapter.

Examining Student Work

During the school year following the immersion experience participants would meet multiple times (ideally three to five) to examine student work related to Systems and System Models and/or Developing and Using Models. Teachers can use work samples to evaluate the alignment of the task and rubric or scoring guide with learning outcomes for the SEP and CCC. Is the task open-ended? Is it at an appropriate level of complexity and abstractness? Using either a protocol they found online or one they developed collectively, teachers can analyze both individual and group work samples to determine how students are progressing in their understanding of systems and in their ability to develop and use models of those systems to construct explanations about a range of scientific phenomena. They can use their analyses to design instruction to help students understand that two systems that appear quite different on the surface, such as the carbon cycle and the human digestive system, share certain commonalities. All sessions could be devoted to examining student work around either the CCC or the SEP, or the group could move back and forth between the two. When deciding whether to spend the entire year focused just on Systems and System Models or Developing and Using Models, consider teachers' familiarity and prior exposure to the practice of examining student work and the NGSS. Teachers who are unfamiliar with one or both may find it beneficial to stay on one theme throughout the entire year. Sessions could be either face-to-face or virtual depending upon the geographic distribution of teachers or other factors that might limit their ability to meet face-to-face.

Summary

Science instruction for gifted learners should be characterized by rigor, the use of complex thinking, problem-based learning focused on sense-making, the structures and tools of inquiry, and analogical reasoning. Professional learning for science teachers of the gifted must equip them to design and deliver that instruction. Professional learning needs to address both teachers' science knowledge and their PCK to enable them to meet the needs of high-ability learners. However, this involves more than merely improving their knowledge of science concepts. Teachers should understand the themes or crosscutting concepts that permeate the sciences and the practices of inquiry by which scientists do their work. Whether or not teachers reside in a state that has adopted the Next Generation Science Standards, the three-dimensional approach to science instruction central to the NGSS provides a framework within which to support high-ability learners in science and design professional learning for their teachers. This chapter argues that a way to bridge the gap between the science education and gifted education literature on professional learning is to design professional learning experiences that emphasize the science and engineering practices and crosscutting concepts from the NGSS. Immersion and examining student work are two professional learning strategies that can be combined to provide sustained opportunities for teachers to improve their science content knowledge and their PCK. Either could be used in isolation or combined with other professional learning strategies; however, using immersion and examining student work in tandem can increase the likelihood that professional learning for science teachers of the gifted will be generative and result in positive changes in their teaching practices to better meet the needs of high-ability learners.

Resources

Adams, C., Cotabish, A., & Dailey, D. (2015). *A teacher's guide to using the Next Generation Science Standards with gifted and advanced learners.* Prufrock Press.

Adams, C., Cotabish, A., & Ricci, M. C. (2014). *Using the Next Generation Science Standards with gifted and advanced learners.* Prufrock Press.

Brunsell, E., Kneser, D. M., & Niemi, K. J. (2014). *Introducing teachers and administrators to the NGSS: A professional development facilitator's guide.* NSTA Press.

Dailey, D., & Cotabish, A. (Eds.). (2017). *Engineering instruction for high-ability learners in K–8 classrooms.* Prufrock Press.

MacFarlane, B. (Ed.). (2016). *STEM education for high-ability learners: Designing and implementing programming.* Prufrock Press.

Next Generation Science Standards. (n.d.). *Video.* Retrieved from https://www.nextgenscience.org/resource-type/video

National Science Teaching Association (n.d.). *NGSS videos.* Retrieved from https://ngss.nsta.org/ngss-videos.aspx

Rhoton, J. (Ed.). (2018). *Preparing teachers for three-dimensional instruction.* NSTA Press.

Schwarz, C. V., Passmore, C., & Reiser, B. J. (Eds.). (2017). *Helping students make sense of the world using Next Generation Science and Engineering Practices.* NSTA Press.

Zembal-Saul, C., McNeill, K. L., & Hershberger, K. (2013). *What's your evidence? Engaging K–5 students in constructing explanations in science.* Pearson.

References

Adams, C. M. (2003). Nurturing talent development in science. In P. Olszewski-Kubilius, L. Limburg-Weber, & S. Pfeiffer (Eds.), *Early gifts: Recognizing and nurturing children's talents* (pp. 19–38). Prufrock Press.

American Association for the Advancement of Science. (1993). *Benchmarks for science literacy.* Oxford University Press.

Council of State Science Supervisors. (2015). *Science professional learning standards.* http://cosss.org/Professional-Learning

Gilbert, J. K., & Newberry, M. (2007). The characteristics of the gifted and exceptionally able in science. In K. S. Taber (Ed.), *Science education for gifted learners* (pp. 15–31). Routledge.

Gubbins, E. J. (2008). Professional development. In J. A. Plucker & C. M. Callahan (Eds.), *Critical issues and practices in gifted education* (pp. 535–562). Prufrock Press.

Johnsen, S. K., & Clarenbach, J. (2017). *Using the national gifted education standards for Pre-K–grade 12 professional development* (2nd ed.). Prufrock Press.

Johnsen, S. K., & Kendrick, J. (Eds.). (2005). *Science education for gifted students.* Prufrock Press.

Learning Forward. (2011). *Standards for professional learning.* https://learningforward.org/standards

Little, C. A., & Ayers Paul, K. (2017). Professional development to support successful curriculum implementation. In J. VanTassel-Baska & C. A. Little (Eds.), *Content-based curriculum for high-ability learners* (3rd ed., pp. 461–483). Prufrock Press.

Loucks-Horsley, S., Stiles, K. E., Mundry, S., Love, N., & Hewson, P. W. (2010). *Designing professional development for teachers of science and mathematics* (3rd ed.). Corwin Press.

Melville, W. (2010). *Professional learning in a school-based community of science teachers.* Sense.

National Academies of Sciences, Engineering, and Medicine. (2015). *Science teachers' learning: Enhancing opportunities, creating supportive contexts.* The National Academies Press. https://doi.org/10.17226/21836.

National Association for Gifted Children, & The Association for the Gifted, Council for Exceptional Children. (2013). *NAGC-CEC teacher preparation standards in gifted education.* http://www.nagc.org/sites/default/files/standards/NAGC-%20CEC%20CAEP%20standards%20%282013%20final%29.pdf

National Research Council. (2012). *A framework for K–12 science education: Practices, crosscutting concepts, and core ideas.* The National Academies Press.

NGSS Lead States. (2013). *Next generation science standards: For states, by states.* The National Academies Press.

Novak, A. M. (2018). What works in professional learning for educators of the gifted: Findings from research and legislation. In A. M. Novak & C. L. Weber (Eds.), *Best practices in professional learning and teacher preparation in gifted education: Methods and strategies for gifted professional development* (Vol. 1, pp. 5–21). Prufrock Press.

Novak, A. M., & Lewis, K. D. (2018). Tools of the trade: Finding the best fit for your professional learning needs. In A. M. Novak & C. L. Weber (Eds.), *Best practices in professional learning and teacher preparation: Methods and strategies for gifted professional development* (Vol 1., pp. 51–69). Prufrock Press.

Odden, T. O. B., & Russ, R. S. (2019). Defining sensemaking: Bringing clarity to a fragmented theoretical construct. *Science Education, 103*(1), 187–205. https://doi.org/10.1002/sce.21452

Robbins, J. I. (2011). Adapting science curricula for high-ability learners. In J. VanTassel-Baska & C. A. Little (Eds.), *Content-based curriculum for high-ability learners* (2nd ed., pp. 217–238). Prufrock Press.

Schwarz, C. V., Passmore, C., & Reiser, B. J. (2017). Moving beyond "knowing about" science to making sense of the world. In C. V. Schwarz, C. Passmore, & B. J. Reiser (Eds.), *Helping students make sense of the world using next generation science and engineering practices* (pp. 3–21). NSTA Press.

Shulman, L. S. (1986). Those who understand: Knowledge growth in teaching. *Educational Researcher, 15*(2), 4–14. https://doi.org/10.3102/0013189X015002004

Taber, K. S. (2007a). Choice for the gifted: Lessons from teaching about scientific explanations. In K. S. Taber (Ed.), *Science education for gifted learners* (pp. 158–171). Routledge.

Taber, K. S. (2007b). Science education for gifted learners? In K. S. Taber (Ed.), *Science education for gifted learners* (pp. 1–14). Routledge.

VanTassel-Baska, J. (2017). Introduction to the integrated curriculum model. In J. VanTassel-Baska & C. A. Little (Eds.), *Content-based curriculum for high-ability learners* (3rd ed., pp. 15–32). Prufrock Press.

VanTassel-Baska, J., & MacFarlane, B. (2008). Science, secondary. In J. A. Plucker & C. M. Callahan (Eds.), *Critical issues and practices in gifted education* (pp. 579–593). Prufrock Press.

CHAPTER 9

Crafting Professional Learning Experiences for Teachers of Gifted Students in Mathematics

Eric L. Mann and Rebecca L. Mann

Introduction

In the fall of 2010, the Conference Board of the Mathematical Sciences (CBMS) held a forum on the content-based professional development of teachers. One of the many comments that stood out in the subsequent report read:

> For generations, high school students have studied something in school that has been called mathematics, but which has very little to do with the way mathematics is created or applied outside of school. One reason for this has been a view of curriculum in which mathematics courses are seen as mechanisms for communicating established results and methods—for preparing students for life after school by giving them a bag of facts. Students learn to solve equations, find areas, and calculate interest on a loan. Given this view of mathematics, curriculum reform simply means replacing one set of established results by another one. . . .

There is another way to think about it, and it involves turning the priorities around. Much more important than specific mathematical results are the habits of mind used by the people who create those results. (CBMS, 2011, p. 8)

In the spring of 2017, the Association of Mathematics Teacher Educators (AMTE) released the *Standards for Preparing Teachers of Mathematics* (SPTM). This 2-year effort, with input from many other organizations, including the National Council of Teachers of Mathematics, the Mathematical Association of America, and the American Statistical Association, culminated in a comprehensive road map of the professional knowledge needed to effectively teach mathematics from Pre-K–grade 12. These standards, combined with the changes in curricular emphasis advocated in the Common Core State Standards for Mathematics (CCSS-M), envision a mathematics classroom environment in which students are encouraged to creatively explore mathematical concepts rather than passively adopt procedures with little or no conceptual understanding of why they work (or when they are appropriate to use).

Both the mathematics and mathematics education communities have noted the shift needed in how school mathematics is experienced. With each advance in technology the laborious (and boring) computational tasks endured by past generations of students are minimized, providing opportunities to explore deeper the patterns, relationships, and concepts underlying mathematics. All students should have the opportunity to explore mathematical topics at a pace appropriate for them. Some mathematically talented students are best served by a faster pace, others may thrive on opportunities to explore topics more deeply, some will be interested in the history of mathematics, and there will be a few whose nontraditional ways of thinking will open new mathematical insight for the teacher and student. Drive-by, one-shot professional learning experiences cannot provide the time and collaboration required for mathematics teachers to develop the habits of mind and skills necessary to embrace changing priorities.

Transforming the Learning of Mathematics

> We have known for some years now . . . that most children's mathematical journeys are in vain because they never arrive anywhere, and what is perhaps worse is that they do not even enjoy the journey. (Whitcombe, 1988, p. 14)

At the beginning of mathematics content courses for preservice teachers, students are often asked to write a brief biography describing their past mathematical experiences. Although there are a few who share positive experiences, usually associated with a specific teacher rather than the mathematical content, the vast majority describe mathematics as a static, difficult, and incomprehensible discipline. Most have forgotten the mathematics they were exposed to in their K–12 experience, and what they do remember is the "mathematics of routine computation and manipulation (usually with some formula proof thrown in). Mathematics was little more than a collection of recipes that students were expected to memorize and practice" (Silver et al., 1990, p. 6).

These beliefs can carry over into the practice of teaching as well. In his chapter on changing the teaching of mathematics, Weissglass (1994) summarized the beliefs and values of mathematics teachers with whom he had worked. A few that resonate here are:
- you must master the content before you can use your brain to think mathematically,
- people learn mathematics by listening to someone talk about it and from doing homework problems,
- mathematics is too difficult to understand on one's own—students need to be told,
- making mistakes is a sign of weakness, and
- it is okay not to be good at math. (p. 68)

This is a very narrow view of mathematics, one that is bounded by rules and is computationally focused. Silver et al. (1990) wrote, "the logical structure implicit in much of mathematical knowledge has seduced us into believing that the hierarchical, simple-to-complex ordering that can be imposed on mathematics is synonymous with mathematics itself." (p. 7). Mathematics is much more; " an evolving, innovative science of patterns, relations, and logical reasoning" (Sheffield, 2017, p. 15). Unfortunately, students often develop this narrow view of mathematics early in their educational experience. In identifying students for an advanced fifth-grade math program, we decided that in addition to looking at performance, we should also interview the students. "Do you like math?" was asked, and the first child interviewed answered with a question, "Do you mean math the class or math the subject?" He loved the study of mathematics but hated his computationally focused math class.

For teachers to instill in their students the mathematical practices called for in the CCSS-M, students need the opportunity to:
- make sense of problems and persevere in solving them,
- reason abstractly and quantitatively,
- construct viable arguments and critique the reasoning of others,
- model with mathematics,
- use appropriate tools strategically,
- attend to precision,
- look for and make use of structure, and
- look for and express regularity in repeated reasoning (National Governors Association Center for Best Practices & Council of Chief State School Officers, 2010).

Teachers need to embrace these practices as well. This is challenging if one has only been asked to do no more than follow directions and solve problems with known solutions, often in the back of the book or in the teacher's edition.

The CCSS-M mathematical practices describe the varieties of expertise that mathematics educators at all levels must seek to develop in their students. The development of deep roots in important "processes and proficiencies" is of long-standing importance in mathematics education. The first of these are the process standards from the National Council of Teachers of Mathematics (NCTM, n.d.) of problem solving, reasoning and proof, communication, representation, and connections. The second are the strands of mathematical proficiency specified in the National Research Council's (2001) report *Adding It Up: Helping Children Learn Mathematics*: adaptive reasoning, strategic competence, conceptual understanding (comprehension of mathematical concepts, operations, and relations), procedural fluency (skill in carrying out procedures flexibly, accurately, efficiently, and appropriately), and productive disposition (habitual inclination to see mathematics as sensible, useful, and worthwhile, coupled with a belief in diligence and one's own efficacy).

For teachers who work with students talented in mathematics (e.g., gifted, high-ability, exceptional mathematical promise, etc.) these practices, processes, and dispositions are critical in creating an engaging learning environment that offers opportunities for both depth and breadth in the mathematical work students are asked to undertake. In their book *Using the Common Core State Standards for Mathematics With Gifted and Advanced Learners*, Johnsen and Sheffield (2012) add a ninth practice: Solve problems in novel ways and pose new mathematical questions of interest to investigate. Providing students the opportunity to struggle with ill-defined problems, experiment with their own invented problem-solving strategies, and pose their own questions to explore develops the productive mathematical dispositions needed for future success in the discipline, as well as dealing with day-to-day problems.

Professional Learning Needs

Teachers of high-ability mathematics students often attempt to meet their students' needs by providing them acceleration in the form of independent study. Students who can interpret and analyze mathematical problems and circumstances quickly and through the use of multiple methods benefit from working with knowledgeable teachers who do more than present them with the next chapter in the book. Although a change in the traditional approach to teaching mathematics is important for all students, it is essential for gifted learners.

To accomplish this change in the way mathematical content is taught can be threatening to the teacher who relies on textbooks and standardized procedures, but this change creates an enriching and more productive learning experience for students and teachers alike. Teaching from a conceptual versus computational perspective, students "solve problems by working from a deep understanding of them . . . [working] from their understanding . . . Once they have developed conceptual methods and have reflected on those methods in notation, they can then appreciate that conventional methods are but one way to solve problems" (Thompson et al., 1994, p. 91). This approach works especially well for gifted learners, as they have a preference for conceptual understanding and their computational skills can often lag behind their understanding of complex mathematical processes (Rotigel & Fello, 2004).

TeachingWorks at the University of Michigan (http://www.teachingworks.org) is working to identify high-leverage practices and content that are central to the task of teaching and essential in the development of well-prepared early career teachers of mathematics. Many of these practices are applicable in multiple disciplines, but of the 19 high-level practices, the second—*explaining and modeling content, practices, and strategies*—emphasizes the importance of being able to analyze and carefully choose the tasks and questions posed to students. To do this effectively, teachers must have a deep understanding of the mathematical concepts involved and how they relate to and prepare students for more advanced mathematics, as well as the skill to evaluate alternative, student-invented problem solving strategies and methods.

In identifying high-leverage content, TeachingWorks looks to those concepts that are foundational to the K–12 curriculum and essential to developing understanding. High-leverage content in mathematics can "include place value, number concepts and operations, fractions and representing and explaining mathematical ideas and relationships" (TeachingWorks, n.d., para. 3). Although these content terms may sound familiar and, as an adult, one may have the necessary skill to work in these areas successfully, unpacking these concepts in ways that support a student's developing understanding requires a specialized knowledge of the content.

Ball et al. (2008) identified this specialized content knowledge as a relatively uncharted area. This work is foundational to the efforts at TeachingWorks with a focus on "demands of practice" that are encountered in teaching of mathematics, calling for "the content preparation of teachers that is professionally based—both distinctive, substantial and fundamentally tied to professional practice and to the knowledge and skill demanded by the work" (p. 405).

Professional Learning Strategies

The National Council of Teachers of Mathematics and Solution Tree Press have jointly published a series of texts, *Common Core Mathematics in a PLC at Work* (https://www.solutiontree.com/products/common-core-math-plc-work.html), that offer a framework for professional learning community (PLC) work at specific grade bands (K–2, 3–5, 6–8, and high school). Recognizing that the CCSS-M require a shift from the traditional low-level cognitive demand tasks to high-level, more challenging tasks that require a deeper understanding of the content, the PLC at Work model advocates a change in instructional emphasis (see Figure 9.1).

- An instructional emphasis that approaches mathematics learning as problem solving (Mathematical Practice 1)
- An instructional emphasis on cognitively demanding conceptual tasks that encourage all students to remain engaged in the task without watering down the expectation level (maintaining cognitive demand) (Mathematical Practice 1)
- Instruction that places the highest value on student understanding (Mathematical Practices 1 and 2)
- Instruction that emphasizes the discussion of alternative strategies (Mathematical Practice 3)
- Instruction that includes extensive mathematics discussion (math talk) generated through effective teacher questioning (Mathematical Practices 2, 3, 6, 7, and 8)
- Teacher and student explanations to support strategies and conjectures (Mathematical Practices 2 and 3)
- The use of multiple representations (Mathematical Practices 4 and 5)

Figure 9.1. High-leverage mathematics instructional practices linked to CCSS mathematical practices. From *Common Core Mathematics in a PLC at Work* (p. 25), by M. R. Larson, F. Fennell, T. L. Adams, J. K. Dixon, B. M Kobett, and J. A. Wray, 2012, Solution Tree Press. Copyright 2012 by Solution Tree Press. Reprinted with permission.

It is difficult to envision what a mathematics classroom with a conceptual focus might be like if one has not had that experience. Borko et al. (2015) designed a PLC grounded in problem solving that they named the Problem-Solving Cycle (PSC). Recognizing that the specialized knowledge needed to teach mathematics effectively is different from that needed in other STEM professions, and that being asked to use instructional strategies that are unfamiliar from those one may have experienced as a student, the PSC is grounded in collaborative work on carefully selected mathematical problems. Once a solution has been agreed upon, teachers then dig deeper by analyzing the underlying mathematical concepts and anticipating correct and incorrect ways a child may approach the problem. In doing so, teachers discuss the mathematics from multiple perspectives and develop ways to support the unique needs for their students in learning the content. This is best done in the context of rich mathematical problems defined as problems that:
- address several critical mathematical concepts and practice,
- are accessible to students with different levels of mathematical knowledge,
- contain multiple entry and exit points, and
- encourage a variety of solution strategies (Borko et al., 2015, p. 6).

This approach aligns well with the NAGC-CEC Teacher Preparation Standards in Gifted Education (National Association for Gifted Children, & The Association for the Gifted, Council for Exceptional Children, 2013), specifically:

- 3.1: Understand the role of central concepts, structures of the discipline and tools of inquiry.
- 3.2: Design appropriate learning and performance modifications for individuals with gifts and talents that enhance creativity, acceleration, depth and complexity in academic subject matter.
- 5.3: Collaborate with . . . professional colleagues . . . to select, adapt and use evidence-based strategies that promote challenging learning opportunities. (pp. 3–5)

Another advantage to the PSC approach is that participants develop a broader view of mathematics. Jilk (2016) noted that if educators hold a narrow, limited view of mathematics it is difficult to notice strengths in their classrooms, especially in students who are not part of the dominant culture. In addition, she noted that "unexamined habits toward teaching [such] as fixing students' problems and misconceptions often gets in the way of being able to reimagine and invent teaching actions that instead focus on accessing and building on students' strengths and multiple ways of understanding" (p. 189). By participating in a problem solving-focused PLC, teachers share their respective strengths while examining the habits that get in the way of developing a student's mathematical ability.

One source of these types of problem-solving activities is the prototype professional development modules (https://www.map.mathshell.org/pd.php) from the Shell Center for Mathematical Education (a collaborative effort of the University of California, Berkeley and the Shell Center team at the University of Nottingham; Mathematics Assessment Resource Service, 2015). Taking an activity-based approach and based on example classroom activities, these modules provide an environment where productive discourse among the participants about ways to strengthen their teaching practices can occur while engaging in problem-solving activities. Following a PLC approach, participants use these experiences as they plan and teach a lesson in their classrooms, reconvening to share their reflections on the lesson and its impact both on their teaching practice and student learning. The introductory material to these modules reads, in part:

> To truly meet the demands of the Common Core State Standards it is not sufficient to simply revise the list of mathematical content covered in the curriculum. The Standards' emphasis on Mathematical Practices require students to

be able to think mathematically, and apply the techniques they have learned to rich problems in diverse contexts. Achieving this requires changes in the way mathematics is taught and assessed in most schools. (Mathematics Assessment Resource Service, 2015)

Accompanying the professional development modules are ready-to-use classroom challenges at all grade bands with supporting videos of students engaged in this work.

Collaborative work in solving rich problems is imperative but not sufficient in a PLC seeking to effect change in the way educators teach mathematics. Elliott et al. (2009) developed a framework for mathematics professional development with an emphasis on the mathematical knowledge needed for teaching. In this framework, the participants are encouraged to "slow down" and explicitly engage in conversation focusing on the mathematical ideas, why they are important, and how they support student learning. All too often, when a reasonable solution is found, there is a tendency to move on to the next task rather than to reflect on the work completed. For educators to develop the skill to converse mathematically and explore their own mathematical thinking, as well as that of others, requires time and a supportive community. Elliott et al. (2009) identified seven "productive sociomathematical norms" that occur when this happens:

- Sharing has a purpose of extending and deepening mathematical thinking.
- Sharing consists of explanations that emphasize the meaning of mathematical ideas.
- Mathematical connections among solutions, approaches, or representations are explored.
- Justification consists of a mathematical argument.
- Justification emphasizes the why and the how methods work.
- Questions push on [for] deepening understanding of mathematical ideas.
- Confusion and error are embraced as opportunities to deepen mathematical understanding—comparing ideas, reconceptualizing problems, exploring contradictions, pursuing alternative strategies (p. 369).

Teachers need this experience to develop their mathematical skills, regardless of the level that they teach; an elementary teacher needs a deep understanding of place value and how it supports the manipulation of numbers in the arithmetic operations students are asked to master, just as a secondary teacher needs an understanding of not only how the fundamental theorem of calculus links the concepts of a function's derivative and integral, but also how this knowledge lays a foundation for more advanced work in mathematics.

One resource the prospective teachers we work with have found helpful as they build their understanding of the mathematics they will teach is the Progressions Documents for the Common Core Math Standards (see http://ime.math.arizona.edu/progressions). These documents, available online in various stages of development, describe the progression of various mathematical topics across all grade levels: elementary, middle, and secondary. Drawing on both educational research and the structure of mathematics, the documents offer students insight into how mathematical thinking and understanding develop and the reasons why topics are emphasized at a specific time and order in a child's development. For many, the discussion in the progression documents is a "light bulb" moment, in which they make connections that should have been made as they progressed through the K–12 curriculum.

Implications

In crafting his Retiring Presidential Address at the end of his term as president of the Mathematical Association of America, Francis Su (2017) focused on two questions: "Why does the practice of mathematics often fall short of our ideals and hopes? How can the deeply human themes that drive us to do mathematics be channeled to build a more beautiful and just world in which all can truly flourish?" (para. 1). His talk explored the relationship between mathematics and five human basic human desires—play, beauty, truth, justice, and love—relationships rarely explored in the K–12 mathematics classroom where "little more than computational skill with the standard algorithms and a textbook to provide practice" is required (Even & Lappan, 1994, p. 128). Depriving any child of a rich mathematical experience is wrong; allowing talent to wither is immoral. Teachers of gifted and talented mathematics students need (1) an enthusiasm for mathematics, (2) the ability to share the beauty and wonder of mathematics with their students, (3) the strength to admit they do not have all of the answers and then model ways for students to find the answers on their own, (4) the flexibility and willingness to work with their students as coinvestigators when the students' curiosity leads investigations in unplanned directions, and (5) the confidence to step back and let the students take responsibility for their own learning of mathematics (Sheffield, 1994, pp. 27–28). These traits take time to develop and are best explored in the collaborative environment of a professional learning community.

Summary

In working with inservice and preservice teachers, we have found that few have been asked to explore the underlying mathematical concepts upon which K–12 curriculum is based. Often, their past experiences focused on replicating a solution method to solve a series of similar problems. Rarely were they asked to think about the structure of the problem or the strategies that might lead to a satisfying solution, explore alternate solution methods, or ask why the method offered was chosen. This may be sufficient to survive a K–12 mathematics course of study as a student but does little to prepare a child for the messy, real-world problems they will encounter in later years, and it is woefully insufficient preparation for the teaching of mathematics.

Effective mathematics teachers have an in-depth conceptual understanding of the mathematics that they teach. Their acceptance of students who use nontraditional methods for solving problems is essential, especially when supporting gifted learners. That acceptance and knowledge is a result of extensive preparation in preservice mathematics programs and continued learning opportunities through properly focused professional learning communities. In answering the question "What does it mean to know mathematics for teaching?", Ball et al. (2005) wrote:

> the mathematical knowledge held and expressed by students is often incomplete and difficult to understand. Others can avoid dealing with this emergent mathematics, but teachers are in the unique position of having to professionally scrutinize, interpret, correct, and extend this knowledge. (p. 17)

Mastering content is important, but if the emphasis is always on practice and never on creative performance, the true nature of mathematics is lost. The gifted student of mathematics needs the opportunity to experience mathematics as described by Halmos (as cited in Albers, 1986):

> [Mathematics] is Security, Certainty, Truth, Beauty, Insight, Structure, Architecture. I see mathematics, the part of human knowledge that I call mathematics as one thing—one great glorious thing.
>
> Mathematics—this may surprise you or shock you some—is never deductive in its creation. The mathematician at work makes vague guesses, visualizes broad generalizations, and jumps to unwarranted conclusions. He arranges and rearranges his ideas, and he becomes convinced of their truth long before he can write down a logical proof. The conviction is not likely to come early—it usually comes after many attempts, many failures, many discouragements, many false starts. (pp. 127, 380–381)

Professional learning communities in mathematics that fail to incorporate the creative beauty of mathematics may help prepare teachers to improve student test scores and move faster through the curriculum, but students will continue on a journey that leads nowhere.

Resources

- NRICH Maths Project, The University of Cambridge
  - Professional learning articles for the elementary classroom teacher: https://nrich.maths.org/9405
  - Professional learning articles for the secondary classroom teacher: https://nrich.maths.org/whatwethink

- Progressions Documents for the Common Core Math Standards, Institute for Mathematics and Education, The University of Arizona: http://ime.math.arizona.edu/progressions
- Related resources:
  - Clements' video on Learning Trajectories: https://thelearning exchange.ca/videos/doug-clements-learning-trajectories (*Note*. Ontario's Ministry of Education offers many other reso-urces to support professional learning activities. For mathematics, visit https://thelearningexchange.ca/project_category/mathematics.)

- Fletcher's videos on Progressions in Early Number and Counting, Operations (Addition, Subtraction, Multiplication, and Division), and Fraction Concepts: https://gfletchy.com/progression-videos

- Shell Center for Mathematics Education, Mathematics Assessment Project: https://www.map.mathshell.org
- TeachingWorks, University of Michigan: http://www.teachingworks.org
- Math for Love's selected resources: https://mathforlove.com/resources
- Johnsen, S. K., & Kendrick, J. (Eds.). (2005). *Math education for gifted students*. Prufrock Press.

References

Albers, D. J. (1985). Paul Halmos. In D. J. Albers & G. L. Alexanderson (Eds.), *Mathematical people: Profiles and interviews* (pp. 121–132). Birkhäuser.

Association of Mathematics Teacher Educators. (2017). *Standards for preparing teachers of mathematics*. https://amte.net/standards

Ball, D. L., Hill, H. C., & Bass, H. (2005). Knowing mathematics for teaching: Who knows mathematics well enough to teach third grade, and how can we decide? *American Educator, 29*(1), 14–22, 43–46.

Ball, D. L., Thames, M. T., & Phelps, G. (2008). Content knowledge for teaching: What makes it special? *Journal of Teacher Education, 59*(5), 389–407. https://doi.org/10.1177/0022487108324554

Borko, H., Jacobs, J., Koellner, K., & Swackhamer, L. E. (2015). *Mathematics professional development: Improving teaching using the problem-solving cycle and leadership preparation models*. Teachers College Press.

Conference Board of the Mathematical Sciences. (2011). *Common standards and the mathematical education of teachers*. https://www.cbmsweb.org/archive/Forum3/CBMS_Forum_White_Paper.pdf

Elliott, R., Kazemi, E., Lesseig, K., Mumme, J., Carroll, C., & Kelley-Peterson, K. (2009). Conceptualizing the work of leading mathematical tasks in professional development. *Journal of Teacher Education, 60*(4), 364–379. https://doi.org/10.1177/0022487109341150

Even, R., & Lappan, G. (1994). Constructing meaningful understanding of mathematics content. In D. B. Aichele & A. F. Coxford (Eds.), *Professional development for teachers of mathematics* (pp. 128–143). National Council of Teachers of Mathematics.

Jilk, L. M. (2016). Supporting teacher noticing of students' mathematical strengths. *Mathematics Teacher Educator, 4*(2), 188–199. https://doi.org/10.5951/mathteaceduc.4.2.0188

Johnsen, S. K., & Sheffield, L. J. (2012). *Using the Common Core State Standards for mathematics with gifted and advanced learners*. Prufrock Press.

Larson, M. R., Fennel, F., Adams, T. L., Dixon, J. K., Kobett, B. M., & Wray, J. A. (2012). *Common Core mathematics in a PLC at work, Grades K–2* (pp. 5–24). Solution Tree Press.

Mathematics Assessment Resource Service. (2015). *Mathematics assessment project: Prototype professional development modules*. University of Nottingham. https://www.map.mathshell.org/pd.php

National Association for Gifted Children, & The Association for the Gifted, Council for Exceptional Children. (2013). *NAGC-CEC teacher preparation standards in gifted education*. http://www.nagc.org/sites/default/files/standards/NAGC-%20CEC%20CAEP%20standards%20%282013%20final%29.pdf

National Council of Teachers of Mathematics. (n.d.). *Process*. https://www.nctm.org/Standards-and-Positions/Principles-and-Standards/Process

National Governors Association Center for Best Practices, & Council of Chief State School Officers. (2010). *Common Core State Standards for mathematics*. http://www.corestandards.org/Math

National Research Council. (2001). *Adding it up: Helping children learn mathematics*. The National Academies Press. https://doi.org/10.17226/9822c

Rotigel, J. V., & Fello, S. (2004). Mathematically gifted students: How can we meet their needs? *Gifted Child Today, 27*(4), 46–51. https://doi.org/10.4219/gct-2004-150

Sheffield, L. J. (1994). *The development of gifted and talented mathematics students and the National Council of Teachers of Mathematics Standards*. University of Connecticut, The National Research Center for the Gifted and Talented.

Sheffield, L. J. (2017). Dangerous myths about "gifted" mathematics students. *ZDM Mathematics Education, 49*(1), 13–23. https://doi.org/10.1007/s11858-016-0814-8

Silver, E. A., Kilpatrick, J., & Schlesinger, B. (1990). *Thinking through mathematics: Fostering inquiry and communication in mathematics classrooms*. The College Board. http://files.eric.ed.gov/fulltext/ED387350.pdf

Su, F. (2017). *Mathematics for human flourishing.* https://mathyawp.wordpress.com/2017/01/08/mathematics-for-human-flourishing

TeachingWorks. (n.d.). *High-leverage content.* http://www.teachingworks.org/work-of-teaching/high-leverage-content

Thompson, A. G., Philipp, R. A., Thompson, P. W., & Boyd, B. A. (1994). Calculational and conceptual orientations in teaching mathematics. In D. B. Aichele & A. F. Coxford (Eds.), *Professional development for teachers of mathematics* (pp. 79–91). National Council of Teachers of Mathematics.

Weissglass, J. (1994). Changing mathematics teaching means changing ourselves: Implications for professional development. In D. B. Aichele & A. F. Coxford (Eds.), *Professional development for teachers of mathematics* (pp. 67–78). National Council of Teachers of Mathematics.

Whitcombe, A. (1988). Mathematics creativity, imagination, beauty. *Mathematics in School, 17*(2), 13–15. https://www.jstor.org/stable/30214447

CHAPTER 10

Using the CLEAR Curriculum Model's Language Arts Units to Support Professional Learning in Gifted Education

Tracy C. Missett, Carolyn M. Callahan, and Cheryll M. Adams

Curriculum designed to engage, challenge, and promote continual intellectual growth in advanced learners lies at the heart of all gifted programming. Without such curriculum, developing a conception of giftedness and methods for identifying gifted learners, as well as implementing strong instructional strategies in the classroom, will not provide appropriate learning experiences for gifted learners. Consequently, unless and until educators are able to develop and deploy a rich and rigorous curriculum for gifted learners, "all of our efforts are largely for naught" (Hertberg-Davis, 2018, p. 249). Nevertheless, most gifted students do not regularly experience rich and rigorous curricula appropriate to their readiness levels, interests, and learning preferences (Hockett & Brighton, 2016). Rather, research shows that gifted students often sit in classrooms covering material they have already mastered while being taught by teachers who have had no training in recognizing and meeting the needs of gifted students. Moreover, many teachers of gifted students lack access to quality curriculum and professional learning opportunities that provide knowledge and understanding of the key features of quality curriculum (Gubbins, 2014).

To ensure that teachers working with gifted learners are prepared to recognize, develop, and deploy curriculum defensible for gifted learners, experts urge taking part in professional learning opportunities addressed to those ends (VanTassel-Baska, 2014). For example, the National Association for Gifted Children (NAGC, 2019) recommended that practicing teachers have specific content knowledge and pedagogical skills in gifted education so that they are able to develop gifted learners' talents for high-level functioning. To that end, NAGC and The Association for the Gifted, Council for Exceptional Children (CEC-TAG) adopted standards for professionals who work with gifted students called the NAGC-CEC Teacher Preparation Standards in Gifted Education (NAGC & CEC-TAG, 2013). The Teacher Preparation Standards identify the knowledge and skills teachers need to effectively identify and serve gifted learners. More specifically, they propose that teachers of gifted learners should be prepared to create curriculum appropriate to meet the needs of diverse gifted children. Similarly, the federal education law known as the Every Student Succeeds Act (ESSA, 2015) emphasizes six criteria for professional learning, proposing that related efforts should be sustained, intensive, collaborative, job-embedded, data-driven and classroom-focused.

Despite calls for educators to engage in professional learning designed to (1) strengthen their understanding of the nature and educational demands of gifted learners, and (2) provide strategies for appropriately responding to the differences between gifted learners and their peers through the implementation of high-quality curriculum, many states and local school districts are reducing budgets for professional development broadly, and in the area of gifted education specifically. Further, typical professional development is often designed and delivered without consideration of the differences among teachers and the children they serve. Faced with such constrained learning budgets, educators must think creatively about ways to experience and take advantage of quality professional development opportunities beyond the limited and typically one-shot workshop offerings of the school district.

In this chapter, we discuss a curriculum model—the CLEAR Curriculum Model—that supports the development of curriculum characterized by evidence-based and appropriate learning experiences for gifted learners (Azano et al., 2018). Currently, six language arts units—two in each grade across grades 3–5—have been created using the CLEAR Curriculum Model (Azano et al. 2016; Callahan et al., 2017; Missett et al., 2016). Using these units together offers teachers a strong and effective substitute for traditional professional learning in an era of minimal funding.

We start by providing an overview of the CLEAR Curriculum Model, including a description of the theoretical underpinnings of the model and its foundational elements. Next, using lesson component examples from the CLEAR language arts units, we discuss the ways in which teachers can use, and have used, the CLEAR language arts units themselves to better understand and respond to professional learning recommendations reflected in the NAGC-CEC Teacher Preparation Standards in Gifted Education and ESSA. We conclude the chapter with recommendations for resources that guide educators on using the CLEAR Curriculum Model to deepen their understanding of the construction and implementation of quality curriculum for gifted learners.

Overview of the CLEAR Curriculum Model

The CLEAR (Challenge Leading to Engagement, Achievement, and Results) Curriculum Model is a synthesis of the strongest and most compatible curricular elements from three well-regarded models in gifted education: (a) the differentiated instruction model (Tomlinson, 1995, 1999, 2001); (b) the Schoolwide Enrichment Model (Renzulli & Reis, 2000, 2014); and (c) the depth and complexity model (Kaplan, 2005, 2018). CLEAR provides a framework for the design and use of authentic, rigorous curriculum appropriate for gifted learners (Azano et al., 2018). Although these models are fully articulated in other texts, the key features of each that lie at the heart of CLEAR are briefly described here to provide the basis for seeing how the units based on the CLEAR framework provide a professional learning experience for the teachers who implement it.

The Differentiated Instruction Model

Differentiated instruction situates the individual at the center of all learning experiences (Tomlinson, 2018) to differentiate based on the individual's unique learning characteristics. Curriculum developed using the differentiated instruction model differentiates for each student in terms of the content to which students are exposed, the processes used to understand the content, and the products students create. In differentiated instruction, a differentiated curriculum is informed through the use of ongoing formative assessments—both formal and informal—which support teachers in recognizing student differences. As such, assessment enables the teacher to monitor student progress. Additionally, teachers use continual formative assessment as the fundamental basis for instructional decision making in terms of a student's readiness level (to determine the appropriate pace of learning), interests, learning profile and preferences, as well as flexible grouping arrangements.

The Schoolwide Enrichment Model

The Schoolwide Enrichment Model (SEM) emphasizes the creative process and encourages the construction and deployment of curriculum that provides students with academic experiences authentic to a discipline (Renzulli & Reis, 2000, 2014). In essence, these experiences situate learners "in the shoes" of a practicing professional in a field. Thus, tasks students engage in and the products they create reflect work on a real-world problem or topic for investigation. Additionally, learning tasks and products created reflect appropriate vehicles to communicate the results of efforts to an appropriate audience, one a professional in the field might choose. The student collects data, synthesizes ideas, or creates new ideas using an appropriate methodology of the field of study to create authentic products that add new knowledge, ideas or products to the field of study. Finally, academic tasks and products reflect student-selected topics of investigation rather than teacher-constructed activities in the SEM.

Depth and Complexity

Depth and complexity employs standards-based curriculum as the basis for advancing academic rigor (Kaplan, 2005). To add depth to the standards-based curriculum, the depth and complexity model explicitly focuses on the big ideas, language of the discipline, details, patterns, and rules within a discipline. These concepts are then coupled with a focus on complexity inherent in a discipline, including multiple perspectives, interdisciplinary connections, unanswered questions, ethical issues, and changes over time. Curricular applications of differentiated instruction employ depth and complexity to facilitate student exploration of challenging content and student application of the processes necessary to develop understanding and expertise at high levels. The depth and complexity model emphasizes the integration of big ideas and essential understandings in order to establish clear learning goals for students. The features of depth and complexity are articulated by a collection of icons, or pictorial representations. Icons explicitly guide teachers regarding the particular lesson organization, literacy focus, discipline exploration, subject analysis, content focus, learning objective, instructional strategy, and focus on student differences (Kaplan, 2018). In essence, they provide teachers with a visual representation of the curriculum features and instructional strategies that support deep and complex learning.

Integration of the Models Into CLEAR

These key elements from the differentiated instruction model, SEM, and depth and complexity model have research-based support in the field of gifted education. They combine in CLEAR to provide a novel and integrated framework for designing high-quality, authentic curriculum appropriate for academically diverse learners, including students identified as gifted (Azano et al., 2018). CLEAR imposes five foundational curriculum elements on the development of rigorous curriculum for gifted learners: (1) Continual Formative Assessment, (2) Clear Learning Goals, (3) Data-Driven Learning Experiences, (4) Authentic Products, and (5) Rich Curriculum. Each element is considered vital to the creation of rigorous and engaging curriculum for diverse gifted learners. More detailed examples of each element are provided later in this chapter.

Integrated throughout CLEAR units are a series of icons. Although many of the icons are derived from Kaplan's depth and complexity model, others have been specifically developed for CLEAR. Icons are particularly useful to a teacher's recognition and use of best practices as icons explicitly draw a teacher's attention to the particular content focus, learning objective, or instructional configuration of a learning activity within a CLEAR unit, and to student differences. Icons serve as a road map to guide instruction throughout a unit (Azano et al., 2018) and as models of the ways the elements of the three frameworks work together and independently in quality curriculum and instruction for gifted learners. As such, they offer professional development to teachers by making explicit best practices in gifted education and curriculum implementation. In Figure 10.1, we explain several icons and how they guide teachers throughout CLEAR units.

To date, six language arts units have been developed using the CLEAR model. There are two third-grade units in *Poetry and Fairy Tales* (Azano et al., 2016), two fourth-grade units in *Fiction and Nonfiction* (Callahan et al., 2017), and two fifth-grade units in *Research and Rhetoric* (Missett et al., 2016). The Poetry and Rhetoric units have received national curriculum awards from NAGC. Additionally, in a study funded by a Javits grant, the Poetry and Research units were implemented in multiple third-grade class-

DISCIPLINE EXPLORATION icons are used to explain how to explore the discipline and where to focus student attention during instructional activities. (DI indicates a principle from the differentiated instruction model; SEM indicates a curriculum principle from the Schoolwide Enrichment Model; and DC indicates a principle from the depth and complexity model.)

	Language (DC) Indicates a task that helps students learn the specific specialized and technological terms associated with a specific area of study or discipline.
	Real World Application (SEM) Indicates a task that applies the language and tools of the discipline in an environment or activity similar to what an expert in the field would experience.
	Big Idea (DC) Indicates the generalizations, principles, and theories that distinguish themselves from the facts and concepts of the area or discipline under study. Big ideas refer to an essential understanding about a topic or discipline that students should take away from the lesson or unit.

LESSON ORGANIZATION icons indicate how to group students for instructional activities.

	Whole Class (DI) Indicates a teacher-led activity with the entire class together.
	Small Group (DI) Indicates an activity during which students are in pairs or small groups of approximately 3–5.
	Independent Work (DI; DC) Indicates an activity during which students individually work, such as when conducting research, writing on a topic of interest, or demonstrating understanding.

Figure 10.1. Icons in the CLEAR curriculum model.

Using the CLEAR Curriculum Model

SUBJECT ANALYSIS icons indicate how a task offers students depth and complexity of a particular topic.	
	Details (DC) Indicates a task that helps students achieve greater depth of understanding through an examination of the specific attributes, traits, and characteristics that describe a concept, theory, principle, and even a fact.
	Patterns (DC) Indicates a task that helps students achieve greater depth of understanding by analyzing the patterns and trends that can be identified in a discipline and in what they are learning.
	Over Time (DC) Indicates tasks that help students achieve a more complex level of understanding by guiding them to consider what they are learning from a historical perspective and to recognize that the passage of time changes our knowledge of things.
FOCUS ON STUDENT DIFFERENCES icons indicate how teachers can differentiate a particular activity as informed by continual formative assessment.	
	Differentiation by Readiness (DI; SEM) Indicates the process of adjusting learning experiences to match individual students' levels of demonstrated achievement and points of development, all of which might vary depending on background knowledge, prior learning experiences, and profile of competencies related to different topics or kinds of activities.
	Differentiation by Interest (DI; SEM) Indicates the process of adjusting learning experiences to match individual students' interests, and guides the teacher to offer choice in learning materials, topics, or groups.
	Learning Profile (DI; SEM) Indicates the process of adjusting learning experiences to match individual students' patterns of strengths, weaknesses, and preferences that determine how information is processed and expressed.
	Twice-Exceptionality (DI) Indicates the process of adjusting learning experiences that focus on strengths of students with disabilities, so that teachers have instructional strategies that promote academic, social, and behavioral gains for twice-exceptional students.

Figure 10.1. Continued.

rooms; students exposed to the CLEAR units showed a significant positive difference on achievement measures (Callahan et al., 2015).

Using the Foundational Elements of CLEAR and CLEAR Units for Professional Learning

As recommended by the NAGC (2019) Gifted Programming Standards, the use of CLEAR language arts units affords specific content knowledge and pedagogical skills in gifted education so teachers are able to develop gifted learners' talents for high-level functioning. Table 10.1 illustrates the alignment between the five foundational elements of the CLEAR Curriculum Model and the NAGC Teacher Preparation Standards. Implementation of CLEAR units also address the six ESSA criteria for professional development proposing that teacher learning efforts should sustained, intensive, collaborative, job-embedded, data-driven and classroom-focused.

Foundational Element 1: Clear Learning Goals

CLEAR units are designed around clear learning goals that are meaningful, important, and well-articulated. Clear learning goals are typically indicated by discipline exploration and subject analysis icons. Establishing clear learning goals in a CLEAR unit is essential because doing so helps to ensure that the level of learning for students is elevated. Clear learning goals are reflected in the big ideas, key knowledge, skills, and understandings within the unit's field of study, and they are ultimately transferable to other learning experiences. As examples, big ideas in the fifth-grade Rhetoric unit are "Rhetoric is an art that can be systematically studied" and "Understanding the interests and values of an audience is key to persuasion" (Missett et al., 2016, p. 125). Big ideas in the fifth-grade Research unit are "Research is an organized and systematic way of finding answers to questions" and "Values, experiences, and motivation contribute to [a reader's] perspective and purpose" (Missett et al., 2016, pp. 26–27). Because the big ideas in both units

Table 10.1
Nexus Among the CLEAR Curriculum Model, the NAGC-CEC Teacher Preparation Standards, and the NAGC Gifted Programing Standards

CLEAR Model	NAGC-CEC Teacher Preparation Standards in Gifted and Talented Education	NAGC Pre-K–Grade 12 Gifted Programming Standards
Data-Driven Learning Experiences; Continuous Formative Assessment	Standard 1: Learner Development and Individual Differences	Standard 1: Learning and Development
Clear Learning Goals, Rich Curriculum, Authentic Products	Standard 3: Curricular Content Knowledge	Standard 3: Curriculum Planning and Instruction
Continuous Formative Assessment	Standard 4: Assessment (4.4, 4.5)	Standard 2: Assessment (2.4)
Clear Learning Goals, Rich Curriculum, Continuous Formative Assessment, Data-Driven Learning Experiences, Authentic Products	Standard 5: Instructional Planning and Strategies	Standard 3: Curriculum Planning and Instruction

share underlying concepts of systems, values, and perspective, as well as skills and essential understandings that are developed in the units, learning goals are aligned and become more transferable for students as they are exposed to the units over time.

CLEAR and National and State Standards. The clear learning goals in CLEAR units also reflect state and national standards, as well as the NAGC (2019) Gifted Programming Standards (see Table 10.1). For example, the key understandings and skills students will acquire in the fifth-grade Rhetoric unit are: "Students will engage in a study of Aristotle's Rhetoric to answer the questions: When do you appeal to one's intellect, emotions, or sense of morality when trying to persuade? Students will learn to identify and analyze a variety of rhetorical devices to better understand the art of rhetoric" (Missett et al., 2016, pp. 127–132). Clear learning goals in the fifth-grade Research unit are: "Students will learn and employ advanced research skills from crafting open-ended research questions to discerning between reliable sources. Using the Big6 research process, created by Michael B. Eisenberg and Robert E. Berkowitz (1987), students carry out their own research study and present findings at a research gala" (Missett et al., 2016, pp. 26–30). Both fifth-grade units also address Common Core

State Standards for English Language Arts, particularly those related to creating texts for purpose, manipulation of audiences by speakers, bias, and understanding the perspective of both speakers and audience members (CCSS.ELA-Literacy.RL.5.1–5.10; CCSS.ELA-Literacy.W.5.1–5.10; CCSS.ELA-Literacy.SL.5.1–5.5; CCSS.ELA-Literacy.RI.5.1–5.10).

Big Ideas and Learning Goals. The iteration of big ideas and learning goals in each lesson is a model that encourages teachers to reflect on every lesson they plan to teach, as well as the importance of what they choose to teach. One teacher noted:

> By [sic] working through the CLEAR unit, it struck me how the "Big Ideas" icon showed up in more areas than just the beginning of each lesson! When I had written curriculum previously, "big ideas" were included at the beginning of a unit or lesson, but often lost within the lesson itself. By having the icons there, it is a great reminder of how the conceptual piece is playing out in instruction. This was a big "aha!" moment for me that I probably wouldn't have noticed had I not been working with the CLEAR unit.

Foundational Element 2—Continual Formative Assessment

Ongoing (continual) formative assessment informs all CLEAR unit activities. For example, Figure 10.2 shows that in the third-grade Fairy Tales unit, teachers ask students to complete an exit card to assess students' emerging understanding of fable, folktale, moral, and plot.

Similar exit cards are included throughout all CLEAR units as one means of informal assessment. These ongoing formative assessments—often indicated by group differences and lesson organization icons—provide explicit directions to teachers for grouping, differentiation of tasks, and/or instructional strategies. The use of continual formative assessment throughout a unit allows teachers to not only monitor student progress, but also collect assessment data to provide profiles of student readiness levels, interests, and preferred ways of learning and expressing learning. Therefore, teachers use assessment data as feedback about students in order to tailor their own instruction to meet the needs of diverse gifted learners. The repeated use of strategies like exit cards throughout the units also reinforces for teachers the way to use assessment to inform their own instruction, thereby providing informal professional development.

> **Exit Card**
>
> 1. Which has a more complex plot: a fable or a fairy tale?
> 2. Did you think there was a moral in "The Frog King (or Iron Henry)?" If so complete the sentence: "The moral of the story is . . . "
> 3. How would you describe what folklore means to a friend who doesn't know that word?

Figure 10.2. Sample exit card. Adapted from *Poetry and Fairy Tales: Language Arts Units for Gifted Students in Grade 3* (p. 173), by A. P. Azano, T. C. Missett, and C. M. Callahan, 2016, Prufrock Press. Copyright 2016 by Prufrock Press. Adapted with permission.

Foundational Element 3— Data-Driven Learning Experiences

Data-driven learning experiences in CLEAR units reflect the recognition that gifted learners have diverse learning needs and characteristics. Consistent with this philosophy, the ongoing formative and summative assessments included in the units provide data to teachers that are essential for purposes of differentiating based on readiness levels, interest, and learning profiles. For example, in the fourth-grade Fiction unit, students take the formative assessment outlined in Figure 10.3 to identify progress toward mastery of the language of the discipline of fiction writing (indicated by the Language icon):

Using student responses as data to inform next instructional steps, teachers do not guess at the level of student progress. Instead, they use the data to group students by readiness and scaffold the complexity of text provided in the next lesson (indicated by student differences icons).

By specifically identifying clear learning goals, measuring progress toward them with data-driven learning experiences, and then aligning them with standards and big ideas through all CLEAR units, teachers' under-

> **Formative Assessment 1**
>
> **Directions:** *Circle* the terms that you know describe characters. *Underline* the terms that you think describe characters. *Cross out* the terms that do not describe characters. Then, write the definitions of any terms that you know.
>
> | | |
> |---|---|
> | Abstract | Round |
> | Antagonist | Sensory |
> | Concrete | Static |
> | Dynamic | Stock |
> | Empathy | Stereotype |
> | Protagonist | |
>
> **Figure 10.3.** Sample formative assessment. From *Fiction and Nonfiction: Language Arts Units for Gifted Students in Grade 4* (p. 60), by C. M. Callahan, T. C. Missett, A. P. Azano, M. Caughey, A. V. Broderson, and M. Tackett, 2017, Prufrock Press. Copyright 2017 by Prufrock Press. Adapted with permission.

standing of how to create effective curriculum deepens with each implementation of the units. One teacher noted:

> Often, teachers develop evaluative criteria and just hand it to the students. However, making students responsible for part of the grading gives them ownership of the work [and mastery of the goals]. Furthermore, the CLEAR unit doesn't just suggest teachers do this, but provides support so teachers understand how to implement a student developed evaluation. Not only was this unit developed for fifth-grade gifted students to learn how to do research, but also for instructors to learn how to teach G/T students! For me, this was key, and I just drank it all in!

Foundational Element 4— Authentic Products

CLEAR units afford multiple opportunities for students to step into the shoes of experts in a discipline in the creation of authentic products. For example, students have poetry readings and create poetry anthologies in the Poetry unit. Students examine and create persuasive rhetorical exemplars, such as eulogies, commercials, and public policy statements, and they then produce a rhetorical endeavor of interest in the Rhetoric unit. In the Nonfiction unit, students create and write a memoir to remember their own life or some part of it. Thus, students apply the knowledge and skills they have acquired to creating a work product comparable to those an expert would create. Typically, Real-World Application and the subject analysis icons accompany these learning experiences to remind teachers that they reflect the work engaged in by experts.

One teacher described her professional growth resulting from the authentic products element of the model as follows:

> One thing that the CLEAR units helped me do was to keep the big ideas in mind at all times and help students see how the details we were working on always pointed to learning on a conceptual level, and making a product an expert would make. When I tried my hand at creating a unit, I had to really think about how a student would act as a practitioner (in my case science), for example, keeping learning authentic stretched my thinking while elevating the quality of instruction.

Foundational Element 5—Rich Curriculum

Taken together, the foundational elements of CLEAR support the creation of high-level, rich curriculum. Units constructed using the model move students beyond the acquisition of discrete facts and shallow understanding in a field, and toward learning that is deep, complex, and transferable. A rich curriculum is also evidenced by a focus on big ideas that again, refer to the core concepts, principles, theories, inquiries, and processes in a field of study. Because big ideas reflect expert and essential understanding in a unit of study, they anchor the discourse and provide a basis for setting curriculum priorities to focus on the most meaningful content. One teacher noted:

> The thing that struck me as the most different aspect of this unit from other units I've taught was the lack of traditional handouts. Any handout was a way to organize or record students' thinking, and everything else is expected to be student-produced. I liked that! I think it just reinforces the fact that this unit is intended for real, in-depth learning that is more similar to what professionals would do. . . . I have been able to incorporate using handouts like this into my own practice! I just threw out a big bunch of worksheets!

Another teacher, after creating her own CLEAR unit, noted:

> It is now clear (yes, pun intended!) to me how to effectively use the icons through studying and using the CLEAR units. For example, it is very intentional about how students are behaving as researchers. The Tools of the Discipline icon shows up frequently reminding teachers (and thus students) they are truly acting as researchers. When I created a lesson and put in the icons, I could immediately see places where I needed to go back and revise to include more complexity. The organization [the units] provide is wonderful as it is easy to see the different facets laid out for each lesson, such as whole-group versus independent instruction and differentiation by readiness, interest, or learning profile.

From the previous articulation of the foundational elements of the CLEAR model, and teacher responses articulating how use of the model supported their professional development, we move to the proposition that using the CLEAR model also addresses the ESSA criteria.

1. CLEAR units provide teachers with sustained exposure to high-quality curriculum. Each of the six CLEAR language arts units is comprised of approximately 15–18 detailed lessons occurring across three grade levels. Throughout the units, the five foundational elements of the model are extensively embedded in classroom learning experiences and make evident the features of high-quality curriculum. This avoids the one-day, stand-alone professional development opportunities discouraged by ESSA and NAGC. Consequently, with each year of implementation of the CLEAR units, teachers have the opportunity to better understand and gain expertise in implementing and creating curriculum reflecting the five foundational elements of the model.

2. CLEAR units focus teachers intensively on the features of exemplary curriculum at a granular level. This is accomplished most effectively through the continual insertion of icons—which are themselves pictorial representations of exemplary curriculum features—throughout the units and their application to multiple and varied learning experiences. For example, the 2E icon provides instructional guidance to teachers with students who possess both gifts and disabilities impacting learning in "real time"—or when a teacher is most likely to need differentiation strategies. Thus, in the Rhetoric unit, students are asked each day to write journal entries identifying personal experiences when they tried to persuade someone to do or believe something. In that case, the 2E icon reminds teachers to differentiate for students with disabilities in written expression, suggesting these students may need a scribe, to orally share, or the opportunity to draw their experiences. Similarly, the Big Idea icons continually guide teachers toward an intensive focus on the most important and meaningful content in the discipline that a lesson/unit addresses. Collectively, the icons provide intensive illustrations of the features of exemplary curriculum implementation that are typically covered in professional development. In addition, "Teacher Tips" offered throughout the units provide explanations of the lesson content as well as insights into strategies for successful implementation.

3. CLEAR units are collaborative in several ways. First, extensive participation of teachers, school leaders, and curriculum experts supported their development. Second, because the units cover three grades, multiple opportunities for discussion and feedback loops among teachers across grade levels are afforded so that teachers can learn from the experiences of teachers who have already worked with the units. Third, CLEAR units recognize that many gifted students are twice-exceptional. Thus, the units allow classroom teachers, gifted education specialists and special education staff to collaborate to deepen their understanding of ways to differentiate instruction for students who are twice-exceptional.

4. CLEAR units are job-embedded in that they are directly usable in the classroom. The units include all necessary materials for full implementation, from worksheets, to web links for all texts, to assessments and rubrics. Additionally, the units are imbued with a wide range of practical tools to advance teacher understanding of effective instructional strategies that are evidence-based. They also deepen a teacher's understanding of strategies for improving student academic achievement or substantially increasing the knowl-

edge and teaching skills of teachers. Teachers can directly observe the ways in which applying the elements of the CLEAR model and the three frameworks (differentiated instruction, Schoolwide Enrichment Model, and depth and complexity) generate high-level responses from students.

5. CLEAR units strengthen teachers' ability to employ instructional strategies that are data-driven. First, the foundational features of CLEAR are themselves supported by research (Callahan et al., 2015). Second, CLEAR units show teachers how to use data in their own classrooms. CLEAR units extensively integrate ongoing formative assessments and mechanisms for using assessment data to inform instruction, which supports professional development in multiple ways. These elements of CLEAR improve teachers' understanding of student learning, as well as their ability to analyze student work and achievement from multiple sources.

6. CLEAR units are classroom-focused because they show teachers how to enact individually what is known about best practices in gifted education. This enables teachers to work toward improved student engagement and outcomes. The focus on the classroom is evident in the place-based pedagogy embedded in CLEAR units. When teachers allow students to engage in tasks related to students' lived experiences, often by making connections between the class material and their community, engagement is enhanced. As an example of place-based pedagogy, the Research unit uses the metaphor of the researcher as explorer. To engage students in thinking of research as exploration, the initial unit activities pose the question of whether Columbus really discovered North America. Initial learning activities in the unit challenge students to consider others who may have discovered the continent. As a reflection of place, teachers in Montana who implemented the Research unit used the state's archeologic record as well as local indigenous oral history to examine the proposition that Native Americans first discovered Native America. This more authentically reflected community beliefs. Similarly, in the folktale unit, students examine the Cinderella story as told by several diverse cultures. These same teachers in Montana incorporated into the lesson the Cinderella story told by the Navajo that is illustrative of the provision in ESSA (2015) to acknowledge indigenous history (Mackey, 2018). These experiences make evident the ways in which use of the CLEAR Curriculum Model supports teachers in their own professional growth in understanding and using best practices in gifted education.

Implications/New Insights

This chapter articulates ways in which the use of high-quality curriculum itself supports professional learning with a particular example. Of course, the success of this approach to professional learning is dependent on some fundamental tenets. First, for any curriculum, including curricula based on the CLEAR Curriculum Model, to be effective as a tool in enhancing teacher skill through professional learning, the curriculum must be of high quality and for gifted learners. As Hockett (2009) and Hockett and Brighton (2016) articulated, high-quality curriculum for gifted learners must first meet the standards for high-quality curriculum in general. That is, high-quality curriculum for gifted learners is based in curriculum principles that include:

- a conceptual foundation in design, organization and implementation;
- a foundation in ideas, principles, and skills fundamental to the discipline of the unit;
- flexibility that reflects variations in students' cognitive ability, interests, and learning preferences;
- an emphasis on guiding students to achieve expertise in the discipline by promoting discipline-based skills and cognitive and metacognitive processes associated with expertise;
- lessons and activities that progressively develop expertise across grade levels;
- emphasis on student outcomes with a particular goal of deep understanding in the discipline;
- relevance and ability to engage students in learning; and
- a balance between breadth and depth.

In addition, high-quality curriculum for gifted learners should be characterized by:

- a conceptual approach to organize or explore content that is discipline based and integrative;
- content and a structure that guides learners in the pursuit of advanced levels of understanding that goes further than the general education curriculum with greater abstraction, depth, breadth, and complexity in content, process, and product;
- the inclusion of sophisticated processes and resources that are reflective of those used by experts, scholars, and practicing professionals in the disciplines;
- an emphasis on problems, products, and performances that are authentic, reflect real-life, and are based on products or outcomes

that reflect student accomplishment of viewing their learning through a new lens, taking another perspective, reflecting new interpretation, extending understanding, and/or creating new products; and
- flexibility to allow for student self-directed learning based on their interests and optimum pace of learning, and varied in instructional approaches, learning resources, content and form, skill levels, and types of learning opportunities.

The CLEAR curriculum has met these fundamental standards, which are reflected in the "A" (Authentic Products) and "R" (Rich Curriculum) dimensions of CLEAR.

The second tenet of using curriculum as a tool to develop teacher skills is that the model or the particular curricular units must be research-based. That is, the key to positive outcomes for gifted learners is that their teachers learn to develop or implement evidence-based curricula in their classrooms. Teachers should be implementing curricula or modeling frameworks that have been subject to experimental testing that demonstrates their effectiveness. In the case of the CLEAR curriculum, we have carried out research across the nation that demonstrates that in classrooms where the CLEAR curriculum is implemented students earn higher scores on standards-based outcome measures (Callahan et al., 2015). These are reflected in the "E" of the CLEAR Curriculum Model (Data-Driven Learning Experiences).

Foundational pedagogical practices of the field are included in basic premises of the CLEAR Curriculum Model and other effective curricula that address the specific needs of gifted students. In addition to those that are reflected in the "C" (Continual Formative Assessment) and the "L" (Clear Learning Goals) of the CLEAR model, the curriculum should be infused with opportunities for tiering, differentiation, and grouping according to appropriate level of challenge, and use multiple teaching strategies that promote deep thinking and self-reflection (e.g., Socratic seminars, tasks at the highest level of Bloom's taxonomy, problem-based learning, etc.).

With CLEAR units or other curricula that meet these basic tenets, teachers can engage students in their classrooms systematically in the type of curriculum implementation that exposes the teachers to best practices and significantly positive outcomes for their students. In addition, in CLEAR units, teachers can explore through real-time practice in the classroom the basic tenets and key elements of the three most respected curriculum models in gifted education. The opportunity for teachers to engage simultaneously (and inexpensively) in professional learning while delivering high-quality instruction to their students is both an effective and an efficient use of teacher and student time. Once teachers have practiced using the models of the units already developed, they are also well-positioned to create their own curriculum using the five foundational elements of the CLEAR Curriculum Model.

Notably, the use of high-quality curriculum as professional learning tools extends well beyond units developed using the CLEAR Curriculum Model. Beyond CLEAR units, educators have available to them a number of curriculum models that would similarly support professional learning. Examples of other curriculum models with developed curricular applications include (but are not limited to) the Mentoring Mathematical Minds Model (Gavin et al., 2009) and the Integrated Curriculum Model (VanTassel-Baska & Wood, 2009). The units developed under these models are research-based and grounded in the pedagogical principles of the field. Many of them have received curriculum awards from NAGC. Teachers can go to the NAGC Curriculum Studies Network for a list of curriculum units that have been determined to be of high-quality (see https://nagccurriculumnetwork.weebly.com/award-winning-units.html).

Summary

The use of evidence-based curricular units that illustrate and model the key elements of three of the most respected curricular frameworks and quality curriculum and instructional principles provide an efficient and effective approach to staff development. The availability of the units based on the CLEAR Curriculum Model allows for personalized staff development that is sustained, intensive, collaborative, job-embedded, data-driven, and classroom focused as outlined by ESSA (2015) and NAGC and CEC-TAG (2013). By clearly incorporating the tenets of quality curriculum with repeated illustrations of the tenets, teachers can first determine the degree to which they already know and understand the principle. Teachers who are quickly able to implement at a high level can proceed expeditiously; those who are learning for the first time will have the opportunity to read more in unit introductions and teacher tips with increasing confidence each time they see a principle in action. In either case, through direct implementation teachers have the opportunity to see the ways in which students respond. Because seeing is believing, they can then generalize to new curricula they may develop or differentiate themselves in ways that are more likely to reflect the NAGC (2019) Gifted Programming Standards and the

NAGC-CEC Teacher Preparation Standards in Gifted Education (NAGC & CEC-TAG, 2013).

Resources

Azano, A. P., Missett, T. C., & Callahan, C. M. (2016). *Poetry and fairy tales: Language arts units for gifted students in grade 3*. Prufrock Press.

Azano, A. P., Missett, T. C., Tackett, M. E., & Callahan, C. M. (2018). The CLEAR Curriculum Model. In C. M. Callahan & H. Hertberg-Davis (Eds.), *Fundamentals of gifted education: Considering multiple perspectives* (2nd ed. pp. 293–309). Routledge.

Callahan, C. M., Moon, T. R., Oh, S., Azano, A., & Haley, E. P. (2015). What works in gifted education: Documented effects of an Integrated Curricular Model. *American Educational Research Journal, 52*(1), 137–167. https://doi.org/10.3102/0002831214549448

Callahan, C. M., Missett, T. C., Azano, A. P., Caughey, M., Broderson, A. V., & Tackett, M. (2017). *Fiction and nonfiction: Language arts units for gifted students in grade 4*. Prufrock Press.

Missett, T. C., Azano, A.P., & Callahan, C. M. (2016). *Research and rhetoric: Language arts units for gifted students in grade 5*. Prufrock Press.

References

Azano, A. P., Missett, T. C., & Callahan, C. M. (2016). *Poetry and fairy tales: Language arts units for gifted students in grade 3*. Prufrock Press.

Azano, A. P., Missett, T. C., Tackett, M. E., & Callahan, C. M. (2018). The CLEAR Curriculum Model. In C. M. Callahan & H. Hertberg-Davis (Eds.), *Fundamentals of gifted education: Considering multiple perspectives* (2nd ed., pp. 293–309). Routledge.

Callahan, C. M., Moon, T. R., Oh, S., Azano, A., & Haley, E. P. (2015). What works in gifted education: Documented effects of an Integrated

Curricular Model. *American Educational Research Journal, 52*(1), 137–167. https://doi.org/10.3102/0002831214549448

Callahan, C. M., Missett, T. C., Azano, A. P., Caughey, M., Broderson, A. V., & Tackett, M. (2017). *Fiction and nonfiction: Language arts units for gifted students in grade 4.* Prufrock Press.

Every Student Succeeds Act, 20 U.S.C. § 6301 (2015). https://congress.gov/114/plaws/publ95/PLAW-114publ95.pdf

Gavin, M. K., Casa, T. M., Adelson, J. L., Carroll, S. R., & Sheffield, L. J. (2009). The impact of advanced curriculum on the achievement of mathematically promising elementary students. *Gifted Child Quarterly, 53*(3), 188–202. https://doi.org/10.1177/0016986209334964

Gubbins, E. J. (2014). Enrichment. In J. A. Plucker & C. M. Callahan (Eds.), *Critical issues and practices in gifted education: What the research says* (2nd ed., pp. 223–236). Prufrock Press.

Hertberg-Davis, H. (2018). Defensible curriculum for gifted learners: Where the rubber meets the road. In C. M. Callahan & H. Hertberg-Davis (Eds.), *Fundamentals of gifted education: Considering multiple perspectives* (2nd ed., pp. 249–251). Routledge.

Hockett, J. A. (2009). Curriculum for highly able learners that conforms to general education and gifted education quality indicators. *Journal for the Education of the Gifted, 32*(3), 394–440. https://doi.org/10.4219/jeg-2009-857

Hockett, J. A., & Brighton, C. M. (2016). General curriculum design: Principles and best practices. In K. R. Stephens & F. A. Karnes (Eds.), *Introduction to curriculum design in gifted education* (pp. 41–62). Prufrock Press.

Kaplan, S. (2005). Layering differential curricula for gifted and talented. In F. A. Karnes & S. M. Bean (Eds.), *Methods and materials for teaching gifted students* (2nd ed., pp. 107–132). Prufrock Press.

Kaplan, S. N. (2018). Differentiating with depth and complexity. In C. M. Callahan & H. L. Hertberg-Davis (Eds.), *Fundamentals of gifted education: Considering multiple perspectives* (2nd ed., pp. 270–278). Routledge.

Mackey, H. (2018). Creating equitable learning spaces for indigenous students. *Equity Dispatch, 2*(5), 1–7. https://greatlakesequity.org/resource/creating-equitable-learning-spaces-indigenous-students

Missett, T. C., Azano, A.P., & Callahan, C. M. (2016). *Research and rhetoric: Language arts units for gifted students in grade 5.* Prufrock Press.

National Association for Gifted Children. (2019). *2019 Pre-K–Grade 12 Gifted Programming Standards.* http://www.nagc.org/sites/default/files/standards/Intro%202019%20Programming%20Standards.pdf

National Association for Gifted Children, & The Association for the Gifted, Council for Exceptional Children. (2013). *NAGC-CEC teacher preparation standards in gifted education.* http://www.nagc.org/sites/default/files/standards/NAGC-%20CEC%20CAEP%20standards%20%282013%20final%29.pdf

Renzulli, J. S., & Reis, S. (2000). The Schoolwide Enrichment Model. In K. Heller, F. Monchs, R. Sternberg, & R. Subotnik (Eds.), *The International handbook of giftedness and talent* (2nd ed., pp. 367–382). Elsevier.

Renzulli, J. S., & Reis, S. M. (2014). *The Schoolwide Enrichment Model: A how-to guide for talent development* (3rd ed.). Prufrock Press.

Tomlinson, C. A. (1995). *How to differentiate instruction in mixed-ability classrooms.* ASCD.

Tomlinson, C. A. (1999). *The differentiated classroom: Responding to the needs of all learners.* ASCD.

Tomlinson, C. A. (2001). *How to differentiate instruction in mixed-ability classrooms* (2nd ed.). ASCD.

Tomlinson, C. A. (2018). Differentiated instruction. In C. M. Callahan & H. L. Hertberg-Davis (Eds.), *Fundamentals of gifted education: Considering multiple perspectives* (2nd ed., pp. 279–292). Routledge.

VanTassel-Baska, J. (2014). Matching curriculum, instruction, and assessment for the gifted. In J. A. Plucker & C. M. Callahan (Eds.), *Critical issues and practices in gifted education: What the research says* (2nd ed., pp. 377–386). Prufrock Press.

VanTassel-Baska, J., & Wood, S. M. (2009). The integrated curriculum model. In J. S. Renzulli, E. J. Gubins, K. S. McMillen, R. D. Eckert, & C. A. Little (Eds.), *Systems and models for developing programs for the gifted and talented* (2nd ed., pp. 655–691). Prufrock Press.

About the Editors

Christine L. Weber, Ph.D., is a professor in the Department of Teaching, Learning, and Curriculum at the University of North Florida, in Jacksonville. She instructs teachers in strategies for conceptual teaching and learning, assessment tools, and meeting the needs of gifted and diverse learners. She has been a member of the Editorial Review Board for *Gifted Child Today* since 1998. Under her leadership, the Florida's Frameworks for K–12 Gifted Learners was developed in 2007 and disseminated to all school districts in the state. Dr. Weber has published numerous articles and presented at state, national, and international conferences. She currently serves as the Representative Assembly for The Association for the Gifted, Council for Exceptional Children (CEC-TAG), and Chair of the National Association for Gifted Children (NAGC) Professional Learning Network. She previously served as Co-Chair of Awards for the NAGC Research and Evaluation Network. Her recent books, with coauthors Boswell and Behrens, include *Differentiating Instruction for Gifted Learners: A Case Studies Approach* and *Exploring Critical Issues in Gifted Education: A Case Studies Approach.*

Angela M. Novak, Ph.D., is an assistant professor in elementary and middle grades education at East Carolina University in Greenville, NC. She teaches undergraduate and graduate courses in education, focusing on assessment practices and gifted education. She also works with the University of Virginia as an adjunct instructor in its master's-level gifted endorsement series. Dr. Novak has worked in public education in the gifted field as a classroom teacher, resource teacher, and central office support. She also spent 5 years in the private, not-for-profit sector of gifted education. Dr. Novak strives to serve gifted children through service to the field of gifted education. For the National Association for Gifted Children (NAGC), she is currently the Co-Chair of the Diversity and Equity Committee, the founding coordinator of the Rural Gifted Special Interest Group, and the Program Chair of the Professional Learning Network, having recently served as Network Chair. Dr. Novak was recently elected to the board of The Association for the Gifted, Council for Exceptional Children (CEC-TAG) as the Membership Coordinator. She serves North Carolina gifted as the Co-Chair of the North Carolina AIG Institutes of Higher Education Consortium and Region 1 Representative to the Board of the North Carolina Council for Exceptional Children.

About the Authors

Cheryll M. Adams, Ph.D., is the Director Emerita of the Center for Gifted Studies and Talent Development at Ball State University. She received her Ph.D. in educational psychology with an emphasis in gifted education from the University of Virginia, her M.Ed. from UVA, and her B.S.Ed. in secondary science from the University of Georgia. She currently teaches online courses in gifted education and has presented widely at local, state, national and international conferences. She is a former member of the Board of Directors of the National Association for Gifted Children and is past Chair of the NAGC Professional Standards Committee. Her publications include 12 coauthored books, 22 book chapters, and numerous other publications. She was the coauthor, the project director, and a principal investigator of Project GATE, Project CLUE, and Project CLUE-Plus, three Jacob K. Javits grants. Previously, she was a math and science teacher for 15 years.

Tammy Burnham, Ph.D., is an assistant professor at Winthrop University. She teaches undergraduate and graduate courses in pedagogy, literacy, practicum, and teacher leadership. Her research interests include supervision, teacher development, at-risk student populations, and motivational psychology. Dr. Burnham can be contacted at burnhamt@winthrop.edu.

Carolyn M. Callahan, Ph.D., Commonwealth Professor of Education at the University of Virginia, developed the Summer and Saturday Enrichment Programs at UVA. For more than 20 years she has been the principal investigator on projects of the National Research Center on the Gifted and Talented (NRC/GT), is currently the co-principal investigator for the National Center for Research in Gifted Education (NCRGE), and has been principal investigator on six Javits grants, including a current grant focusing on rural gifted students. Her work with the NRC/GT, NCRGE, and Javits projects has focused on curriculum development and implementation. As part of her work with the NRC/GT she was co-evaluator for the U.S. Department of Education of the Javits program and conducted a national survey of gifted and talented programs. She has conducted evaluations of grant projects including several Javits grants, state-level programs, and local-level gifted programs. She has been recognized as Outstanding Professor of the Commonwealth of Virginia and Distinguished Scholar of the National Association for Gifted Children. She also has served as President of NAGC and The Association for the Gifted, and as editor of *Gifted Child Quarterly*. Dr. Callahan has published more than 200 articles and 50 book chapters on topics in gifted education, with one of those publications considered the definitive book on evaluation. She is the coeditor of *Critical Issues and Practices in Gifted Education*.

Kimberley L. Chandler, Ph.D., is the Chief Academic Officer for Essex County Public Schools in Virginia. Her professional background includes teaching gifted students in a variety of settings, serving as an administrator of a school district gifted program, and providing professional development training for teachers and administrators. Her research interests include curriculum policy and implementation issues in gifted programs, the design and evaluation of professional development programs for teachers of the gifted, and gifted education services in rural settings. Previously, Dr. Chandler served as the editor and contributing author of numerous curriculum materials from the Center for Gifted Education at William & Mary. She has served as Guest Editor of the *Journal for the Education of the Gifted* for special issues focusing on international issues in gifted education and learning resources. She coauthored (with Tamra Stambaugh) *Effective Curriculum for Underserved Gifted Students* and coedited (with Cheryll M. Adams) *Effective Program Models for Gifted Students From Underserved Populations*.

Kim A. Cheek, Ph.D., is an associate professor in the Department of Teaching, Learning, and Curriculum at the University of North Florida in Jacksonville, FL. She is also the Elementary Education Curriculum

Area Director. Dr. Cheek has a Ph.D. in science education from Durham University in the United Kingdom, as well as master's degrees in elementary education and the geosciences. She teaches graduate and undergraduate STEM courses and supervises Ed.D. students. Dr. Cheek previously taught elementary and middle school as a regular education classroom teacher and a special educator. Her primary research interest is in improving student understanding of science concepts that occur at unfamiliar spatial and temporal scales. She has also conducted research on the use of the coaching cycle to improve teacher candidates' ability to ask higher order questions in science.

Karen D. Jones, Ph.D., is an Assistant Professor of Educational Leadership at East Carolina University. Previously, she has worked as an elementary teacher, as well as a campus and district-level administrator. Her research focus is on preparing principals to be successful with diverse populations.

Bronwyn MacFarlane, Ph.D., is Professor of Gifted Education at the University of Arkansas at Little Rock (UALR). She has been recognized with the Early Leader Award from the National Association for Gifted Children (NAGC), the UALR College of Education Faculty Excellence Award in Research and Creative Endeavors, and more. She has served as college associate dean, gifted program academic dean, and in nationally-elected NAGC positions, and has taught more than 20 university courses and gifted and foreign languages in K–12. Her dissertation focused on Advanced Placement foreign language teacher perceptions and differentiated instruction. She has authored many publications and has delivered more than 150 presentations to state, national, and international audiences. She is the national columnist of "The Curriculum Corner" for NAGC's *Teaching for High Potential* magazine. She served as guest editor for the *Roeper Review* special issue about STEM and Gifted Education Curriculum. Her books include *Specialized Schools for High-Ability Learners: Designing and Implementing Programs in Specialized School Settings* (2018) and *Second Language Learning for the Gifted: Connection and Communication for the 21st Century* (2017 with Joyce VanTassel-Baska and Ariel Baska). Her 2016 edited book, *STEM Education for High-Ability Learners: Designing and Implementing Programming*, was the first book of its kind to specifically bring together a discussion of the critical elements needed for delivering comprehensive STEM educational programming to develop high-ability talent in the STEM fields. She also coedited *Leading Change in Gifted Education: The Festschrift of Dr. Joyce VanTassel-Baska* (2009 with Tamra Stambaugh).

Eric L. Mann, Ph.D., is an associate professor in the Mathematics Department at Hope College in Holland, MI. After completing a military career in the Air Force, he taught elementary and middle school for 7 years before entering the doctoral program in educational psychology at the University of Connecticut with emphasis in gifted and mathematics education. Dr. Mann served on the faculty at Purdue University's Institute for P–12 Engineering Research and Learning and the Gifted Education Resource Institute before accepting his current position, where he works with preservice K–8 teachers to develop the specialized mathematical content knowledge they need to teach.

Rebecca L. Mann, Ph.D., joined the faculty at Hope College in 2013 after serving as clinical assistant and associate professor at Purdue University. She completed her Ph.D. in educational psychology with emphasis in gifted education and special education at the University of Connecticut, for which she received the National Association for Gifted Children's Doctoral Student Award. Prior to her doctoral studies, she worked for 17 years as an elementary and middle school classroom teacher, as well as a gifted resource teacher in Colorado and New Hampshire. In 2001 she was named the New Hampshire Educator of the Year of the Gifted.

Tracy C. Missett, Ph.D., is the Director of the Saturday and Summer Enrichment Program at the Curry School of Education, University of Virginia. Dr. Missett received her Ph.D. and B.A. from the University of Virginia, her J.D. from the University of California, and her M.A. from Teachers College, Columbia University. Dr. Missett has engaged in research with the American Psychological Association and the National Research Center on the Gifted and Talented (NRC/GT) on the effectiveness of the CLEAR Curriculum Model. Dr. Missett has published multiple peer-reviewed journal articles and book chapters on topics in gifted education, including those related to the CLEAR Curriculum Model. Dr. Missett has also received two curriculum awards on language arts units developed using the CLEAR Curriculum Model (Poetry and Rhetoric) from the National Association for Gifted Children.

Emily Mofield, Ed.D., is an assistant professor in the College of Education at Lipscomb University where she teaches gifted education and doctoral research courses. Her background includes 15 years of experience teaching gifted students and leading gifted services. Emily currently serves as the National Association for Gifted Children Chair for Curriculum Studies, and she has coauthored numerous award-winning gifted curricula. She is also the author/coauthor of several research publications related to achievement motivation and collaborative teaching practices. Dr. Mofield received the NAGC Hollingworth Award for excellence in gifted education research and the 2019 Texas Association for the Gifted and Talented's Legacy Book Award for *Teaching Tenacity, Resilience, and a Drive for Excellence* (with Megan Parker Peters). Emily regularly leads professional learning addressing the social-emotional needs of gifted learners and implementing effective differentiation strategies for advanced learners for school districts, conferences, and special groups.

Mary Cay Ricci, M.S.Ed., is an education consultant and speaker, and a former elementary/middle school teacher and central office administrator in Maryland. She is the *New York Times* best-selling author of *Mindsets in the Classroom: Building a Growth Mindset Learning Community*. She has also authored *Ready-to-Use Resources for Mindsets in the Classroom*, *Mindsets for Parents* (with Margaret Lee), *Create a Growth Mindset School*, and *Nothing You Can't Do!: The Secret Power of Growth Mindsets*. She was an adjunct professor at Johns Hopkins University Graduate School of Education for 8 years.

Mary L. Slade, Ph.D., is a professor in the Department of Early Childhood Education in the College of Education at Towson University in Towson, MD. Mary has taught in higher education since 1990, focusing teaching and scholarship on gifted education. Previously she taught in elementary, middle, and high schools as a fourth-grade, gifted education, and English teacher. Dr. Slade served several terms on the Board of Directors of the National Association for Gifted Children and received the Early Leader Award from the organization. Currently, Mary is on the Board of Directors for the North Carolina Association for Gifted Children. Over the past 25 years, she has presented more than 200 professional learning programs in Pre-K–grade 12 education, as well as more than 175 professional papers. Dr. Slade has published widely in gifted education, including more than 25 articles, book chapters, and reports, as well as three books.

Hope (Bess) E. Wilson, Ph.D., is an associate professor of education at the University of North Florida, where she teaches graduate and undergraduate courses in assessment, educational psychology, and statistics. She graduated with a Ph.D. in gifted education from the University of Connecticut. Her research focusing on early childhood giftedness has been published in *Gifted Child Quarterly*, *Journal of Advanced Academics*, *Journal for the Education of the Gifted*, and *Roeper Review*, and she is the coauthor along with Jill Adelson of *Letting Go of Perfect: Overcoming Perfectionism in Kids* (Prufrock Press, 2009). She was the 2017 Early Leader

Award recipient for the National Association for Gifted Children. She is an associate editor for the *Journal of Advanced Academics,* and chair of the Research and Evaluation Network for NAGC. She is a founding board member of the Innovation Collaborative, a nonprofit organization working at the intersections of the arts, sciences, and humanities.